In the Shadow of the Statue of Liberty

In the Shadow of the Statue of Liberty

Immigrants, Workers, and Citizens in the American Republic, 1880-1920

Edited by **Marianne Debouzy**

University of Illinois Press
Urbana and Chicago

First University of Illinois Press Edition, 1992

Manufactured in the United States of America
1 2 3 4 5 C P 5 4 3 2 1

This book is printed of acid-free paper.

Library of Congress Cataloging-in-Publication Data

A l'ombre de la statue de la Liberté. English
In the shadow of the Statue of Liberty : immigrants, workers, and citizens in the American Republic, 1880-1920 / edited by Marianne Debouzy. — 1st University of Illinois Press ed.
p. cm.
Translation of: A l'ombre de la statue de la Liberté.
ISBN 0-252-01924-5 (cl). ISBN 0-252-06252-3 (pb)
1. Immigrants—United States—History—Congresses. 2. Working class—United States—History—Congresses. 3. United States Emigration and immigration—History—Congresses. 4. United States Social conditions—1865-1918—Congresses. I. Debouzy, Marianne. II. Title.
E184.A1L66 1992
973.91dc20 91-44-54
CIP

Contents

Introduction

In 1986 the Centennial of the Statue of Liberty was celebrated in the most extravagant fashion. Not only was the press filled with eulogies of America as a land of freedom[1] but the "cultural mystique of unlimited opportunities and success, freedom and equality",[2] which recent historical scholarship has shown to be far removed from the realities, thrived with renewed vigor. The occasion, however, also provided labor and immigration historians with the opportunity to engage in a more sober reappraisal of the period, one manifestation of which was a colloquium held in Paris in October 1986. "Looking backward" to 1886 the participants set out to examine what kind of freedom workers and immigrants actually enjoyed in the United States at the time and to explore the complexities of the age as revealed by the events of that particular year.

Their reflexion was spurred by the fact that 1886 was a crucial date in American social history for more than one reason: the year of the inauguration of the Statue of Liberty was also that of the Haymarket trial wich stands as a landmark in the history of the repression of the labor movement. Could the issue of freedom at the time be reduced to either one or the other of these two symbolic events?

The papers presented in this volume which come out of the Paris colloquium take up several themes closely connected with the issue of freedom. The year 1886 is taken as a symbolic reference date, but since it marks as well a crucial turning point in American social history, the colloquium came to focus on the nature of the changes taking place in the 1880s and 1890s – changes in the collective representations of America, changes in immigrant and worker experience as well as developments in political ideology, civil liberties and the notion of citizenship.

Part I deals with the representations of America as a land of freedom that prevailed among European immigrants and more specifically among radicals at the end of the nineteenth century.[3] In his book *European Socialists and the American Promised Land* (1970) R. Lawrence Moore opened up this line of inquiry, but the papers in this volume differ in that they explore the point of view of immigrant workers rather than that of outside observers and social thinkers. Part II confronts these representations of the "model Republic" with the experience of freedom that immigrant workers had once they were in the United States.

Our understanding of this experience has been greatly increased by recent scholarship and in particular by recent research on migrations viewed in a transatlantic perspective. By placing "immigration in its larger context, an Atlantic economy with segmented labor markets, some segments of which have been internationalized",[4] Dirk Hoerder and other scholars have brought into focus aspects of immigration up to now largely ignored. The contributors to this volume make it clear that the transatlantic perspective is indispensable if we are to grasp the significance of the social and political history of immigrants in the United States. One school of historians has described their experience essentially as a process of uprooting; subsequently the retention of cultural traits was stressed. To-day there is a growing awareness of the fully transatlantic dimension of their experience, i.e. of the interaction between social movements, intellectual influences and militant networks in the old and the new world. This approach proves to be particularly rewarding in the case of immigrant radicalism on which Part III focuses.

Why radical immigrants? When dealing with the issue of freedom in American society at the end of the nineteenth century, it is clear that much of the debate on the nature of American society, its future and more especially the hopes of the labor movement, was carried on by radical immigrants outside or inside organizations, parallel to, in conjunction or in competition with American reformers and radicals. These immigrants belonged to different national groups, some of which have long remained quite invisible (like the French), others of which have been lumped together indiscriminately as "illiterate peasants" (e.g. Sicilians, Hungarians). The papers in Part III challenge this vision.

Key issues in the debate were the rights of workers, the place of the labor movement in the larger society, the relationship of workers to politics and the state. This debate took place in a society whose ideological framework had been shaped by the Republican tradition, itself a legacy of the American Revolution. The exact nature of this ideology has been a subject of controversy among historians in recent years and the conflicting interpretations that have emerged are echoed in the first section of Part IV. Republicanism which meant different things to different people, rested on the notion of citizenship. As Republicanism underwent considerable reinterpretation at the end of the nineteenth century, so did the concept of citizenship. Labor leaders interpreted it in ways that fitted the aspirations of skilled workers; judges in ways that buttressed the social order; while radical immigrants of the various political persuasions, wary of the attempt to settle the problem of the status of the worker by an appeal to his status as citizen, remained divided about what it meant. Section 2 of Part IV explores the relationship between the two in the changing political context of the late nineteenth century and early twentieth century.

The role played by the courts in redefining freedom and citizens' rights became obvious with the anti-labor judicial activism of the 1880s which reached a climax with the Haymarket trial. In spite of the fact there was "firm" legal basis for finding the Chicago anarchists guilty (i.e. conspiracy law enabled the judges to convict them) workers became aware that labor was threatened and so was freedom of speech. They protested through the labor press and manifested their opposition to the hangings. In the two years following the Haymarket trial labor engaged in vigorous political activity, initiating local political experiments (labor reform parties) in many cities. But the movement was soon to collapse.

By the turn of the century, the hope once entertained by some labor organizations and militants that American society would be a "workingmen's democracy" had died. A new definition of national identity emerged based on a changed ideology of citizenship. Citizenship became highly selective and the result, one of the papers suggests, was a crucial decline in working-class political participation (Part IV, section 3).

The papers in this volume cannot claim to provide definitive answers to all the questions raised; they can only aim to unravel some of the threads which run through the theme of freedom. The various contributions have been grouped thematically but the order of presentation adopted should not conceal their basic interconnectedness.

Notes

1. Cf "Freedom First", *Time*, June 16 1986, p.32: "Freedom is the essential American virtue because the United States, uniquely, is a nation populated by the free choice of its inhabitants. Except, of course, for those who were brought to America in slave ships." Cf also "Promise of America", *U.S. News and World Report*, July 7, 1986; "The Lady's Party", *Time*, July 14, 1986.

2. Dirk Hoerder, Introduction to *Labor Migration in the Atlantic Economies*, Westport, Conn. Greenwood Press, 1985, p. 3.

3. Dirk Hoerder has pointed to the ambiguity of the term "immigrants" and suggested that "migrants" and "migrant laborers" would be more adequate terms. *Ibid.*, pp. 8-9.

4. *Ibid.*, p. 3. Cf also Frank Thistlethwaite, "Migration from Europe Overseas in the Nineteenth and Twentieth Centuries", *XI*[e] Congrès International des Sciences Historiques. Rapports, Stockholm, 1960, pp. 32-60.

Acknowledgements

The invaluable help of a number of people made the publication of this volume possible. I wish to express my heartfelt thanks to Madeleine Rebérioux, Professor at the University of Paris VIII, who provided the initial impetus for the project. Through her initiative, a grant was obtained from the Ministry of Culture in 1985 that served to fund the Paris colloquium held in October 1986. I am deeply indebted to Jacques Debouzy, John Atherton, Charles Sowerwine, Jean Chase, Helen Chenut, Nancy Green, Larry Portis and Alice Thorner who improved the quality of the book through careful reading and criticism.

I am grateful to Michel Dreyfus and Gérard Noiriel who read the manuscript in its entirety and made helpful suggestions.

My thanks are due as well to Mme Pauly, Déléguée Générale aux Célébrations Nationales.

Finally, I owe many thanks to Annie Sabatier and Shara Chennaf at the Presses Universitaires de Vincennes.

One of the very first persons invited to the colloquium was Herbert Gutman; this volume is dedicated to his memory.

I

The Image of the Model Republic and Its Metamorphoses

Part I deals with representations of America as the land of freedom among Germans, Italians and Swedes. The richest sources for these representations, as many of the papers underline, are to be found in the letters written home by emigrants and in the articles printed in the labor and radical press both in the U.S. and in the homeland. These images, with their strong political connotations, provide excellent terrain on which to explore the special place America occupied in the radical imagination.

Dirk Hoerder argues persuasively that in nineteenth century Germany "America" was not simply a destination but a "construct" made up of several images. In the early decades of the century the vision of American democracy as a model Republic was essentially a middle class vision, one that appealed to reformers and revolutionaries. (It was the case as well in Italy according to Vecoli). German migrant workers took over this middle class vision and made it their own – which can lead us to ask whether the same sort of transfer did not take place in other European countries. To what extent did such visions shape workers' expectations? The different papers suggest that in the late nineteenth century the construct "America" varied with each social group and that a comparative approach is required to do justice to the complexities. A given image could be simply borrowed from a commonly held world outlook, or it could be a novel construct. Or again existing images could be reinvested with a different class connotation.

Vecoli stresses the fact that the representation of America was partly shaped by the accounts immigrants gave of their experience in the U.S.. The image of America in the Italian press was linked to the bad treatment and discrimination Italians were often victims of. Important too was the vitality of the radical tradition among Italian immigrants (and here another question arises: why such vitality?). Finally representations of America fed on the culture of origin. They depended upon national styles and specific cultural references, they expressed a peculiar sensibility through selected words and symbols. A typology of representations could well be elaborated on the basis of national and cultural criteria. Moreover representations of America changed over time. With American society undergoing deep transformations, labor and radical papers proliferated and the radical imagination reshaped the image, though the myth of America as the promised land retained its appeal. In all three cases, German, Italian and Swedish, the mood of the radical press – at home and among immigrants – changed from admiration to criticism, indignation and denunciation. By the close of the century, the myth of America as a land of freedom was being subjected to systematic critique.

What caused the image to change? It fluctuated with political events and economic cycles in the U.S. and at home, but also with the political strategy of radical groups. The different phases through which the image passed raise further questions: Were the crucial moments which brought about change identical in all countries? To what use were the representations of America put by the different radical groups? Did the function of these representations vary with specific occasions? Changing views brought about changes in symbols. The form of a symbol might remain the same while its content or connotations were transformed, as with the ironic use of the "free country" image in the Italian radical press. Or the symbol itself might change as when the Statue of Liberty went through a succession of metamorphoses and suggestions were made for its replacement by other emblematic figures. The study of these representations points to the need to explore further the networks and channels through which they circulated. Images were often relayed from one socialist or radical paper to another: thus the German–American socialist paper *Der Sozialist* was a source for the Swedish socialist *Socialdemokraten* (Tedebrand). There were constant contacts and exchanges between correspondents of immigrant papers and those who wrote for papers in the homeland. An image formed by one group might spread and become a stereotype used by all groups, or on the contrary keep its unique political or national quality.

A final question might be raised: what was the impact of these representations? What influence did they have on immigrants and on people at home? While the papers in Part I do not claim to offer definitive answers, they do show that the 'negative' representations of America did not stop migrants from immigrating and did not dispel their illusions or expectations. They certainly gave emotional coloring to the ongoing debate concerning America. Proof of the liveliness of the radical imagination, they provided critics of America with forceful images and compelling symbols in their fight against bourgeois democracy.

German Immigrant Workers' Views of "America" in the 1880s

Dirk Hoerder

"America" – the land of opportunity? Or "America" as a place of exploitation, degrading living conditions and police attacks on striking workers? Before entering into a discussion of the expectations of workers who planned to migrate, the sources of information available to them and their experiences and views after migration, we have to take a close look at the destination: "America".

Increasingly in recent years Canadians have pointed out that North America happens to contain two states and that the one we are usually talking about when dealing with nineteenth century migration is the United States of America (an imperialist term in itself). But we are not concerned with present-day debate about correct denotations of states. Rather we are asking: Did prospective migrants planning their transatlantic voyage aim at a particular political entity, with bourgeois-democratic structures and presumably higher wages and better job opportunities? If so, did they mean the United States of America?

The Image of "America" and the State "U.S.A."

A German saying, repeated in songs, proclaimed "Auf nach Amerika" — "Let's go to America".[1] In several Eastern European languages the saying was different: "za chlebom" (Slovak) — "to bread".[2] No state is mentioned; a very basic economic goal, to have enough food, is pursued. While the latter term cannot be reinterpreted for ideological purposes to imply desirable political structures, such an interpretation is easy for the former. Prospective East European migrants may have had information about political and social advantages of the United States compared to the Czarist empire or the Habsburg (dual) Monarchy — and we know that some were well informed — there was no doubt that migration was intended to improve a standard of living that in many areas was at subsistence level. On the one hand, research in the East and Southeast European countries emphasizing the loss of population and mentioning political exiles of the revolution of 1848/49 has only occasionally kept in focus the image of people moving in search of a living. On the other hand, research on German migrants has emphasized the importance of the Fortyeighter political refugees and those expelled under the anti-socialist laws. In this latter context, people moving to the big cities of the new world in search of a living have rarely been cited. Only the peasant, who settled frontier areas and contributed to a sturdy "American" farming population, have not been neglected by scholars. The artisans, the skilled and unskilled workers among German migrants, went unnoticed by filiopietistic scholars. However, statistics show that even in the 1840s only one third of the new arrivals to the U.S. were farmers. During the last of the three great waves of German migration, in the 1880s and early 90s, two-fifths of the total German migrants reached American shores and few farmers were among them.[3]

Nevertheless, the image of people moving from German autocracy to the land of the free has a kernel of truth in it. Fortyeighters were outspoken and attracted attention: a considerable number of them attained positions of prominence in the German-American ethnic community, a few entered American political circles; most important for our argument, they edited liberal and labor periodicals.[4] (The parallel migration of Czech and Hungarian Fortyeighters merits similar attention.)[5] Their influence alone, however, does not explain the prominence of the image of a free country. The roots of this image may be found in the debate over the American Declaration of Independence and over the Constitution that deeply influenced the European liberal political circles throughout the Age of Revolution. American political institutions were the reference point for many debates on republican goals among European reformers and revolutionaries.[6] This "orderly" transition from one political status to another became the model for most middle-class reformers, a transition which was assiduously contrasted with the bloodshed of the French Revolution. The plebeian democratic tradition that emerged from the latter have for long remained unnoticed by scholars both in the U.S. and in Germany[7] who have largely ignored the extensive literature on America as a land of democratic institutions and the preconceptions to which it gave rise.

In Eastern Europe, where the American Revolution also served as a point of reference, the appeal was less broad, given the degree of literacy and the more limited size of reformist political elites.

The more sophisticated scholarly studies of this image of America point out that contemporary admirers of the newly formed United States of America knew little about the social and economic realities of the new nation despite their extensive knowledge of the founding texts. (This explains the disenchantment of German Fortyeighter immigrants.) Thus "America" became a construct emerging in the minds of European reformers, a middle-class image which in turn had an impact on the working classes. It then underwent a process of transformation in the decades after the Civil War. In addition to denoting a more desirable state of political affairs, it implied more desirable conditions in general. The first change of meaning is vividly illustrated by a German author writing about settlement and farming opportunities in the newly opened territories of Siberia, who entitled his book "Ein anderes Amerika" —the other America.[8] The nature of this other America is illustrated by the German saying, "to plan cities the American way", to produce "on an American scale."[9]

Thus, during the nineteenth century, an abstract construct of "America" developed, which tended to become a kind of secular religion. The other new world was not a paradise in a state of eternal bliss, but a world in which, through choice, hard work and the ability to make the best of opportunity, one's personal condition could be improved. This construct was reinforced by letters from immigrants who explained that one did not have to doff one's cap when asking for a job.[10] There were taxes, but not the multitude of preying officials, tithe-sucking church structures, and haughty princelings characteristic of the old world.[11] The image might have been cast in less positive terms – but the unsuccessful write less often and often not at all. In the minds of many prospective migrants – and in the minds of those remaining at home – "America" did not mean a country, it meant a better world.

I have argued elsewhere that the category "state" or "nation" is relatively unimportant for processes of acculturation. The essential fact is that people move from one ethnic culture and one set of wage earning patterns into another labor market of markedly different characteristics and into another ethnic enclave far removed from that with which they are familiar. Migrants follow their hopes, which direct them to places where they have reason to believe they will find jobs – Budapest, Vienna, Paris, America: "Vienna was looked upon as a kind of Eldorado and people sent their children to make their fortune there."[12] In France, novels indicated that young male villagers could make their fortune in Paris.[13] But research on Paris, on German villages and on small Hungarian as well as Sicilian towns suggests that it was essentially the unbearable structures and emotional problems at home that pushed people out; measured against them any destination seemed an improvement. "America" was only the best-known of such better worlds, a world which happened to send out recruiting agents, to have a Statue of Liberty placed in its main port of arrival and to cultivate an ideology that combined material opportunity and the blessing of liberty. It is at this point that the image "America" and the nation "U.S.A." came together. People migrated to a myth-enshrouded "America" and found themselves in a political entity called the "U.S.A." where they could exercise the right to vote or join political machines, where political institutions seemed more responsive than did those in the old country.

German Trade Unions and Social Democrats View "America"

German-speaking social democrats in Europe and in America were in relatively close contact during the years of the anti-socialist laws (1878-1890), when no party periodicals could be published in Germany. There is less evidence concerning the German trade unions during this period since the umbrella organization, the Allgemeiner Deutscher Gewerkschaftsverband (General German Trade Union Federation) was established only in 1890 and did not publish its *Correspondenzblatt* for medium- and lower level functionaries before 1891. We will, therefore, deal with trade union views only briefly. The *Correspondenzblatt* reported regularly on the annual conventions of the American Federation of Labor. Though criticism was voiced concerning some AFL positions, the reports show a basic admiration for this large organization. The growth of the AFL greatly impressed the fledgling German unions. By the mid-nineties however, the tone of the reports changed. More and more criticism of conservative AFL-policies was voiced and later AFL cooperation with the National Civic Federation was viewed with derision. Articles in the *Correspondenzblatt* also dealt with working and living conditions in the United States: Potential migrants were warned that higher wages were balanced by the fact that living costs were also higher. The reports of the social democratic press were more detailed and more critical. The attitude of the social democratic press was in fact close to that of German-language labor periodicals in the United States, since many articles appearing in the German press were reprinted from the German-American press or were authored by the same persons.[14] In the 1880s the *Sozialdemokrat*[15] characterized U.S. society as dominated by capitalism, especially in the form of monopolies and — quoting the *New Yorker Volkszeitung* — said that nowhere in the world were differences between exploiters and exploited so wide. However, some positive aspects received mention; for example, agriculture was said to be more productive and advanced in the U.S. than in Europe. Such evaluation, it should be noted, was not limited to the relative degree of success of peasants or farmers, but contained an element of international competition. The interest in a better standard of living was closely entwined with an interest in the division of the world's resources. In view of the advanced position of the U.S. in some fields, the *Sozialdemokrat* quoted Goethe: "Amerika, du hast es besser"- America, you are better off. But this praise for the achievements of the real "America" was paralleled by an implicit recognition that "America" was a goal to be achieved everywhere in the world: "Ein politisch und sozial befreites Deutschland, das ist unser Amerika" – a politically and socially liberated Germany, that is our America.[16]

The *Sozialdemokrat* voiced the latter position when discussing emigration. It stated clearly that the German migrants were mainly agricultural and industrial workers who migrated because of need. Emigration was opposed because it detracted attention from the causes of miserable social conditions, since it thinned ranks of the discontented, and since the most energetic part of the population was lost to the country.[17]

The dichotomy between positive and negative aspects continued throughout the reporting of the *Sozialdemokrat*. When the struggle for the eight-hour day gained momentum in the U.S., it was time to quote Goethe once again, but when German labor migrants to the new world reported that because of the U.S. economic crisis many of them were continuing their journey on to Brazil, the *Sozialdemokrat* commented that "emigration is often a change for the worse."[18]

By the end of the decade the *Sozialdemokrat* reflected admiration for technical innovation, thus contributing to the image of a more dynamic society. Critical analysis, however, followed swiftly: mechanization meant unemployment and reduced wages on the one hand, increasing productivity on the other. Therefore the role of unskilled workers would gain in importance and they might be used as strikebreakers. Or, as the *Sozialdemokrat* recognized, in contrast to most AFL unions, unskilled workers would have to be organized too. All attempts to further the goals of the working classes in the United States – on this issue social democratic and trade union periodicals agreed – depended on the entry of the workers' organization into the arena of political life. There was no criticism of bread-and-butter struggles. They were an important aspect of workers' day-to-day resistance to exploitation, but they would not improve the situation permanently. Political strategies and a political consciousness should be developed among members of U.S. unions since (according to the *Sozialdemokrat*) wage slavery is worse than chattel slavery. Sometimes the hope was expressed that people would be exasperated enough to change the social structures. The German term used is "aufräumen" meaning "to clean up", "to bring order to".[19]

An essay by Philipp Rappaport (Indianapolis) published in *Neue Zeit* summarized the situation by arguing that even during the Haymarket persecution freedom of speech and of the press was comparatively broader in the U.S. than in any European country. But he contrasted this advantage with the hierarchical structure of U.S. organizations, especially the trade unions and political institutions. The Knights of Labor suffered from the influence and accommodationist position of Powderly; the U.S. President was more powerful than the King of England. Americans themselves succumbed to myths. Since the founding period a national pride had developed, which while it might have been justified at the start, now led to self-conceit (Dünkel). Americans regarded everything alien as inferior; the Constitution had become the incarnation of political wisdom, "and this feeling of superiority is encouraged from above so that – and this is hardly an exaggeration – the poorest devil carries his suffering more easily, because it is American suffering."[20]

While this may be an overstatement, it points to a number of issues that have not been investigated by migration researchers. Does migration and the process of acculturation lead to an overblown pride in achievements? This is said of Americans[21] and of the people of Berlin, a city of in-migrants. Does the creation of new societies or of industrial centers lead to insecurities because the forces of tradition, the experience of generation, cannot function as legitimizing factors? The letters and the newspaper articles written by German migrants do not point in this direction.[22] Sources concerning East European migrants, Poles and Lithuanians, show how impressed they were by everything getting bigger and bigger and quicker and quicker. Some felt anxiety, others admiration.[23] This question remains open. In conclusion, we may say that German workers toying with the idea of migration could obtain realistic and detailed information about the United States. In addition to the discussion of the image of "America" the social democratic and trade union press contained comparisons of wage levels and living expenses. Whatever their hopes and their respective personal images, potential labor migrants had access to a broad range of information through the labor press and through letters.

German Migrants in the United States

The view German immigrants held of their new surroundings varied greatly according to their social position. Newspapers for middle-class German-Americans portrayed the United States as a country with political and cultural shortcomings, but one that basically fulfilled their aspirations. A tendency to emphasize the German cultural contributions to the new nation is marked.[24] Letters give a somewhat more differentiated picture but since the selection preserved is heavily biased towards male members of farming and urban middle-class communities, the positive aspects dominate. They include references to increased workpace, periods of unemployment, and difficulties in gaining a foothold in commerce or in agriculture, but a basic theme is: by hard work any individual can make his (or her) own way.[25] The labor press of the 1880s, on the other hand, draws a basically negative picture of exploitation and wage slavery. It is worth noting that German diplomats – little interested in the aspirations and demands of workers – came to similar conclusion looking from the top down.[26] Few of them had a positive opinion of American institutions, many called the United States a plutocracy, a country where money ruled.[27] "America is no longer a new country" the *New Yorker Volkszeitung* (*NYVZ*) argued in 1881. Democratic and republican ideals were but a veil to hide the reality of wage slavery. Statistics were marshalled to show the low standard of living which workers had to accept and the high degree of exploitation to which they were subjected. Working conditions in East Coast cities differed little from those in Germany. In fact, monopolies were oppressing workers more than the policeman's club did in Germany.[28]

On the whole, conditions in the United States became increasingly similar to those in Europe: paupers and millionaires, starvation and extreme luxury, a growing class of speculators and idlers living off dividends on both sides of the Atlantic. Corruption was judged to be worse than in Russia; the pace of work, because of the high speed of machinery, faster than in England. The New York police, compared to that in Berlin, was corrupt, brutal and deeply involved in criminal rackets. During strikes or workers' meetings it was an organ of the employing classes. The *NYVZ* sometimes exposed police scandals years before the English-language press took notice. But only then did the governmental "Lexow Committee" take action. Thus criticism voiced in the German-language ethnic press — and this probably holds true for other immigrant groups' newspapers — remained unheard in the "host" society.[29]

The rapid development of technology and of capital concentration received particular attention. In the United States the usage of new machinery, the adaptation of inventions for everyday production, and the division of labor had progressed much further than in Germany or Europe. Federal or state legislatures were unable to control or regulate the monopolies.[30] The whole development necessitated, according to the *NYVZ* a new strategy for the labor movement in general and for workers in particular. Judging that "the art of exploitation has been developed to its highest level in America", the *NYVZ* noted the increasing production and higher wages. But as to the postulated advantages for workers and the interest of big industry in promoting the physical, intellectual, moral and financial well-being of its workers, the *NYVZ* was skeptical. By offering good wages, better housing, reading rooms and evening courses, capitalists ultimately wanted total submission on the part of their workers. In this way a state of "benevolent slavery" would be instituted.[31]

The general attitude of immigrant workers as represented in the *NYVZ* was, economically speaking, that the U.S. was ahead of Europe with regard to productivity, nominal wages, degree of exploitation, mechanization and monopolization. With respect to the political system, even in view of massive police repression, the U.S. still offered asylum to political refugees from Europe. But this was a difference of degree not of substance. Migrants came, according to the *NYVZ*, not because of prosperity in the U.S., but because of social problems in Europe.[32]

One important topic that received regular attention in the columns of the *NYVZ* was immigration, just as migrant workers received regular attention in European labor newspapers and union periodicals. The attitude was ambivalent: on the one hand, workers were advised not to lure their friends to the U.S. by private letters. It was not workers whose interests lay in further immigration, but steamship and railroad companies in particular, and capitalists in general, who needed cheap workers and strikebreakers.[33]

On the other hand, people had to leave Germany/Europe. In that case it was preferable to go to the United States rather than to the German colonies ruled in the Prussian spirit. Any restrictions on immigration would demean the principles of granting political asylum to refugees and would therefore be a disgrace for the republic.[34] It should be noted that the German socialists in cases of need referred to republican principles, even when elsewhere they argue that these had long been thrown overboard by the captains of industry, monopolists and other rulers.

In 1881 the *NYVZ* was critical of the political consciousness of German and other European migrants. During the decades from the 1830s to the 1850s politically conscious immigrants had come to American shores. They had had a chance to earn a living or even to achieve a modest level of prosperity. But by the 1870s and early '80s most immigrants had been conditioned in Europe into submissiveness, promonarchical attitudes and bigotry. They had no chance to improve their lot in the U.S., because even the West was in the hands of monopolists and because workers in the cities competed against each other. Thus, even with great personal sacrifice and through hard work nobody could achieve "independence".[35] As to the role of the labor movement under these circumstances, it was argued that socialists should fight for better conditions in their countries of origin and that only the politically persecuted should migrate. In the United States, workers would have to strengthen their organizations and teach migrants about the political and economic situation. Secondly, they would have to intensify their struggles for a shorter workday, so that additional immigrants would exert less competitive pressure for scarce jobs.[36]

Five years later the *NYVZ* still recognized concrete reasons for migrations to continue. They were mainly "push"-factors: European despotism, hopes for improved social conditions, simple curiosity, opposition to the draft system, but also avoidance of criminal prosecution. The basic causes were still the desolate economic and confining social conditions in the homeland. The socialists suggested a remedy for the immigration problem: abolish capitalism in Europe – then there would be no further need for emigration; and, to make doubly sure, abolish capitalism in the United States, then additional immigration could easily be observed. However, since this development was not to be expected in the near future, the German socialists turned to what they considered a problem: Polish, Slovak, Jewish and Italian immigrants were said to be a "common nuisance".[37] In 1887 the *NYVZ* noted that the new immigration was coming under increasing criticism from native-born Americans and old immigrants and that, while the granting of political asylum should not be restricted, its present form only served the capitalists. Cautiously the paper added that migration also increased internal commerce and populated the empty wilderness areas. Those coming (Poles, Slovaks, Italians, Belgians) were, however, imported by the monopolists, and still had to work off their prepaid tickets in the factories. These new immigrants came in poverty, they were a helpless proletariat and would remain proletarians all their lives. Upward mobility and the achievement of an independent means of livelihood was for them impossible.[38]

Thus the German socialist immigrants shared the problems many European and North American labor movements had with labor migration. They felt superior to the Southern and Eastern European new immigrants, and having come largely from the skilled trades[39] they still harbored hopes of gaining an independent or at least a secure living with their skills.

Whether this attitude can be interpreted as a desire to move into the middle class is open to serious doubt. "Independence" was a term that was much used among migrating workers, but which has received little scholarly attention. Setting up shop was a widely accepted means to escape poverty under certain conditions. Widows of drowned sailors in village communities opened small stores to be independent of authorities and not to be a burden on the community. Black-listed members of the German Social Democratic Party received a small amount of money to set up shop (or buy a pair of horses and a wagon) to be "independent" of employer persecution and not to be a drain on Party aid funds.

On the whole migrants who, before leaving, could inform themselves to some degree —(in the 1880s the social-democratic and union press had to be publihed abroad)— about "America" experienced in the United States what they had been told to expect. The slight advantage in political liberties was counterbalanced by the apathy of large sections of the working classes; higher nominal wages were counterbalanced by higher living costs and a quicker workpace. The expectations once associated with "America" were no longer realistic. Most of those migrants whom we can trace through labor newspapers in the last quarter of the nineteenth century did not experience a free society, while earlier letters from the second and third quarters of the century, coming mainly from villagers and small-town residents, indicated a feeling of liberation from numerous social constraints.

Migration to a "free" Society?

Up to the time of the Civil War many or most German migrants — at least those who left records for historians — seem to have experienced the new society as permitting considerably more economic and political freedom. Freedom was invoked most frequently by refugees from the revolutions of 1830 and 1848. In the United States, it was reported by these and other immigrants, there were no swarms of petty officials, little or no police, no involuntary tithes for church and priests, no deference to higher officials, princelings and other aristocrats.

Migrants of the last wave of German newcomers, 1880-1893, experienced a different society. The police had become a class institution, small capital had little chance against big capital. In the United States, there was at times the opportunity to earn higher wages. But to do so generally meant accepting even greater exploitation. This situation did not — so it seems from the labor press — lead to disillusionment since most migrants came with few illusions. The often repeated statement from the pre-Civil War period, that any person willing to work hard could make his way and become self-sustaining was no longer heard from lower-class migrants in later decades — and they comprised the vast majority of the new arrivals of this period.

Emigration, at this time, was politically motivated in the sense that neither Germany nor the United States were countries of "freedom" for the workers, but in the United States struggle for better conditions remained possible, while in Germany the anti-socialist laws prevailed from 1878 to 1890. The right to vote in the U.S. was not necessarily a sign of a free society, especially since working-class voters and candidates of groups to the left of the Democratic Party in particular witnessed numerous election frauds.

Emigration, at this time, was economically motivated in the sense that job opportunities were considered slightly better in the U.S. than at home at the time of departure. The nominally higher wages for some skilled workers were of less importance than the increasing number of unskilled ones. In view of the higher living costs probably only unattached young males ("prime workers" — to paraphrase earlier advertisements for black slaves) could earn more in terms of purchasing power. That social security and support networks of kin and village or neighborhood community were absent, was obvious to migrants. America is for the healthy and strong — the weak ones had better remain at home, this was a current theme in letters and newspapers giving advice to migrants.

While it seems that the comparisons of the *NYVZ* between economic conditions in Europe and the United States were a little too bleak — as revealed in its own assessment of the causes of emigration — in our opinion, the slight improvement in economic standing cannot explain the whole flow of migration. Rather, it seems that under changing economic conditions at home and under the impression of being part of a relatively surplus population, large sections of the population in the age bracket from 15 to 30 seriously considered the possibility of moving elsewhere. That is roughly speaking, emigration affected those from the age at which they were capable of supporting themselves (or when they faced the draft) to the age at which many had gone from being single to being married, becoming part of a new family unit. In this age bracket we argue — on the basis of the still fragmentary evidence — migration was less a move toward greater opportunities than a move away from constraining social relations. It was an attempt to take one's fate/future into one's own hands. Freedom did not mean freedom from want and oppression, it meant freedom from being shunted along well-worn paths into a dreary timelessness that could hardly be called a future. It meant the opportunity to seek a future off the beaten track, to be responsible for one's decisions. The quest for "independence" pursued by migrants from many cultures seems to be little more than being at liberty to leave when circumstances become unbearable. Historians have interpreted this as "flight" rather than "struggle" and I am still not convinced that this interpretation is entirely wrong; but subjectively many migrants saw this as their personal "freedom". Migrants do not move to a "free" society, they "free" themselves from the old. Perhaps the concept of "day-to-day" resistance of chattel slaves — slow work, disregard for the upkeep of tools and farm animals — can be transferred to those proletarians who can no longer experience artisanal or skilled workers' pride in their product. Their day-to-day resistance is to drop work and to migrate. Many migrated to America. Given the demand for unskilled workers there, the chances to move ahead were probably greater. And of those for whom the move meant further descent and abject poverty we know little. They did not write letters and much of the labor press did not deign to take notice of the "lumpen proletarians".

Migrants perceived new hierarchies of values in the U.S.: the "almighty dollar" as supreme arbiter of status; the accelerated pace of work; the lack of job security and tradition-honored obligations. These conditions were designed to produce a system of "the survival of the fittest". Migrants comparing this to their old values were dissatisfied. But many where proud that they were strong, and they all strove for dollars. Thus no basic critique of the new constraints developed among the majority of migrants. Socialists and militant unionists were the exception. In fact, the migrants mitigated the system by establishing mutual-aid societies and creating communities and kinship networks that counteracted the pure-and-simple (or pure-and-brutal) capitalist system and its specific forms of harassment, exploitation and degradation.

Notes

I am grateful to Horst Rößler for his help in analyzing the newspapers *Sozialdemokrat* and *New Yorker Volkzeitung*.

1. German emigrant songs extolling "America" are reprinted in Lutz Röhrich, "Auswandererschicksal im Lied", *Hessische Blätter für Volks- und Kulturforschung* 17 (1985), 71-109.

2. Paul Krause, "Labor Republicanism and *"Za Chlebom"*: Anglo-Americans and Slavic Solidarity in Homestead", 143-169 in D. Hoerder, ed., *"Struggle a Hard Battle" -Essays on Working-Class Immigrants* (DeKalb, Ill. 1986); Victor Greene, *The Slavic Community on Strike* (Notre Dame 1968), 28-29.

3. *Historical Statistics of the United States: Colonial Times to 1970*, 2 vols. (Washington, D.C. 1975), series C 89-119, 120-137.

4. A. E. Zucker, ed., *The Forty-eighters: Political Refugees of the German Revolution of 1848* (New York 1950); Heinzpeter Thümmler, *Sozialistengesetz* § 28. *Ausweisungen und Ausgewiesene 1878-1890* (Berlin-Ost 1979).

5. Cf. Richard Schneirov, "Free Thought and Socialism in the Czech Community in Chicago, 1875-1887", 121-142 in Hoerder, ed., *"Struggle a Hard Battle"*; P. Krause, "Labor Republicanism", *ibid*., 154.

6. Jaroslav Pelenski, ed., *The American and European Revolutions, 1776-1848: Sociopolitical and Ideological Aspects* (Iowa City 1980); *La Révolution Américaine et l'Europe* (Paris 1979); *The Impact of the American Revolution Abroad* (Washington, D.C. 1976); Horst Dippel, *Germany and the American Revolution 1770-1800* (Chapel Hill 1977); Erich Angermann, "Der deutsche Frühkonstitutionalismus und das amerikanische Vorbild", *Historisch Zeitschrift* 219 (1974), 1-32; Eckhart G. Franz, *Das Amerikabild der deutschen Revolution von 1848/49* (Heidelberg 1958); Aladár Urbán, "A lesson for the Old Continent. The Image of America in the Hungarian Revolution of 1848/49", *New Hungarian Quart.* 17 (no. 63), (1976), 85-96; Zofia Libiszowska, "American Thought in Polish Political Writings of the Great Diet (1788-1792)", *Polish-American Studies* 1 (1976) 41.

7. For German-Americans Bruce Levine has begun to work on this question: "In the Heat of Two Revolutions: The Forging of German-American Radicalism", 19-45 in Hoerder, ed., *"Struggle a Hard Battle"*.

8. Otto Heller, *Sibirien, ein anderes Amerika* (Berlin 1930).

9. In the 1850s a particularly large house in the city of Barmen was called "Groß Amerika": Klaus Goebel and Günther Voigt, eds., *Die Kleine, mühselige Welt des jungen Hermann Enters* (Wuppertal, 3rd ed. 1979), 28. Walter Köpping, ed., *Lebensberichte deutscher Bergarbeiter* (Frankfurt/M. 1984). 110.

10. This particular remark was made by a German immigrant in 1861 (Wolfgang Helbich ed., *"Amerika ist ein freies Land..." Auswanderer schreiben nach Deutschland*, Darmstadt 1885, 116); by a Swedish immigrant, 1903 (David M. Katzman and William M. Tuttle Jr., *Plain Folk. The Life Stories of Undistinguished Americans*, Urbana Ill., 1982, 33); by a Swiss technician (cited in Hannes Siegrist, "Images of Host Countries: The U.S. and German in the press of Swiss Technicians (1904-1935)", in Harzig/Hoerder, eds. *The Press of Labor Migrants*, 565).

11. Helbich, *"Amerika"*, 32, 35; Hans Herder, ed., *Hessisches Auswandererbuch* (Frankfurt 1983), 21, 22 passim.

12. Heinz Fassmann, "A Survey of Patterns and Structures of Migrations in Austria, 1850-1900", 69-93 in D. Hoerder, ed., *Labor Migration in the Atlantic Economies* (Westport, Ct. 1985), 79; F.G. Kürbish and R. Klucsarits, eds., *Arbeiterinnen kämpfen um ihr Recht* (Wuppertal n.d.), 86, 94.

13. Isabelle Bertaux-Wiame, "The Life History Approach to the Study of Internal Migration: ...Paris...",186-200 in Paul Thompson and Natasha Burchardt, eds., *Our Common History: The Transformation of Europe* (London, 1982), 189; on Hungary see research in progress by Julianna Puskas; on Sicily see research in progress by Donna Gabaccia; cf. generally Gert Raeithel, "Go West". *Ein Psychohistorischer Versuch über die Amerikaner* (Frankfurt/M. 1981).

14. D. Hoerder and Hartmut Keil, "The American Case and German Social Democracy at the Turn of the Twentieth Century, 1878-1907", in *Why is there no Socialism in the United States? / Pourquoi n'y a-t-il pas de socialisme aux &am.tats-Unis?* édité par Jean Heffer et Jeanine Rovet, Paris, EHESS, 1988, pp. 141-165.

15. The following paragraphs are based on a close reading of the *Sozialdemokrat* for the years 1880, 1885, 1890.

16. *Sozialdemokrat*, 24 Oct. 1880, 16 Jan. 1881.

17. *Ibid.*, 16 Jan. 1881.

18. *Ibid.*, 23 July 1885.

19. *Ibid.*, regular column "Sozial Politische Rundschau", 1890; 22 Feb., 11 July, 28 Nov. 1880.

20. *Neue Zeit* 7 (1889), 63-69, esp. 66.

21. The travel literature of the nineteenth century again and again pointed to the fact that Americans continuously extolled the virtues and advantages of their country. See among many others *A Russian Looks at America. The Journey of Aleksandr Borisovich Lakier in 1857*, ed. and transl. by Arnold Schrier and Joyce Story (Chicago 1979) and the summary of German travel reports: Gerhard Armanski, Renate Grunert, Marianne Suchan, "Aufbruch in die Neue Welt. Entstehung des deutschen Amerikabildes im Spiegel der Auswanderer- und Reiseliteratur", *Dollars & Träume* 4 (Sept. 1981), 19-48, 5 (Mærz 1982), 135-151.

22. Letters collected by the Bochum Immigrant Letters Project, Wolfgang Helbich with Ulrike Sommer and Bettina Goldberg.

23. D. Hoerder, ed., "Bremen als Auswandererhafen: Briefe polnisch Auswanderer 1890 und 1891" *Beiträge zur Sozialgeschichte Bremens* 7

(1984), 139-177, esp. 157,159 passim: Antanas Kaztauskis, "From Lithuania to the Chicago Stockyards", *Independent* 57 (4 Aug. 1904), 241-248.

24. See for example *New Yorker Staats-Zeitung*.

25. I am grateful to the Bochum Colleagues (cf. note 22) who have shared their collection with me.

26. The following analysis is based on a close reading of the *New Yorker Volkszeitung*, 1881, 1885, 1887, and of the special anniversary issued reprinted in D. Hoerder and Thomas Weber, eds., *Glimpses of the German-American Radical Press* (Bremen 1985). See also Renate Kiesewetter, "Die Institution der deutsch-amerikanische Arbeiterpress in Chicago", *ibid.*, pp. 179-214.

27. Dirk Hoerder, ed., *"Plutokraten und Sozialisten" Berichte deutscher Diplomaten und Agenten über die amerikanische Arbeiterbewegung, 1878-1917* (München 1981).

28. *NYVZ* 16 March, 18 April, 1 July, 9 Aug. 1881, 6, 24 May 1887.

29. *NYVZ* 14 Feb., 18 April, 1 July 1881, 6, 24 May 1887. Thomas Weber, Die Berichterstattung der "New Yorker Volkszeitung" hinsichtlich der örtlichen Polizei im Zeitraum von 1886-1892, unpublished state examination thesis, 1985. See also Sidney L. Harring, *Policing a Class Society: the Experience of American Cities, 1865-1915* (New Brunswick, N.J., 1983). – For views on political institutions in general see Hartmut Keil's paper for this symposium.

30. *NYVZ* 14 May 1885, 4, 17 Feb., 3, 10, 24 March, 20 April, 30 May, 4 June 1887.

31. *NYVZ* 1, 2, 9, 15 May, 10, 14 Nov. 1885.

32. *NYVZ* 13 May 1881.

33. *NYVZ* 20 Jan., 26, 28 Feb., 2 May, 30 June 1881. For the views of German unions on migrant labor see Hans-Peter Winter, Analyse der Ausländerpolitik der deutsch Gewerkschaften, thesis Universit. of Erlangen-Nürnberg 1980; Martin Forberg, Freie Gewerkschaften und ausländische Industriearbeiter, 1890-1918, M.A. Thesis, University of Münster, 1985.

34. *NYVZ* 24 Sept. 1881, 16 April 1887.

35. *NYVZ* 30 June, 1 July 1881, 4 Jan. 1882.

36. *NYVZ* 25 April, 10 June 1881.

37. *NYVZ* 1, 2, 7, 8 May 1887.

38. *NYVZ Ibid.*, 11 Feb., 16 April, 18 May 1887.

39. The many union reports in the twenty-fifth anniversary issue of the *NYVZ* in 1903 came almost exclusively from unions of skilled workers.

"Free Country": The American Republic Viewed by the Italian Left, 1880-1920

Rudolph J. Vecoli

From the eighteenth century to the present, the United States has been held up as an example, positive or negative, by Italian reformers and revolutionaries. In 1784, Vittorio Alfieri's ode, *L'America Liberata*, contrasted an Italy bound in chains to the free republic across the Atlantic. The American Revolution powerfully influenced the aspirations of the Risorgimento. Espousing the rights of man, the United States served as a model for a republic of Italy. During the struggle for unification, hundreds of exiles took refuge in America. While contact with antebellum realities, particularly slavery, chilled the ardor of some, most appear to have been confirmed in their enthusiasm for the American republic. The Civil War and the emancipation of blacks removed the remaining doubts of those like Federico Garlando who believed that the dreamed-of utopia had been realized in the New World.[1]

Indeed, the idea of a *nuovo mondo* deeply imbedded in the Italian imagination was not easily scotched. Not only were intellectuals affected by its mythic power. Many peasants

---

I wish to acknowledge the assistance of Linda Watson in the preparation of this essay.

and workers were moved to emigrate by these images of *la terra promessa* and *Cuccagna.*[2] This utopian vision found expression in schemes for establishing agricultural colonies. As late as 1890, such a colony in the Middle West "where immense lands almost free lie fallow" was proposed in the socialist *Cuore e Critica.*[3] Although this venture was stillborn, increasing numbers of immigrants pursued their own notion of the promised land; however, they were seeking work in industrializing America rather than homesteads. Their United States was radically different from either the ideal republic of the *litterati* or the Cockaigne of the *contadini.* From their experiences would be fashioned new images which would drastically alter the view of America from Italy.

A sharply critical portrait of the United States emerged from the writings of the Italian left from the 1880s on. Within a few years, they had transmuted the term "free country" to an ironic usage suggesting the contradiction and hypocrisy between the professed ideals of the republic and the realities of capitalism. At the turn of the century, Napoleone Colajanni, sociologist and reformer, wrote:

> I, who have had the same enthusiasm for American institutions, confess that to strengthen my republican faith, which remains unshakeable, I would not today, as I would have some twenty years ago, seek examples and contrasts in the United States to condemn the monarchies in Europe... The times of Washington, Franklin, Madison, Jefferson, etc., have faded; to the enthusiasm of Tocqueville and Laboulaye have succeeded the bitter criticisms of Henry George, James Bryce, and a hundred others.[4]

Among the hundred others were those of Colajanni's countrymen who, during the recurring periods of repression, sought political exile in the United States. A new breed of radicals, anarchists and socialists, for whom a united Italy, even a republic, was not the end, they aspired to the overthrow of capitalism and the establishment of the worker's commonwealth. Viewing American democracy through various ideological lenses, they elaborated a wide-ranging critique of its institutions, social conditions, and pretensions which was disseminated among the growing immigrant population and the working classes of Italy.[5]

The failed insurrections of the seventies resulted in the dispersion of the internationalists in Europe and the Americas. By 1885, they had formed the *gruppo communista an-*

archico Carlo Cafiero in New York City, and their correspondence began to appear regularly in Italy. A letter in *Il Paria* of Ancona bearing the title "*Le delizie della repubblica... Americana*", described the concentration of wealth and poverty in this country "where the King is elected for four years." Other articles on child labor and political corruption appeared under the caption, "Oh! Le repubbliche!"[6]

The execution of the Chicago anarchists in 1887 was seized upon by Italian radicals as exposing the myth of America as a land of liberty. They participated in the protests which swept the European continent. *Il processo degli anarchici di Chicago* was published that same year in Italy.[7] It was said – with some exaggeration – that peasants and artisans throughout Italy "speak the names of Parsons, Spies, Lingg, Fisher, and Engel with even more admiration than our fathers of Young Italy gave to the name of Mazzini or Garibaldi." On November 11, the date of the executions, Peter Kropotkin observed that there was not a city in Italy worth naming "where the bloody anniversary was not commemorated by enthusiastic crowds of workers."[8] From 1890, *Primo Maggio*, which recalled the Haymarket tragedy, was celebrated as an affirmation of international working-class solidarity. In the "Little Italies" of the United States, the observance of *la pasqua dei lavoratori* (the Easter of the workers) took on a quasi-religious quality with the martyrs of Chicago as Christlike figures. This annual ritual reinforced the radicals' conviction that the bourgeois republic was capable of as fierce repression as the worst European tyranny.[9]

L'*Anarchico*, the first radical Italian-American publication, cited the Haymarket case as evidence that justice could not be obtained under bourgeois laws:

> Here, *in the land of liberty*, as ironically we hear repeated everyday by the Yankees, we see seven individuals condemned to death, guilty of having freely expressed their opinion. Here, where all the idiots think they are in the most free and democratic country in the world, we see the autocracy of the dollar reigns over everything.[10]

Noting the repressive measures taken against anarchists, the publication observed that for political exiles, coming to the United States was "like changing the sheets but not the bed." Flaunting the banner of violent social revolution, l'*Anarchico* defiantly proclaimed: "Viva the *free land* cry the Yankees; down with the Land of servility, of hypocrisy and of the God Dollar, cry we Anarchists."[11] Circulating widely in Italy, that its damning view of America was embraced by some was revealed in a letter from the *gruppo degli studi sociali* of Casale Monferrato:

> We of this part of the old world, still saturated with ancient superstitions, prejudices and injustices, which always keep humanity enslaved, we who believed ourselves to be the only oppressed, exploited and vexed; we see that even in this new world in which it appeared that the most ample liberty was reserved to the worker, the thinker, the writer, the purest absolutism, arrogance and cynicism of the capitalist bourgeoisie is in full vigor. We see that you have nothing to envy of this old Europe... We have a common enemy to combat, the bourgeois hydra of the hundred heads.[12]

The exploitation of the Italian immigrants, particularly the abuses to which they were subjected by the *padroni*, became a major theme of the radical indictment of America. Articles such as "Italiani a Nuova York" in *La Questione Sociale* of Florence told of their plight: "You in Europe cannot in truth have an idea of the extraordinary number of brokers, speculators, and agents who follow the worker here to take the shirt off his back and the bread out of his mouth."[13] The writer described a few of "the thousands of ways in which the capitalists milk the worker of his meager earnings". The 1890s was a decade of intense persecution of the Italians, who were victims of lynchings, race riots, mass arrests and expulsions. *La caccia agl'italiani* of Aigues-Mortes had its reprise in New Orleans, Altoona, Cripple Creek, and a score of other places. In *Il Grido degli Oppressi* of New York, Francesco Saverio Merlino, a leading light of the Italian left, exposed this maltreatment: "Each day, thousands upon thousands of Italian workers are assassinated by brutal contractors, condemned to work as forced labor, robbed of their pay."[14] Articles by Merlino describing these outrages appeared in American and Italian publications.[15] An article on the squalor of the Italian quarter of Mulberry Street which he inspired appeared first in the *New York Herald* and then was reprinted in the *Critica Sociale* of Milan under the title "Vergogne Italiane in America" (Italian Shame in America), with a comment that the abject slavery in which the immigrants lived and worked in America should serve as a warning to those considering emigration.[16]

Pietro Gori, who succeeded Merlino as the apostle of anarchism among the Italians in the United States, founded *La Questione Sociale* in Paterson and gave hundreds of lectures on a nationwide tour. Poet and playwright, Gori wrote *Senza Patria*, a melodrama about a family forced to emigrate because of poverty and injustice. The play opens with the reading of a letter from an immigrant son:

> America is not the country of Cockaigne. One needs to work like a beast of burden. It is a republic, that's true; but there is who is above and who is beneath, who commands and who obeys; who eats without working and who works without eating or almost; presidents, cops, tax-collectors, gallows and electric chairs, as or perhaps worse than in civil Europe.[17]

Yet he concludes by urging his family to emigrate: "It is not a patria which we find in America but it is a little more bread." First performed in San Francisco, *Senza Patria* became a standard in the repertoire of the radical theatre. While the warnings of Merlino and Gori did not deter the millions who came in America, they may have alerted some to the snares and delusions awaiting them.

The nineties were years of economic crisis and social upheaval in both Italy and the United States. Repression following the *Fasci Siciliani* and the *Fatti del Maggio* resulted in the exodus of anarchists and socialists to the four corners of the earth. Major figures such as Errico Malatesta, Giacinto Menotti Serrati, Dino Rondani, Luigi Galleani, to name a few, came to North America. Meanwhile, thousands of quarry workers from Tuscany, weavers from Piedmont, peasants from Reggio-Emilia, and artisans from Sicily, among others who had participated in the uprisings, arrived. From their ranks were formed the cadres of the Italian radical movements in the United States. In the years which followed, scores of newspapers of a socialist or anarchist persuasion were published, and in their pages the left critique of America was elaborated and intensified.[18]

For the anarchists, both organizational and anti-organizational, all of the authoritarian institutions of state, church, and private property had to be destroyed to make way for freedom. Reacting to the bloody suppression of strikes, *La Questione Sociale* called for revenge against the "bourgeois assassins". Acting upon this exhortation, Gaetano Bresci, a silk worker from Paterson, returned to Italy and shot King Umberto I. The concerted wrath of the Italian and American authorities descended upon the presumed center of anarchist conspiracy. Paterson was the scene of indiscriminate police raids, searches, and arrests. Quoting the Declaration of Independence, *La Questione Sociale* protested these violations of constitutional rights.[19] But it was the assassination of President William McKinley by an alleged anarchist in 1901 which unleashed the full fury of reaction against the Italian radicals.

Giuseppe Ciancabilla, an extreme anti-organizational anarchist, in *L'Aurora* of Spring Valley, Illinois, observing that being a king or president had its occupational hazards, greeted the event with the headline "La Disgrazia del Signor William McKinley" (The Misfortune of, etc.).[20] Speculating on the motives of the assassin, Ciancabilla came up with a goodly dozen, including the grievances of millions of workers exploited, starved, and beaten by "the capitalist imperialist friends of McKinley." Forced to move to Chicago by mob violence, he continued his unabashed propaganda in *La Protesta Umana*. Commenting on the anti-anarchist bill before Congress, Ciancabilla declared that it surpassed anything "the inquisitorial genius of old Europe had been able to conceive." While it was natural for the bourgeoisie to defend itself, he was nauseated by "the hypocrisy of this country where liberty is strangled in the name of liberty, in which not even the democratic and socialist press protests such measures and still they praise this land of Washington as the most free on earth."[21]

Ciancabilla's excoriation of the American republic was surpassed only by Luigi Galleani, the dominant personality among the anti-organizational anarchists. For almost two decades in his *Cronaca Sovversiva*, he denounced, ridiculed, and impaled the United States with his mordant rhetoric for its crimes against humanity. As did other critics, he contrasted the reality of America with its professed ideals, quoting from the Declaration of Independence and the Bill of Rights:

> Repudiating its ideal of human fraternity, the new country has denied equal rights under the Constitution to Negroes; slammed

> the door shut in the face of the pariahs of the Far East; blessed the most ignoble of all aristocracies, that of fraud and money; subjected science and progress to the Bible; made bordellos of its courts; raised the gallows for human rights...[22]

If the celebration of the Fourth of July should recall the nation to its founding principles, Theodore Roosevelt would be condemned to infamy and the "fat, cossack, and pious republic would be a remote and dark memory."

Anarchists such as Ciancabilla and Galleani, who rejected all forms of authority and believed in absolute liberty for the individual, tested the limits of freedom in the United States and found the constraints maddening. But other Italian radicals also discovered Americans' narrow tolerance of ideas which challenged the existing order. Angiolina Algeri writing from Boston, Pennsylvania, expressed her anger at the denial of civil liberties to those who advocated the rights of workers:

> From the most ignorant to the most cultivated clown one hears nothing but the acclaiming of the liberty of this much praised land, but if you ask them what they mean by "Free Country", they do not know what to answer. If you ask them is it liberty to prohibit with police violence the peaceful speech of our comrade Emma Goldman, they tell you that she has no right to speak because she is an anarchist... This land is free to the point of denying postal privileges and thus condemning to a sure death, any newspaper which seeks to illuminate the poor human beast of burden and to instill in him a little consciousness of his rights.[23]

The suppression of Italian radical newspapers was part of an anti-anarchist campaign launched by President Theodore Roosevelt in 1908. The killing of a priest in Denver, an attack on the Chicago chief of police, and a bombing in Union Square, triggered a "Red Scare." Roosevelt ordered an investigation of anarchism, the barring of anarchist publications from the mails, and the deportation of alien anarchists.[24] *La Questione Sociale* fell under this interdict. The police broke up a protest meeting in Paterson and prohibited future meetings. When told this action was unconstitutional, the mayor replied: "Constitution or no constitution, the anarchists must not speak." In a manifesto, *Il Gruppo La Questione Sociale* lamented that the country "which is proud of the gigantic monument which rises at the mouth of the Hudson, on the one hand guarantees the liberty to write our thoughts, while on the other it strangles our voice and breaks our pen. Under the bronze skin of the Statue of Liberty is hidden, insidious and wicked, St. Ignatius Loyola."[25]

The author of the manifesto was probably Ludovico Caminita, the editor of *La Questione Sociale*, who in a pamphlet entitled *Free Country!* also exploited the symbolism of the Statue of Liberty:

> Before that monument the emigrant forgets the distant patria and with it the sorrows experienced; he opens his heart to the sweetest hopes and he is impatient to touch and kiss the promised land... Oh, the hard reality of things! What bitter disillusionment future experience brings to the ingenuous immigrant! The Declaration of Independence and the first and fourteenth amendments to the Constitution proclaim liberty, but they are pieces of paper. In reality of daily life, the United States are the very antithesis of liberty and equality. America is more of a country of slavery than Italy, France, Germany, and perhaps, of Russia herself.[26]

The attack on the radical press evoked an angry response from the Italian socialists as well. *Il Proletario* complained that when a newspaper criticized the liberty of the *padroni* to exploit the workers, the liberty of government to shoot workers, the liberty of politicians to cheat workers, then the liberty of the impudent publication was suppressed.[27]

In a long article, "La Libertà in America", *Il Proletario* commented that the republic had decided to follow in the footsteps of Holy Russia. New York City Police Commissioner Theodore A. Bingham's proposal to establish a secret service to ferret out blackhanders and anarchists was denounced as a violation of the Constitution. Reprinting the text of the Declaration of Independence, it observed that its authors would rebuke the modern day republic "for the spectacle of a group of do-nothings and plunderers who enjoy the wealth of the nation while the enormous majority works, sweats, and suffers and fails to secure from its labor its daily bread."

> They [the Founding Fathers] reproach the Republic for having suppressed freedom of speech and the press, freedom of thought and religion, and freedom of assembly... In the face of this state of perversion of the government and its rapid degeneration toward despotism, they proclaim the right of the people to overthrow the government and to provide for a new order where

> tyranny is not possible. Given this provocation to civil war, the President is advised first to recover and destroy by fire this subversive declaration and second to eliminate from History the fifty-five revolutionaries who signed it.[28]

Returning to the subject some years later, *Il Proletario* declared that "the myth of liberty and of the American conscience is a bluff, a fraud, and a lie." But it was the American people themselves rather than the capitalists who were responsible for this state of affairs. They were characterized as idiots and eunuchs who allowed themselves to be governed by pirates and highwaymen. The deaths of thousands of workers in labor conflicts were soon forgotten while the proletarian throng went to church and thanked God for belonging to the most free and elect country in the world. "Is this a Republic? Is this a civil people?" Only in the Industrial Workers of the World was there life, youth, and energy; all the rest was an immense cemetery of rotting moral corpses.[29] Dr. Nicola Barbato, a leader of the *Fasci Siciliani* in exile, also directed a biting diatribe at the American people for its cowardliness and passivity:

> There is no form of violence on the part of the authorities which they do not submit to passively; one day an anarchist newspaper is suppressed; another day the entry of an Italian socialist newspaper is prohibited; then the most elementary rights of the workers are denied and it is declared a crime to boycott goods, until finally the reactionary instinct even assumes the defense of czarism. While a shopkeeper education makes this people practical and adapted more than we Europeans for the daily struggle for existence, it is opposed to the development of a civic conscience. The more evolved worker, he of the famous trade union, has only one dream, to become a millionaire with the aid of God and the robust fiber which he believes is his as a member of the greatest race in the world.[30]

One senses that these bitter denunciations stemmed from a deep sense of impotence and alienation. Confronted with an obdurate American conservatism, oftentimes all the Italian radicals could do was rant and rave. Through their writings of these decades there runs the red stripe of class warfare. For anarchist and socialist alike, strikes were the battleground between capitalists and proletariat. These struggles which posed a challenge to power and profits revealed the true nature of the American republic. Homestead, Latimer, Goldfield, McKees Rock, Lawrence, Paterson,

Ludlow, and scores of other strikes were battles in the class war, and among the participants and victims were often Italians. As *Il Proletario* put it, "the spilling of proletarian blood is the story of triumphant American capitalism."[31] Gunmen, state militias, and federal troops were called in to break strikes, and workers were shot, clubbed, and jailed. The result was liberticide. Describing the miners' strike in Colorado, Suprema Magnanai Tedeschi observed that the Constitution had been trampled, martial law declared, *habeas corpus* suspended, mass arrests without warrants made, newspapers suppressed, and labor leaders expelled. "We are in the land of capitalism oligarchy," she declared, "democracy has failed exactly where we expected its complete triumph."[32] The frequent use of injunctions not only denied workers the fundamental right to strike, but a person also could be prohibited from walking down a street, from talking with certain persons, from carrying a camera, from frequenting certain places. Again this state of affairs was compared to the despotism of Holy Russia, but the czarist tyrants did not pretend to govern in the name of liberty and democracy. C.F. Ciampa concluded that the form of government, whether monarchy, republic or democracy, did not matter; for the worker bourgeois regimes were all the same. Liberty for the worker in the United States was the "liberty to die of hunger."[33]

Anticlericalism, a pervasive theme of the Italian left, not only expressed a philosophical atheism, but also drew upon an historic antipathy toward the Church and her priests. For Italian radicals, the liberation of the workers from the influence of the clergy was an essential task of the revolutionary movement.[34] From *L'Anarchico* on, the subversive publications maintained a running attack upon priests, depicting them as gross, venal, and lecherous. For the freethinkers, the much vaunted separation of church and state in the United States proved to be a delusion. Americans, including workers, they discovered, were on the whole a pious, churchgoing people, and this was particularly true of Irish Catholics, who considered the scurrilous treatment of the clergy blasphemous. Nor was militant atheism acceptable. Lorenzo Casas described this paradox:

> Of all the countries of the world, the Republic of the United States is without doubt the nation which offers the greatest re-

ligious freedom, on the condition though of professing some religion; but if you are an atheist religious freedom does not exist for you.[35]

He observed that the religion of Jesus was even more prosperous in the republic than in Catholic Spain. In exercising freedom of speech and press, the Italians soon discovered that attacks upon priests and the Church were not tolerated. Those who heckled street-corner evangelists or disrupted religious processions were likely to be roughly handled by the police and arrested. Carlo Tresca's *La Plebe* of Pittsburgh was denied second-class postal privileges and Tresca himself was jailed for libel for having accused a cleric of sexual misconduct. *La Parola dei Socialisti* of Chicago protested: "We are nauseated by this much trumpeted liberty which raises the Irish priests to the dignity of grand inquisitors against the heretics...".[36]

L'Asino, a socialist publication of Rome which included salacious accounts of priestly seductions with lurid illustrations, circulated widely among the immigrants, much to the dismay of the Catholic hierarchy. Following the Denver shooting of a priest, in response to protests of the papal nuncio, *L'Asino* was denied entry into the country as a pornographic publication. A New York edition was promptly issued, and its readers were urged to support the journal "in these dark moments for the freedom of the press and speech."[37] American socialism tinged with evangelical Protestantism shied away from such overt and vulgar attacks upon men of the cloth. Italian radicals were disgusted by such a mix of religion and revolutionary politics, and their virulent anti-clericalism tended to isolate them from the American left.[38]

In his study, *European Socialists and the American Promised Land*, R. Laurence Moore noted the failure of Marxists to protest the wrongs being done to blacks.[39] To the contrary, whether it was because Italians were also regarded as an inferior race and subject to mob violence, or because racial injustice presented a conspicuous gap in the moral armor of the republic, Italian radicals consistently expressed horror at the barbaric treatment of blacks. Their publications reported lynchings in lurid details. Anarchists such as Galleani mocked the self-righteousness of Americans who expressed indignation at the persecution of the Jews in

Russia while they "denied blacks work in their factories, justice in their courts, protection in their laws, and pity in their hearts."[40] The pretext of the protection of the virtue of white women for racial atrocities was not given much credence. In an insightful reflection on the role of sexuality in American race relations, one writer commented:

> Who do they think they are as a race, these arrogant whites? From where do they think they come? The blacks are at least a race, but the whites... how many of them are bastards? How much mixing is their "pure" blood? And how many kisses have their women asked for from the strong and virile black servants? as have they, the white males, desired to enjoy the warm pleasures of the black women of the sensual lips and sinuous bodily movements? But the white knights care little for the honor and decency of the black women, whom they use and abuse as they please. For these, race hatred is a national duty.[41]

Noting that employers exploited racial hatreds to pit workers against each other, he concluded that the proletariat's motto should be: "Not race struggle but class struggle."

Following World War I, a period of heightened racial violence, the Italian radicals gave increased attention to the plight of blacks. *Cronaca Sovversiva* observed that prejudice and the Jim Crow system made of the Emancipation Proclamation a scrap of paper and not only in the South, since racial bigotry was nationwide. The paper contrasted Wilsonian rhetoric with this brutal fact:

> In the year 1918, which marked the victory of civilization democracy over barbarism, in the United States of America, which of civilization and democracy is the precursor and crusader... two hundred and twenty-four citizens were lynched![42]

Guardia Rossa, which included several articles about lynchings, observed that while the war had been fought to liberate oppressed peoples, in the United States "the people of Ethiopia are still flogged like the slaves of the ancient Roman empire."[43] These writings are unusual for their empathy with blacks and their forthright rejection of racism. One would like to know to what extent such views extended beyond the radical leadership to the ranks of the Italian workers.

As agitators, labor organizers, and journalists, the immigrant revolutionaries were the targets of repression which denied them civil liberties and swept them into jails. Given the frequency of such cases, an almost constant agitation was carried on to rescue comrades from "bourgeois justice". Defense committees were organized, meetings held, funds raised. Nor were these efforts restricted to Italian radicals. The fates of Moyer, Haywood, and Pettybone of the Western Federation of Miners, of the McNamara brothers, of the Russian revolutionary Janoff Pouren, among others, were closely followed in the subversive press, and appeals made to save them from capitalist vengeance.[44] The threat to deport Mexican revolutionaries elicited this protest from *Il Proletario:*

> Even on this occasion the Government of the United States has forgotten the principles of Washington and Jefferson and the hospitality due political refugees; it has denied the right of asylum and it has disowned the tradition of this country to help the victims of tyranny.[45]

But it was on behalf of its own political prisoners that the Italian left mobilized all its forces. When an Italian woman was killed during the Lawrence strike in 1912, two of the strike leaders, Joseph Ettor and Arturo Giovannitti, were arrested as accomplices. Their trial evoked a groundswell of protest from the radical parties of the United States and Europe. The Italians, especially the syndicalists and their organ, *Il Proletario*, waged a vigorous campaign to liberate the "hostages of the battle of Lawrence." An Italian Defense Committee called for simultaneous protests throughout the country and a general strike if necessary.[46] Extending the campaign to Italy, manifestos sent demanding freedom for Ettor and Giovannitti were affixed to walls. A committee was formed in Ripabottoni (Campobasso), Giovannitti's *paese*, to rally nationwide support. Its manifesto declared that the millionaires of the American republic were seeking to avenge their defeat in the Lawrence strike which denied them the power "to oppress the poor starving workers." Protest meetings, the circulation of petitions, the reporting of trial proceedings, a debate in the Chamber of Deputies, all served to make this a *cause célèbre* in Italy.[47] The popular Florentine socialist poet, Idalberto Targioni, wrote a long poem on the case, "Ettor e Giovannitti e l'Emigrazione transoceanica," itself a significant document of the transformation of the Italian view of America.[48] Targioni's verses describe the hard life of workers in the Lawrence mills, the strike, the murder of Anna Lo Pizzo, the trial and liberation of Ettor and Giovannitti. He scoffed at those who claimed that this proved the fairness of bourgeois justice; rather it was fear of the aroused working class which secured their freedom. As *Il Riscatto* of Messina put it, "the international proletariat had snatched the young prey from the claws of the American bourgeoisie."[49]

The arrest of Carlo Tresca on murder charges during the Mesabi miners' strike of 1916 triggered an analogous protest movement. For months on end the case commanded the front pages of *L'Avvenire* (Tresca's journal), *Il Proletario*, and other newspapers. Once again rallies were held, petitions collected, subscriptions initiated. Despite the war, the left in Italy also mounted a massive agitation pro Tresca. As Adriana Dada reports:

> In the months between the end of August and December 1916 (the date when Tresca was released), each day in some part of Italy, socialists, syndicalists, anarchists, met to protest against the United States and for the liberation of Carlo Tresca.[50]

A publication of the Bergamo Chamber of Labor, "Per la liberazione di Carlo Tresca," described the working conditions in the mines which resulted in the strike and attributed the killing to the "gunmen" ("a characteristic institution of the republic of the dollar") employed by the "Steel Trust."[51] Several caricatures by Giuseppe Scalarini regarding the case appeared in *Avanti!*, the organ of the Italian Socialist Party.[52] In one of them, Tresca was depicted as caught in the web of a giant spider. A booklet, *Per Carlo Tresca. Un episodio della Lotta di classe in America... Solidarietà internazionale*, by Arturo Caroti circulated widely.[53] Caroti, a socialist deputy and former labor organizer in the United States, provided a detailed account of the mining industry of Minnesota, the Steel Trust, the strike, and Tresca's arrest. He observed that the class struggle in America was developing much more brutally and ferociously than in Italy because of the contradiction between the myth of democracy and the reality of industrial slavery. The democracy which had existed in the Unites States was dead and buried; a plutocracy now ruled. Although Tresca was also freed, his case, like that of Ettor and Giovannitti, was not viewed as a vindication of the American legal system. Rather in both instances the champions of the workers were seen as having been rescued by the international proletariat.

Moreover, both served to focus attention on exploitation of labor, the class struggle, and government repression in America.

The satisfaction of the left in Tresca's liberation was to be short-lived. Writing in late 1916, Giuseppe Cannata, a theorist of syndicalism, prophesied a coming "reign of terror":

> The capitalist reaction like an inexorable wave advances across America; it overturns and breaks in its fury upon the free men who oppose its march; it hurls itself with ferocious anger against the exponents of militant unionism because it senses in them its major danger.[54]

With the entry of the United States into the war a few months later, the wave did break in all its fury on dissidents of every stripe. Under the banner of the "One Hundred Per Cent Americanism", public authorities and vigilantes hunted out everything and everyone which smacked of disloyalty. Anarchists, socialists, Wobblies were lynched, beaten, jailed and deported. Among them were the most militant of the Italian radicals. *Il Proletario* took note: "The capitalism of this bestarred republic, behind the mask of patriotism, has begun to put into practice the systematic lynching of all who directly or indirectly obstruct its work of exploitation..."[55] Through assemblies and publications, the subversives protested, denounced, and defied their persecutors, but to no avail. Yet they could taunt the patriots of being themselves subverters of democratic ideals:

> Are we or are we not in free America? Unfortunately the word "Liberty" has become a myth. America has been dishonored. The statue of Liberty which rises proudly in the bay of New York and announces to the old world the sunset of the barbarous and reactionary era, is about to become the symbol of despotism and injustice... Having come to America, alleged land of liberty and bread, we have instead encountered a crowd of greedy speculators, of spies and corrupt judges capable of violating all the rights and guarantees of the Constitution.[56]

The "Red Scare" which followed the war intensified the crusade against alleged "Bolsheviks". Systematic persecution as well as internal conflicts reduced the radical movements, including the Italian, to shambles. However, the intransigents rallied and responded with revolutionary rhetoric and bombs. Galleani warned that while the best-known anarchists might be deported, others would remain to prepare for the coming social revolution with knife and dynamite.[57] Bombings in the spring of 1919, on the eve of Galleani's own deportation, appeared to fulfill his prediction. His followers, Roberto Elia and Andrea Salsedo, bade him farewell in their journal *Domani:*

> The republic of lynching can now live tranquilly! It has one enemy less... We will continue our work here defying as always the rags and arrogance of the *padroni* of this delicious *free country* later we will join you, perhaps...[58]

In *Domani* and then *L'Ordine,* they continued their attacks upon "Free America...The Slaughterhouse of all Liberties."[59] The war had torn the veil of hypocrisy which had covered the American "savages of the blue eyes," unleashing a brutal repression which equaled that of the Holy Inquisition. Elia was deported in August 1920, but Salsedo either jumped or was pushed to his death from a Park Row building while in the custody of the Department of Justice.

The United States had not heard the last from Galleani. Resuming publication of *Cronaca Sovversiva* in Turin, he sent several thousand copies to American subscribers under the masthead, *A Stormo!* When news of Salsedo's death reached Galleani, he raged against the United States:

> This monstrous colossus, this republic of the heart of anthracite, with the forehead of ice, with the goiterous throat; this statue of cretinism... whose hands are armed with a whip, from whose lips are suspended a knife and a revolver...[60]

Galleani's colossus bore no resemblance to Bartoldi's. *Cronaca* also reported under the rubric, "Flowers of Democratic Liberty," on the continuous reaction in the United States, the denial of civil liberties, the violent suppression of strikes, the arbitrary arrests and detentions, the deportations. Thus had Wilson's war made the world "safe for democracy."[61]

Meanwhile, Antonio Presi, editor of *Il Proletario,* sent an appeal to all the anarchist and socialist newspapers in Italy to agitate for the release of the political prisoners of America:

> Here we live completely under a reign of terror, the reaction against the vanguard of the proletariat has surpassed all precedent. Deportations, lynchings, are the order of the day as are arrests en masse.[62]

Presi went on to say that those in prison or on Ellis Island awaiting deportation were immigrant workers who had "come from Europe in search of bread somewhat less bitter and liberty less restrictive, but alas, what illusion, what a foolish thought for a European worker!" Citing the crimes of American capitalism from the execution of the Haymarket anarchists on, Presi declared that he did not hate the American people, but did "hate profoundly the hypocrisy of American capitalism which has the impudence to proclaim itself the most democratic and humane in the world."

In May 1920, Tresca published an issue of *Guardia Rossa* devoted to "The White Terror in America" which reprinted accounts of the lynching of blacks, police brutality toward strikers, denials of freedoms of speech and assembly, etc. Reflecting on this record of injustice and inhumanity, Tresca confessed his profound disillusionment with the United States:

> When the ship which transported us to America passed before the historic, colossal Statue of Liberty there was a joyous rush to the side; all eyes were fixed on that torch of light, seeking to penetrate the breast of that woman, symbolizing the most dear of human aspirations "La Libertà," to see if there was a heart within which beat for all of the political refugees, for all of the slaves of capital, for the disinherited of the world.[63]

And Tresca too dared to hope that in this bourgeois democracy he would find a greater degree of justice and freedom; but after sixteen years,

> Now I am disillusioned... Perhaps I will pass again, still a pilgrim of the faith, before that statue. Like so many of my comrades — perhaps I will be DEPORTED before these vibrant pages will be read by the Italian workers who suffer, aspire, struggle. Oh! that torch will no longer shine the light it did!
>
> Now I am disillusioned. The land of Jefferson and of Lincoln has but chains, prisons and torture for whosoever thinks, feels, aspires for a tomorrow of justice, of fraternity, of liberty. I have combatted: I have had my wrists bound by your handcuffs; I have felt on my shoulders the weight of your clubs; I have tested the severity of your prisons and your jailers. O bourgeois republic! Like so many I came to love you. And now...

For Bartolomeo Vanzetti and Nicola Sacco, America proved a disillusionment as well. Arriving at age twenty, "ignorant of life and somewhat of a dreamer," Vanzetti had encountered here "all the brutalities of life, all the injustice, the corruption in which humanity struggles tragically." Sacco testified that he "was crazy to come to this country because I was liked a free country," but he discovered "there was all the difference, because...I could live free (in Italy) just as well."[64] For Sacco and Vanzetti, their American calvary ended with their execution on August 23, 1927. The impact of their deaths upon the Italian radical movement and indeed upon radical movements of the world rivaled that of the hanging of the Chicago anarchists four decades earlier. The electrocution of Sacco and Vanzetti fulfilled the radicals' worst nightmare and confirmed their hatred of America as a ruthless capitalist society which was the antithesis of a free country.

Within the span of a half century, the view of the United States from the Italian left had shifted dramatically from the very model of republicanism to the epitome of the evils of capitalism. The experiences of Italian radicals in America played a crucial influence in bringing about this change among their comrades in Italy as well as among many of the immigrants. Their radical critique reached an extensive audience through the spoken as well as written word. Powerful orators such as Galleani and Tresca addressed tens of thousands while their writings reached hundreds of thousands. In evaluating the radical critique, one must assuredly take into account the ideological predispositions of these disciples of Bakunin and Marx. Yet one suspects that the harsh realities to which they were reacting were all too true. Through their writings we hear voices of anger and anguish from the subterranean brutalities of industrializing America. This perspective provides a salutary corrective to the current tendency to write a sanitized history of immigrants in terms of facile patterns of adjustment without the blood, the sweat, and the tears.

One might find surprising the frequent citation of American crucial texts (much more than of Marxist or Bakunist sources) to indict the "bourgeois republic." Yet to quote the Declaration of Independence or the Constitution was, so to speak, to condemn the Americans out of their own mouths. But I believe the Italian radicals were not simply citing these documents as a rhetorical ploy; rather they were expressing genuine disillusionment. Like other immigrants they wanted to believe that America offered a real alternative to old Europe. When they discovered it was no different or even worse, they reacted, as Tresca suggests, like disappointed lovers. In the radical critique, the Statue of Liberty served as the icon of the hopes and aspirations of the immigrants to which was juxtaposed the cruel truth of their lives as workers. In the centennial year of the Statue of Liberty much was made of it as the symbol of freedom and opportunity; little was said of promises betrayed and dreams unfulfilled. Among other things, the critique by the Italian radicals serves as a welcome *amaro* to counter the cloying sentimentality of a Reaganesque version of immigration history.

Notes

1. Alexander DeConde, *Half Bitter, Half Sweet: An Excursion into Italian-American History* (New York, 1971), 1-17, 36-58; Howard R. Marraro, *American Opinion on the Unification of Italy, 1846-1861* (New York, 1932), 165-185; Joanne Pellegrino, "An Effective School of Patriotism", in Francesco Cordasco (ed.), *Studies in Italian American Social History*, (Towata, NJ, 1975), 84-104; Andrew J. Torrielli, *Italian Opinion on America as Revealed by Italian Travelers, 1850-1900* (Cambridge, MA, 1941), 32, 72-108. Giuseppe Mazzini who had earlier expressed reservations about the American republic was convinced by the outcome of the Civil War and the abolition of slavery that the United States had become a "Nation-Guide" destined to lead the progressive forces in the world. Joseph Rossi, *The Image of America in Mazzini's Writings* (Madison, Wis., 1954), 150-151.

2. Emilio Franzina has suggestively explored the sources of such images in emigrant letters, popular literature and folk culture, "Le culture dell'emigrazione. Immagini di 'nuovo mondo' in Italia e forme di socializzazione dei lavoratori italiani all'estero", in *La Cultura operaia nelle società industrializzate* (Milan, 1985), 279-338.

3. Grazia Dore, *La democrazia italiana e l'emigrazione in America* (Brescia, 1964), 183-185. As G. Baribotti explained the scheme, if "many socialists of good will who have a little money should emigrate with a good number of hardworking laborers associating themselves in a socialistic form of production and the establishment of basic industries, they could create a successful center frow which the idea would radiate to the old world".

4. *Latini ed Anglo-sassoni* (Rome, 1906). Quoted by Torrielli, *Italian Opinion*,108.

5. Arnaldo Testi, "L'immagine degli Stati Uniti nella stampa socialista italiana (1886-1914)", in Giorgio Spini, et al., *Italia e America dal Settecento all'Età dell'Imperialismo* (Marsiglio Editori, 1976), 313-348. A thor-

ough study based on the socialist press in Italy which was very helpful in the preparation of this paper.

6. *Il Paria* (Ancona), July 26, 1885; August 17, 30, 1885.

7. *L'Anarchico* (New York), February 1, 1888. *Il Paria* commented that the American millionaires who thought they could repress the worker's movement by killing a few individuals were sowing dragon's teeth. December 5, 1886.

8. The above quotes are from Paul Avrich, *The Haymarket Tragedy* (Princeton, NJ, 1984), 354, 409, 412.

9. Andrea Panaccione (ed.), *Sappi che oggi è la tua festa...per la storia del* 1° maggio (Venice, 1986), 73-126.

10. April 14, 1888.

11. May 12, 1888.

12. May 12, 1888.

13. August 26, 1888.

14. June 5, 1892.

15. See, for example, "Italian immigrants and their Enslavement," *Forum*, 15 (April 1893), 183-190, and "La colonia Italiana di New York," *Tribuna dell'Operaio* (Firenze-Prato), July 9, 1892.

16. Ida M. Van Etten, *Vergogne Italiane in America*, trans. Umano (Milan 1893).

17. Pietro Gori, *Senza Patria* (Buenos Aires, 1899). This edition was dedicated "Ai Lavoratori Italiani d'America."

18. Rudolph J. Vecoli, "The Italian Immigrants in the United States Labor Movement from 1880 to 1929," in B. Bezza (ed.), *Gli Italiani fuori d'Italia. Gli Emigrati Italiani nei movimenti operai dei paesi d'adozione 1880-1940* (Milan, 1983), 257-306.

19. George W. Carey, "The Vessel, the Deed, and the Idea: Anarchists in Paterson, 1895-1908," *Antipode*, 10-11 (1979), 46-58; and "*La Questione Sociale, an Anarchist Newspaper in Paterson, N.J. (1895-1908)*," in Lydio F. Tomasi (ed.), *Italian Americans: New Perspectives in Italian Immigration and Ethnicity* (New York, 1985), 289-298.; A.J. Scopino Jr., "Class Consciousness and Italian American Anarchism, *La Questione Sociale*, 1895-1902," (unpublished paper).

20. September 14, 1901

21. *La Protesta Umana*, I (March 1902), 61; (December 1902), 348-349.

22. "4 Luglio 1776," *Cronaca Sovversiva*, July 6, 1907, reprinted in the collected essays of Galleani, *Aneliti e Singulti* (Newark, N.J., n.d.), 23-26.

23. "Lettera dagli Stati Uniti," *Il Pensiero* (Rome, VII (December 1909), 347-348.

24. *New York Times*, March, April 1908, passim. In his message to Congress, Roosevelt declared: "The anarchist is the enemy of humanity, the enemy of all mankind, and his is a deeper degree of criminality than any other. No immigrant is allowed to come to our shores if he is an anarchist and no paper published here or abroad should be permitted circulation in this country if it propagates anarchist crimes." April 10, 1908. See also Robert Goldstein, "The Anarchist Scare of 1908, a Sign of Tensions in the Progressive Era," *American Studies*, XV (1974), 55-78.

25. *Ai Compagni, ai Simpatizzanti e agli Amici della "Questione Sociale"*, (March 25, 1908); *Ai Compagni*. Both in Nettlau Archive, U.S. J-Italianen, International Institute of Social History, Amsterdam.

26. *Free Country!* (n.p., 1908?). The text is in Italian.

27. *Il Proletario*, November 13, 1908. Research in *Il Proletario* was greatly facilitated by the abstracts of this publication prepared by Mario De Ciampis, one-time editor of the newspaper. "History of *Il Proletario*", Pasquale Mario De Ciampis Papers, Immigration History Research Center, University of Minnesota.

28. *Il Proletario*, April 9, 1908; February 26, July 9, 1909.

29. *Il Proletario*, March 23, 1913.

30. *Il Proletario*, September 25, 1908.

31. *Il Proletario*, September 21, 1901; December 15, 1907; March 1, 1908; May 31, June 7, July 26, 1913.

32. "La Lotta di classe nel Colorado," *Il Socialismo*, III (July 10, 1904), 152-153.

33. *Il Proletario*, May 26, 1900; October 9, December 18, 1904.

34. Rudolph J. Vecoli, "Prelates and Peasants: Italian Immigrants and the Catholic Church," *Journal of Social History*, 2 (Spring 1969), 217-268; Malcolm Sylvers, "L'Anticlericalismo nel Socialismo Italiano (dalle origine al 1914)," *Movimento Operaio e Socialista*, XVI (April-September 1970), 175-189.

35. "Il tradunionismo e lo spirito del popolo americano," *Il Pensiero* (Rome),III (January 1, 1905), 13-14.

36. *La Parola dei Socialisti*, April 4, 1908; *Il Proletario*, November 13, 1908.

37. *L'Asino (Rome)*, XVII (July 5, September 27, 1908).

38. *Il Proletario*, August 23, 1913.

39. R. Laurence Moore, *European Socialists and the American Promised Land* (New York, 1970), 39. An excellent study, it föcuses upon Germany, France, England and Russia, but does not include Italy.

40. *Il Proletario*, January 26, 1902; August 28, 1907; Luigi Galleani, "La legge del taglione," *Cronaca Sovversiva*, September 25, 1915, in *Aneliti e Singulti*, 299-304; *La Protesta Umana*, I (December 1902), 349.

41. *Il Proletario*, June 4, 1909.

42. *Cronaca Sovversiva* (Turin), I (January 17, 1920).

43. *Guardia Rossa* (New York), ca. April 1920, 18, 20, 21.

44. *Il Proletario*, February 2, 1907; September 25, November 27, 1908; March 12, June 11, 1909; May 12, 1911.

45. *Il Proletario*, June 25, 1909.

46. *Il Proletario*, May 18, 25, August 24, October 5, November 30, 1912.

47. "Arturo Giovannitti," Casellario Politico Centrale, Archivio Centrale dello Stato (hereafter cited CPC,ACS), f. Municipo di Ripabottoni, Comizio Pro Ettor e Giovannitti; *Il Riscatto* (Messina), for example, followed the case closely: August 31, September 14, 21, October 19, November 30, 1912. See also Testi, "L'Immagine," 335-336; and Fernando Fasce, "Un episodio di solidarietà internazionale: 'Lotta operàia' e gli

I.W.W.," in *Italia e Stati Uniti dall'indipendenza americana ad oggi (1776-1976)* (Genoa, 1978), 327-340.

48. *Ettore e Giovannitti e l'Emigrazione transoceanica* (Florence, 1912). The poem begins by depicting the arrival of the travel-weary immigrants who find awaiting them "the bourgeoisie of the *dollaro*, ferocious, exploitive, and arrogant, with dripping jaws, who will suck them with ever-growing greed." I am indebted to Paolo Cresci for making available to me a copy of this publication. On Targioni see Libertario Guerrini, "Un poeta estemporaneo, Idalberto Targioni," *Movimento Operaio*, VII (May-August 1955), 3-4, 511-530.

49. *Il Riscatto*, November 30, 1912.

50. Adriana Dada, "I radicali italo-americani e la società italiana," *Italia Contemporanea* (June 1982), n. 146-147, 133-135.

51. "Carlo Tresca," CPC, ACS, Busta 5208, fas. 5618. This is a large file on the agitation in Italy pro Tresca.

52. *Avanti!*, August 30, September 2, 10, 1916; *L'Avvenire*, December 1, 1916.

53. (Milan, 1916).

54. *Il Proletario*, December 21, 1916.

55. September 15, 1917, but also the issues for September 27, October 6, and November 10, 1917.

56. *Il Proletario*, July 14, 1917.

57. *Cronaca Sovversiva*, July 18, 1918.

58. I (June 30, 1919), 7.

59. *Domani*, I (October 15, 1919); *L'Ordine*, I (October 31, December 1, 1919, January 15, 1920).

60. "Tutto l'obbrobrio! ", *Cronaca Sovversiva*, June 12, 1920, reprinted in *Aneliti e Singulti*, 358.

61. January 17, 31, February 14, 1920.

62. *Iconoclasta* (Pistoia), I (April 1, 1920), 65-67.

63. *Guardia Rossa*, 1. A strikingly similar allusion was made by Giuseppe Iannarelli, a *paesano* of Tresca and an organizer for the Workers' International Industrial Union, speaking in Niagara Falls in June 1917: "When the Italians enter this country they see the Statue of Liberty and they breathe freely thinking to themselves that they have at last left the autocratic government and are in the land of the free. Shortly after their arrival they realize their mistake, they become slaves to the capitalists who own them soul and body." Report of Agent 40S, *U.S. Military Intelligence Reports: Surveillance of Radicals in the United States, 1917-1941* (Microfilm ed., University Publications of America), Reel 1, Document 10110-56.

64. Bartolomeo Vanzetti, *The Story of a Proletarian Life* (Boston, 1923), 18. Robert P. Weeks (ed.), *Commonwealth vs. Sacco and Vanzetti* (Englewood Cliffs, N.J., 1958), 105, 120. I am indebted to Paul Avrich for calling Sacco's statement to my attention.

America in the Swedish Labor Press, 1880s to 1920s

Lars-Göran Tedebrand

In various articles I have recently discussed the connection between strikes and political radicalism in Sweden and emigration to the United States.[1] I have also dealt with the image of America among Swedish labor migrants.[2] In this paper I will discuss more thoroughly the image of America in the Swedish labor press 1880s to 1920s.

The mass emigration from Sweden occurred at a time when the great majority of the Swedish population was active in traditional sectors of the economy. However, the number of industrial workers in towns and in rural industries increased very rapidly in Sweden at the end of the nineteenth century. Workers in industry, mining, and crafts amounted to 96,000 in 1870, to 189,000 in 1890, and to 400,000 in 1900. During the first two decades of the 1900s, industry accounted for somewhat more emigration than did agriculture. The metal and mechanical engineering trades made up the largest branch of Swedish industry and accounted for a large share of emigrants.[3] Another important emigrant group was formed by sawmill workers from northern Sweden. Many emigrants were craftsmen, such as tailors and shoemakers. As a whole, emigration had the greatest effect on trades and industrial branches which were the most sensitive to fluctuations in economic cycles.

The accelerated transformation of Swedish society at the end of the nineteenth century was a prerequisite for the establishment and growth of radical and socialist movements and also trade unions. In 1889, the *Sveriges socialdemokratiska arbetarparti (The Swedish Social Democratic Labor Party)* was founded, and in 1898 the *Lands-organisationen (The Swedish Confederation of Trade Unions)* was established. Despite the numerical growth of the working class, the organizational structure of the labor movement remained weak in Sweden before World War I. The number of organized workers did not exceed 100,000 until after the turn of the century. The mobilization of the masses in the growing cities and industrial areas was, for a long time, largely channeled into the so-called popular movements *(folkrörelser)* such as the temperance movement and the free churches. These voluntary associations had more than 300,000 members in 1900 and played a decisive role in the political democratization of society before 1920.[4]

The organization of the industrial workers made only slow progress, partly due to the animosity of employers towards organized labor, partly to the wide geographical dispersion of industrial units, and lastly to the rural background of the early industrial labor force. Many workers, organized in the free churches, showed antipathy towards the young socialist labor movement, because it was considered atheistic. However, there were exceptions to this rule: some workers attached to the free churches played a very active role in the first large strike in Sweden — the strike of the sawmill workers in the Sundsvall district in northern Sweden in 1879.[5]

Repeated crises in the export industries during international depressions and the struggle for higher wages, better working conditions, and the right to organize led to more than 3000 registered strikes in Sweden betwen the 1870s and World War I. The whole came to a climax in the general strike of 1909, in which 220,000 workers participated.

The rising number of strikes over a period of time is a good measure of the growing tension between the working class and the upper levels of the plutocratic Swedish society before World War I. The labor movement regarded emigration as a symptom of the inability of the class society to take care of its citizens. When strikes or socialist activity led to black-listing and rejection by the community, emigration to America was an attractive alternative for those involved. The strength of the emigration alternative was dependent upon the degree of repression against the workers by the employers and society at large, and upon the existence of a tradition of emigration in the local community. The general situation on the Swedish labor market must of course also be stressed as having been influential.[6]

These were the conditions that led to Swedish emigration to America. What did the Swedish immigrants find there, and how were their political attitudes shaped by their experience?

Swedish socialist and trade union activity in America

Around 1880 the Swedish immigrants settled primarily in the Middle West, while around 1900 they were widely distributed in the industrialized states to the East, such as New York and Massachusetts, and in the lumber areas in the states of the West Coast. Although there was a strong influx of Swedish immigrants to urban and industrial America after 1900, the ethnic and cultural "Swedish-America" has always had a clear middle class bias, concentrated in the Middle West. Fear of "socialism" and trade unions is often said to characterize the majority of Swedish-Americans. It is generally assumed that most Swedish-Americans have had a long Republican voting history, only broken by the Great Depression when they began to support Franklin D. Roosevelt and the New Deal. This assumption, however, is not quite true, not even for the Swedes in the Middle West. Many Swedish-Americans were influenced by the Grange, The Farmers'Alliance, the Populists, and the Nonpartisan League. The Swedish-born Minnesota Congressman Charles A. Lindbergh, son of a former member of the Swedish parliament and father of the pioneer aviator, had established a reputation as a staunch Republican progressive prior to World War I. The Swedish-born publisher Swan J. Turnblad, owner of *Svenska Amerikanska Posten* in Minneapolis, the largest Swedish paper in America, backed the Democratic Party. It must also be mentioned that the so-called farmer-labor politics in Minnesota in the 1920s was backed by many Americans of Swedish descent.

As already mentioned, the early Swedish immigrants had an agrarian background and no experience of labor politics and unionism in Sweden. The aspirations of the immigrants were dominated by petty bourgeois standards. The class consciousness of the rural workers was also hampered by vertical ties in Swedish agrarian society. When, for instance, the collection in support of the striking Swedish iron molders in 1905 made only slow progress in Cedar Rapids, Iowa, the Swedish immigrant C.J. Olsson, despaired of the Swedish-American workingman's lack of proletarian consciousness. He wrote in a letter: "There are many Swedes in this city who do not know what a strike is or what the organization means and they do not want to have it explained to them either".[7]

Many urban and industrial workers participating in the later Swedish mass emigration had experienced the tensions and the repressions of expanding industrial capitalism before leaving for America. Some of the pioneers of Swedish socialism and trade unionism emigrated to America. The confrontation with industrial America was no shock to them; many of them were well prepared to take part in the struggles of the American working class. Nonetheless, we must remember that the radical Swedish-American labor movement only attracted a small minority of Swedish immigrants. Most Swedish-Americans regarded with embarrassment and indignation their radical countrymen, who channelled their activities into their own clubs and newspapers. Many emigrating Swedish socialist pioneers and blacklisted workers ceased political activity after their arrival in the U.S..

However the importance of the radical Swedish-American labor movement and its press cannot be underestimated.[8] The Socialist Labor Party (SLP), founded in 1877, published several ethnic newspapers. The Scandinavian one was called *Den nye tid (New Times)* and was edited and published in Chicago. The newspaper had many successors. All in all, about 60 socialist papers have been published in Swedish-America. Although socialism has recently been called "an exotic parenthesis" in the history of the Swedish-American press, radical newspapers played a significant role in articulating the views of radical immigrants and in promoting contacts between the young Swedish labor movement and socialist immigrants.[9]

During the 1880s, a Scandinavian socialist club was founded in New York. One of its leading figures was the shoemaker David Westerberg, born in Gothenburg in 1825 and personally acquainted with Karl Marx whom he had met in England during his "Gesellenwanderungen". *Skandinaviska Socialistklubben (The Scandinavian Socialist Club)* was very active in the 1880s and recruited about 50 subscribers to *Socialdemokraten (The Social Democrat)*, the first socialist newspaper in Stockholm, and from 1889, mouthpiece of the Swedish Social Democratic Labor Party. The New York Club also played an active role when the *Skandinaviska Socialistiska Arbetarförbundet, SSFA (The Scandinavian Socialist Labor Society)* was founded in 1894. This All-Scandinavian socialist organization in America began to publish the newspaper *Skandinavisk-amerikanske Arbetaren (The Scandinavian-American Worker)*. Its first editor was Erik Nordman, born 1852, immigrant in 1888, and once a member of the editorial board of *Socialdemokraten.*[10] After the exclusion of the Danish-Norwegian section in 1896, the newspaper became solely Swedish. The name was abridged to *Arbetaren (The Worker)*, which was the most longlived socialist newspaper in Swedish-America. It was not given up until 1928.

In 1904, the SSFA became a section of the Socialist Labor Party. By 1909, the SSFA had 1500 members and 40 clubs. During the general strike in Sweden that year, it raised funds in support of the Swedish organized workers (more than 200,000 Swedish Crowns were collected in America between July 1909 and June 1910.)

Some of the appeals of the Swedish Social Democratic Party concerning the question of universal suffrage were published in *Arbetaren.* From 1915, the SSFA sent editorial material every month to the socialist parties in Scandinavia. There were also substantial contacts between organized labor in Sweden and the Swedish-American radicals in New York. During the lock-out of the organized Swedish molders in 1905, a meeting was held in New York on June 14th. The organizing committee declared that "from the latest issues of the Swedish labor newspapers and from letters received so far it is clear that there is a life and death struggle between organized labor and organized Capital in Sweden just now". On October 21st a concert and ball for the benefit of the locked-out molders was held.

The Swedish molder C.J. Miller (Möller), born in Lund in southern Sweden in 1875 and an immigrant to the U.S. in 1901, was the link between the organized molders in Sweden and their colleagues in America. He had become a socialist during a two-years' stay in Germany and Switzerland 1899-1900. Miller published articles in *Gjutaren (The Molder)*, the mouthpiece of the trade union of Swedish molders, in which he commented on the American labor market. (The correspondence between Miller and J.E. Blomkvist, the editor of *Gjutaren* has been preserved).

In 1910 another competing organization was founded, *Skandinaviska Socialistiska Förbundet, SSF (Scandinavian Socialist league)*, connected to the Socialist Party of America, established in 1901. SSF's first club was formed in Chicago in 1904. All 13 founders of the Chicago-club had formerly belonged to the young labor movement in Sweden. The mouthpiece of SSF was *Svenska Socialisten (The Swedish Socialist)* founded by A.A. Pattersson in Rockford, Illinois, in 1905. From 1911 the newspaper was published in Chicago. SSF reached its peak membership in 1917/18 when 3735 members were registered. In 1919 there was a break between SSF and the Socialist Party of America. Three years later SSF was united with SSAF to *Förenade Skandinaviska Socialistförbundet (The United Scandinavian Socialist League)*.

Joe Hill is the most well-known of the Swedish immigrants who took part in the radical American labor movement.[11] But other more anonymous Swedes joined the Industrial Workers of the World (IWW). As a matter of fact, in 1911, when Joe Hill was feverishly active as an agitator and balladeer, the IWW published a Swedish newspaper called *Revolt*. It was a monthly published in Chicago. Swedish wobblies also published the periodicals *Alarm* and *Nya Världen (The New World)*. The former was edited in Minneapolis and the latter in Chicago. The editor of *Alarm*, Carl Althén, was arrested in September 1917 and in August 1918 sentenced to 20 years hard labor. After the intervention of the Swedish government, he was released in November 1922. In January 1923, Althén went back to Sweden.

Socialist immigrants were nowhere so strong and influential as in New York in the 1890s. Nonetheless the Scandinavians, especially the Swedes, perhaps played a more important role among the organized workers of Chicago at the end of the nineteenth century. By 1900, Chicago was the third largest "Swedish" city, only surpassed by Stockholm and Gothenburg. 10.8 per cent of the members of the trade unions were Scandinavians in 1886.[12] The Germans dominated many trades. The Swedish ethnic group seems to have played a considerable role among the organized painters of Chicago.[13] One of the most influential local unions was *Scandinavian Local Union no. 194 of the Brotherhood of Painters and Decorators of America*, founded in 1890.

One of the founders was Karl Adolf Hedlund, former Chairman of the Swedish trade union of painters. No. 194 had 1056 members in 1902 and 1997 members in 1909. The considerable social and educational activity of the union, which joined the Socialist Party of America, is mirrored in the national mouthpiece of the painters: *The Painters and Decorators' Journal*. Local union no. 194 had a fairly strong position at times. One of the members, Gustaf Karlsson, former member of the painters union in Stockholm, wrote in a letter in 1912: "the union decides whom the employer shall hire or fire". Such revelations did not go unnoticed by Swedish socialists and workers who did not emigrate.

The image of America in Sweden

The different concepts that have been associated with America in Sweden since the beginning of the mass emigration in the 1840s have induced scholars to study ideas such as democracy, freedom, equality and idealism. Efforts have been made to evaluate American culture, American social life and American mentality.[14] When one analyzes Swedish views of American society in the nineteenth and twentieth centuries it is of importance to distinguish between various viewpoints, particularly between the prevailing upper and middle-class attitude, the attitudes of the rank and file emigrants and of the growing working-class movement.

Swedish "bourgeois" opinion toward the end of the nineteenth century – with certain notable anglophile exceptions – was oriented toward Wilhelmine Germany, a result of the outcome of the Franco-Prussian War. It was strongly critical towards many aspects of American life, which, it was held, encouraged boss rule and cultural philistinism. The Swedish-American author and journalist Vilhelm Berger (1867-1938), immigrant in 1896, talked about "the contempt for America among the educated classes". This pro-German attitude gradually disappeared. Germany's defeat in World War I, and what was regarded as a growing communist threat to traditional middle-class values, played an important role in this process. The vitality of American capitalism can be said to have attracted large segments of the Swedish middle classes in the twentieth century.

Returning emigrants, "yankees", and letters were important in the dissemination of information about America. It is impossible to systematize the kind of information and the image of America given by those channels, as could be done with information given in newspapers. However, it is quite clear that the decision to emigrate among industrial and urban workers in Sweden was based on the predominantly positive information about the American labor market which was spread by returning immigrants and letters from America. The Swedish rank and file had a positive attitude towards the opportunities in America compared to those in Sweden. This "American fever" was a collective phenomenon confirmed by the many autobiographies of Swedish workers published by Nordiska Museet (The Nordic Museum) in Stockholm at the end of the 1940s.

Even the leading Swedish socialist pioneer August Palm (1849-1922), founder of *Socialdemokraten* and *the Swedish Social Democratic Party*, had a very positive view of America. After a trip to the USA he published a book in 1901 in wich he stated that America "is a land with resources, a large country, where everyone is offered opportunities and no one in possession of energy and stubborness will be ruined".[15]

An outspoken critical attitude towards America can be found in the letters of the radical minority among the Swedish immigrants. This attitude is often combined with reproaches against Swedish countrymen for a lack of class consciousness. In 1905 Karl-Johan Ellington described America as the "proletarian hell". "Keep your mouth shut, proletarians, and when you get stiff from rheumatism, go to hell and cook your back legs in the sulphur cauldrons".[16] Another socialist critic, Fredrik Karlsson, wrote in February 1892 from Chicago to the newspaper *SocialDemokraten* in Stockholm :

> It is apparent that the stream of immigration, because of the World Exposition, will be drawn in large part to Chicago in the near future. It would therefore perhaps not be inappropriate to devote a few words to conditions here in this place... It appears to be as though most of the Swedes here should be very satisfied with their new homeland, which is easily explained since they generally, at least up to the present, have had the needs of their stomachs fulfilled. And sadly enough, the majority of our countrymen still have, strictly speaking, no other needs... It would be desirable for some of those who come here who maintain that socialism is inimical to culture. They could here see what kind of culture their own ideal society is capable of producing. Where masses of children are brought up on streets just to satisfy the bourgeoisie's lust for making money. Where art and science are ignored since they do not produce enough profit. Where one can with justice speak of hostility toward culture.[17]

America in the Swedish press

The majority of the Swedish workers read liberal and conservative newspapers at the end of the nineteenth century. However a social democratic press appeared in the 1880s.[18] The first social democratic newspaper was "*Folkviljan*" *(The People's Will)*, founded in Malmö in southern Sweden in 1882. It was followed by *Socialdemokraten* (The Social Democrat) in Stockholm in 1885. In 1889, Hjalmar Branting, the leader of the Swedish social democrats, became editor-in-chief of this paper. The period 1899-1909 was a golden age for the starting of social democratic newspapers in Sweden; more than 20 newspapers were founded during the first decade of the twentieth century.

The liberal press

No comprehensive study has hitherto been made of a fast-growing information about America in the Swedish urban or provincial press during the era of mass emigration.

However, at the *Emigrantregistret för Värmland (The Emigration Institute for the Province of Värmland)* in Karlstad in western Sweden, all articles and advertisements in the local press in which the name "America" has been mentioned have been registered. In table 1 we present the number of articles and advertisements about "America" (Swedish background, conditions in America, culture and other impulses and so on) in the liberal newspaper *Karlstads-Tidningen* 1890 and 1900. *Karlstads-Tidningen* was founded in 1879 and appeared three times a week. The newspaper must be characterized as one of the leading liberal provincial newspapers in Sweden at the end of the nineteenth century. The editor-in-chief from 1890-1939 was Mauritz Hellberg (1859-1947). Hellberg represented a radical and progressive liberalism. Before the founding of the social democratic *Värmlands Folkblad* (1906), *Karlstads-Tidningen* was read by the organized workers in the province of Värmland. The most common reader however was a farmer, an artisan or a member of the petty bourgeoisie in Karlstad.

Table 1 Articles and advertisements about America in *Karlstads-Tidningen*

	1890	1900
Articles	424	436
Words/Article	234	253
Advertisements	64	53
Words/Advertisements	66	

source: *Karlstads-Tidningen* 1890 and 1900.

The newspaper followed in some detail questions of interest for the liberal opinion in Sweden: discussions about tariff protection, agrarian populism, the death penalty discussion and the achievements of the temperance movement. The great opportunities of the Swedish immigrants in America were stressed in the "Letters from America" to the editor. However, the readers were well-informed about unemployment in America, the struggle for the 8-hour day, the strikes in the coal mines, the persecution of union members and the activities of the police force towards organized labor. The First of May demonstration in Chicago in 1890 which gathered 25,000 people was repeatedly discussed. The uneven distribution of wealth in America was underlined.

The newspaper also expressed a critical attitude towards American foreign policy at the turn of the century.

On the whole it must be said that *Karlstads-Tidningen* gave a realistic picture of the American labor market. A more distinct focusing on and a more outspoken critical attitude towards the situation of labor in America can be found in the young Swedish socialist press. Our analysis will be focused on the information about America 1886-1894 and 1913-1927 in the leading socialist newspaper, *Socialdemokraten* (non-orthodox marxian)

The socialist press

A case study of information about America 1886-1894 in *Socialdemokraten*, the leading organ of the Social Democratic Party, has been made by Fred Nilsson.[19] The circulation of *Socialdemokraten* did not exceed 4000 copies during the first years. However, the circulation increased rapidly and the newspaper's information was probably more widely spread among workers, mainly in Stockholm, than the circulation figures indicate, since information about the American labor market was passed on by its readers in factories, hiring halls, and associations, especially the trade unions. As far as information about America is concerned, *Socialdemokraten* depended upon American newspapers and periodicals, letters from emigrated party members and, to a limited extent, upon its own correspondents in America. There are some examples of prominent socialist publicists leaving Stockholm for America, and, as already has been mentioned, in at least one case, Erik Nordman, the editorial activity was continued in America.

The few reports in *Socialdemokraten* from the years 1886-1887 on the whole give a negative picture of existing conditions in America: it was difficult to get a job and wages were low. A few successful strikes were regarded as a positive factor. After the hanging of the anarchists in Chicago in November 1887 the tone of the newspaper was very bitter and was, for example, expressed in a poem by Atterdag Wermelin, a Stockholm writer who had emigrated in 1887.

During the following years, 1888-1889, the newspaper did not give a more attractive picture of the American labor market. It is dominated by reports of a number of unsuccessful strikes, wage cuts, and extensive unemployment. An important source for *Socialdemokraten* during these years was the German newspaper *Der Sozialist* in New York

In 1890, however, very little is said about unemployment in America. Special attention is paid to trade union activities often leading to strikes, of which at least a few ended favorably for the workers. Information about wages and working hours have made a favorable impression on Swedish workers during that specific year. The discussion concerning the 8-hour day in America in 1890 must have been regarded as especially advanced among the Swedish workers since the demands for the 10-hour-day had just started in Sweden by that time.

From 1891 onwards, reports about the American labor market are again pessimistic: unemployment, wage cuts, and violent labor conflicts dominate the news. The peak is quite naturally reached with the Homestead Strike in 1892, which was noted in *Socialdemokraten* as an example of the powerlessness of the American labor organizations. Reports of mass unemployment are more and more frequent during the following year, with the panic of 1893. In 1894 the picture of America as a country of bankruptcies and shutdowns is total, while industrial and urban emigration from Sweden symptomatically reached a low point that year. In 1894, over 7000 Swedish-Americans returned home. The Pullman strike in particular raised many important issues. At stake was the right of industrial workers to organize unions, to declare boycotts, and to strike.

The overall view of American society in *Socialdemokraten* 1886-1894 was without illusions. Class struggle and repression of organized labor in America were stressed. However, conditions on the Swedish labor market at times appeared to be even worse, and the attractiveness of America then increased, even among workers within relatively strong trade unions and with socialist views. The editors therefore considered it important to inform potential emigrants among the readers in some detail about conditions in America. The high degree of realism in the information provided is striking.

When discussing the image of America in the Swedish socialist press at the beginning of the twentieth century, one notes first of all that the old "liberal" image of America as a land of political freedom, justice, and religious tolerance already began to fade during the period of mass emigration. Moreover the early twentieth century was characterized by political and economic advances for the Swedish working class, which reduced the relative differences between Sweden and America. The Social Democrats entered the governing coalition in 1917 and legislation favorable to the working class was passed, for example, accident and old-age insurance, as well as the eight-hour working day in 1919. A growing segment of the Swedish working class also acquired new standards when it came to judging social and political conditions in Sweden as compared with abroad. The working-class movement was, in theory at least, under the influence of marxism and expressed a clear aversion towards the type of capitalist society for which America could be considered the prototype.

The following discussion is based on the issues raised in *Socialdemokraten* 1913-1917, 1920, 1923-1925 and 1927.[20] During these years, the newspaper received its information from other Swedish and Swedish-American newspapers, from news agencies, especially *Svensk-Amerikanska Nyhetsbyrån (The Swedish-American News Agency)*, and, to a lesser degree, from its own correspondents. The majority of the material dealt with conditions in Swedish America, the growing cultural and personal contacts between Sweden and America, presidential campaigns, natural catastrophes, strikes, unemployment, wages, the discussion concerning total prohibition and the power of "alcohol capital" in the big cities, immigration and quota laws. The hardships of immigrants created by the "Americanization crusade" were observed. All this information will not be systemized in this context. The subsequent analysis will mainly be focused on the reports concerning labor and socialism in America.

In the *Socialdemokraten* from 1913 to summer 1917, a period in which the socialists in Sweden still were excluded from political power, it can be observed that emigration was used as a proof of the shortcomings of the class society. The socialist press and the socialist members of the Swedish parliament opposed every restriction in the right to emigrate proposed by the government and the military during World War I. The colorful socialist author and politician

Fabian Mansson (1872-1938) said that "no one can wonder that the workers do not long to stay in a country where the organizations of the employers so ruthlessly oppose every modest request from labor" (18/4 1917). On the other hand the socialists criticized the opinion expressed by professor Gustav Sundbärg in 1913 that "the tyranny of the trade unions" against unorganized workers promoted emigration. The *Socialdemokraten* reminded its readers of the fact that emigration had long been strongest from agrarian districts with a weak or nonexistent labor movement. The newspaper also talked about "the involuntary exile promoted by the blacklists of the employers" (15/10 1913).

The situation on the American labor market was eagerly followed. Referring to the conditions revealed during the strikes of the coal miners in West Virginia in summer 1913 the *Socialdemokraten* wrote: "If the trusts will rule they will bring about a terrorism worse than the Russian" (3/7 1913). The working conditions within certain branches of American industry were described as horrible. The *Socialdemokraten* was especially concerned about the low wages and poor working conditions in the wood pulp factories. The policy of the purchasers of labor to prevent unionism by employing workers of different ethnic backgrounds at the same place of work was stressed (15/8 1913).

After a visit to the U.S., professor Helge Bäckstrām (1865-1932), a socialist member of the Swedish parliament emphasized in an article that mass immigration hampered the activities of the labor movement in America (29/10 1913). He also noticed the separation between the political and trade union branches of the American labor movement, a strange phenomenon to a Swedish observer. It is therefore not surprising that the mouthpiece of the Swedish social democrats in 1914 published an article in favor of the Burnett-Dillingham bill. In this article, the opponents of immigration restriction were divided into three categories: steamship companies, catholics and employers hiring unskilled workers.

Following World War I, the organized working-class movement in Sweden became especially critical of certain tendencies in American society. In 1920 the *Socialdemokraten* published many articles concerning the labor market, labor conditions and socialism in America. The newspaper was concerned about the Red Scare of the postwar years or what was called "fear of bolshevism" "and red hysteria" in the US (8/1 and 5/2 1920). The prosecution of socialist deputies in New York induced the newspaper to talk about "the homelessness of liberty of thought in America". The arrest of strike leaders during the railway strike was observed (17/4) as well as the measures taken by the authorities to prevent May Day demonstrations (3/5).

The improvement of the American labor market 1923-24 led to a last peak in Swedish immigration (31,984 immigrants). Reports on this new "American fever", especially in the forest and saw mill districts in northern Sweden, were numerous in the *Socialdemokraten* as well as in articles concerning the labor market in America. Several articles dealt with the unsatisfactory conditions on Ellis Island ("The tragedy on Ellis Island", 17/5 1924) and the quota laws. Swedish-American newspapers were initially skeptical of the quota laws of 1921 and 1924 but did gradually accept them.[21] The *Socialdemokraten* must be said to have been in favor of the restrictions. The newspaper published (11/2 1924) an article by its correspondent in America Ruth Englund, in which it was argued that the workers of America backed the restrictions while those who opposed them were to be found among the industrialists who wanted a cheap labor force. The protests against the quota laws at the beginning of 1924 were also mentioned in the article. The statement of New York Jews that Jesus and his Apostles would have been forbidden to go through Ellis Island was cited.

The reaction to the quota law question expressed by the *Socialdemokraten* was in accordance with the views of the SPA. On June 6, 1923, the *Socialdemokraten* published an extensive interview with the socialist congressman Victor Berger, editor of *The Milwaukee Leader*, under the headline "Immigration weakens the labor movement in the US". Berger especially attacked the communists, their ethnic sympathizers and their newspapers. As is well-known, Berger shared some of Samuel Gompers' reactionary attitudes towards immigration. However, Berger's emphasis on the close co-operation between the SPA and the trade unions was attractive to the Swedish social democratic press.

Emigration from Sweden dropped to a modest level in the late 1920s. Political conservatism in America and the weakness of the socialist movement were noticed with growing preoccupation in the *Socialdemokraten*. The only hope was inspired by farmer-labor politics in Minnesota that to some extent resembled the later co-operation between the social democrats and the farmers' party in Sweden in 1932. On July 25, 1925, the leading Social Democratic publicist and politician, Arthur Engberg (1888-1944), wrote in the *Socialdemokraten:* "American capitalism is, in our eyes, one of the most ruthless that exists anywhere in the world... and the situation of the American proletariat is nothing less than frightful". It is also well known that the attitude of the entire organized European working class was utterly critical of America in connection with the execution of Sacco and Vanzetti in Boston on 1927. The *Socialdemokraten* published no less than 21 articles concerning the Sacco-Vanzetti case in August 1927. The depression and high unemployment during the early 1930s naturally reinforced this dark picture of America within the Swedish working-class movement. Many workers who had emigrated in 1923-24 returned around 1930, often disillusioned about the future of American society.

Notes

1. L.-G. Tedebrand, *Strikes and Political Radicalism in Sweden and Emigration to the United States* in Dirk Hoerder (editor), *American Labor and Immigration History, 1877-1920s : Recent European Research.* University of Illinois Press, 1983, pp. 221-234. Slighty revised and illustrated L.-G. Tedebrand, *Strikes and Political Radicalism in Sweden and Emigration to the United States* in *The Swedish-American Historical Quarterly* July 1983, pp. 194-210.

2. L.-G Tedebrand, *The Image of America among Swedish Labor Migrants* in Christiane Harzig and Dirk Hoerder (editors), *The Press of Labor Migrants in Europe and North America 1880s to 1930s.* Publications of the Labor Newspaper Preservation Project. Bremen, 1985, pp. 547-560.

3. S. Carlsson, *Chronology and Composition of Swedish Emigration to America* in H. Runblom and H. Norman, *From Sweden to America. A History of Migration.* Uppsala, 1976.

4. Sven Lundkist, *Folkrörelserna i det svenska samhället 1850-1920 (Popular Movements in Swedish Society 1850-1920).* Uppsala, 1977.

5. Tedebrand (1983) and especially Anders Norberg, *Sundsvallsstrejken 1879 - ett startskott till den stora Amerikautvandringen ? (The Sundsvall of Strike 1879 - a Starting-shot for the large Emigration to America ?)* in *Historisk Tidskrift* no. 3, 1978, pp. 263-282.

6. Tedebrand (1983).

7. Arbetarrörelsens arkiv (archives of Swedish Labor Movement).

8. Cf. Henry Bengtsson, *Skandinaver på vänsterflygeln i USA (Scandinavians in the left Wing in the USA)*. Stockholm, 1955 and Per Nordahl, De sålde sina penslar. Om några svenska målare som emigrerade till USA (They sold their pencils. Swedish Painters and Decorators en USA). Kristianstad, 1987. For the Swedish-American Press see J. Backlund, *A Century of the Swedish-American Press*. Chicago, 1952 ; M. Brook, Radical Literature in Swedish-America : A Narrative Survey in *The Swedish Immigrant Press in America 1914-1945*. Chicago, 1966 ; A.F. Scherstam, *The Relation of Swedish-American Newspapers to the Assimilation of Swedish Immigrants*. Rock Island, The Augustana College Library Publications, 15, 1935.

9. U. Beijbom, *Utvandrarna och Svensk-America (The Emigrants and Swedish-America)*. Stockholm, 1986 p. 186.

10. F. Nilsson, *Emigrationen från Stockholm till Nordamerika 1880-1893. En studie i urban utvandring (Emigration from Stockholm to North America 1880-1893. A Study in Urban Emigration)*. Stockholm, 1970, pp. 234-235.

11. One of the best studies on Joe Hill is G.M. Smith, *Joe Hill,* Salt Lake City, 1969.

12. H. Keil, *The German Immigrant Working Class of Chicago, 1875-90 : Workers, Labor Leaders, and the Labor Movement* in Hoerder (1983), p. 163.

13. Nordahl (1987).

14. H. Elovson, *Amerika i svensk litteratur 1750-1820. En studie i komparativ litteraturhistoria (America in Swedish Literature 1750-1820)* Lund, 1930 ; N. Runeby, *Den nya världen och den gamla. Amerikabild och emigrationsuppfattning i Sverige 1820-1860 (The New World and the Old. The Picture of America and Concept of Emigration in Sweden 1820-1860)*. Uppsala, 1969 ; L. Wendelius, *Bilden av Amerika i svensk prosafiktion 1890-1914 (The Image of America in Swedish Prose Fiction 1890-1914)*. Uppsala (printed in Motala), 1982.

15. A. Palm, *Ögonblicksbilder från en tripp till Amerika (Snapshots from a Trip to America)*. Stockholm, 1901, p.243.

16. H.A. Barton, *Letters from the Promised Land. Swedes in America. 1840-1914*. Published by the University of Minnesota Press, Minneapolis, for the Swedish Pioneer Historical Society. New Berlin, 1975, p.219.

17. Barton (1975), pp. 206-220.

18. S. Hadenius, l. Weibull and J.-O. Seveborg, *Socialdemokratisk press och presspolitik 1899-1909 (The Social Democratic Press and Press Policy in Sweden 1899-1909)*. Stockholm, 1968.

19. Nilsson (1970), pp.206-229.

20. I owe a debt of gratitude to the American Library at the Department of History, University of Uppsala for permission to borrow excerpts from *Socialdemokraten*.

21. S. Lindmark, *Swedish America 1914-1932. Studies in Ethnicity with Emphasis on Illinois and Minnesota*, Uppsala, 1971, p. 155.

II

The Immigrant Experience

1. Ellis Island: Experience at the Gate

The first confrontation between hope and reality took place at the gate. The image of America migrants had in their heads often faded when they set foot on the "island of tears", especially when they belonged to an "unwanted" group. This was the case with South Slavs whose reception at Ellis Island Ivan Cizmić describes in his article. The situation can be seen as an illustration of the conventional wisdom turned upside down. Immigration rules supposedly barred from entry into the U.S. immigrants who were not endowed with the qualities supposed to make good citizens. But the Americans implementing the laws were often corrupt and exploited the regulations for their personal profit. The fact of official representatives of the American Republic blackmailing 'new' immigrants was highly paradoxical. At the same time the experience of South Slavs and the way they were discriminated against throws into relief the ambivalent attitudes of recently Americanized immigrants towards newcomers. We are told about the way they behaved in their official roles: for instance, a Hungarian used his newly acquired authority on Ellis Island to persecute and abuse Hungarian immigrants, while another official in a high position, who was born in Dubrovnik, insisted on denying the very existence of discrimination. Whether typical or not, these attitudes are part of the mechanisms of integration.

Cizmić's paper then focuses on the role the newspaper *Narodni list* played in defending South Slav immigrants. The attempt to create a prospective association shows a growing awareness of their rights among immigrants at the time. This awareness —which was shared by other groups (see Fasce's paper on Italian workers)— expressed itself in campaigns designed to encourage citizenship. Whereas Part III probes the different meanings of citizenship for different groups, here we see what it meant to recently arrived "new" immigrants. It was equated with the empowerment of a vulnerable group.

2. Experience in the Factory

After they had passed through the gate, work became a central fact in the life of immigrants. The problem of historians is to get an insight into the subjective dimension of this experience. Adam Walaszek's study of letters written by

Polish emigrants and confiscated by Czarist censorship is an attempt to evoke this dimension. His careful reading of the text enables him to make a number of observations. The first difficulty for these Poles who worked mostly in big industry was how to make sense of the organization of work in that kind of setting. Through the letters one sees them trying to get their moorings, to understand what was going on. To do this they made comparisons with their experience in the old country. Thus they used a variety of agricultural metaphors to describe their industrial work. By contrast with their own rural universe and their experience as peasants in the old world, the organization of industrial work seemed totally arbitrary to them. Though they were familiar with hard work, industrial work was far more wearing, because of its pace and of its meaninglessness. They experienced work in America as antithetic to freedom (no leisure, no holidays), to culture (no communication, no knowledge of the language), to sociability (absence of kin and of friends), to security (lack of regular work/unemployment). Thus work contradicted the expectations of many of them, though, of course, to some, the experience of paid work appeared as a liberation from tyrannical masters.

In general, there was only one positive thing about work: it meant wages in the form of money. Work was not something to be proud of, only something that enabled you to survive and to reach a goal: return home and buy land. As can be seen from Catherine Collomp's paper in Part IV this kind of work was indeed non-work in the eyes of some labor leaders; it did not enable immigrants to forge any kind of social identity; it did not even identify them as workers.

Walaszek's paper gives us an insight into the experience of industrial work for immigrants just off the boat or at any rate recently arrived, whereas Ferdinando Fasce's paper describes what it was for those who had been in the U.S. for some time. He deals with the experience of Italians (and other immigrants) employed by the Scovill Manufacturing Company located in Connecticut, at the time of World War I. The Poles were valued only for their physical strength and they felt "like cattle". As for the Italian workers, they were being "socialized" by the firm that needed a stable labor force, which meant they became targets for employers' propaganda. Work was turned into an instrument of ideological manipulation. Workers were assimilated to the "army that stays at home" and encouraged to be more productive. Efficiency and loyalty to the firm being the best way to show one's allegiance to one's new homeland, particularly during wartime.

The experience described by Fasce ties in with the problem of citizenship dealt with by Catherine Collomp, Linda Schneider and Nick Salvatore in Part IV. Through its appeals to loyalty and patriotism, the firm was creating a new model of citizenship. This 'citizenship' soon became 'contested terrain'. After World War I the firm's reconversion policy produced massive layoffs and a new form of work organization. Immigrant workers became aware of the contradiction between the authoritarianism they were subjected to in the workplace and the democratic rhetoric employers used as justification. Workers then appropriated the rethoric to counter the employers' attacks. They appealed to American workers to fight for Democracy, to kick out the new "kaiser", the new "czar", the new "Van Hindenburg". Their European political experience was put to use to increase their understanding of the factors tending to destroy their freedom. At the same time emerged a new awareness of their relationship to their adopted homeland: their sense of a debt owed the new world was giving way to the feeling that it was America that should have a sense of obligation towards immigrants.

The Experience of South Slav Immigrants on Ellis Island and the Establishment of the Slavonic Immigrant Society in New York

Ivan Cizmić

The Statue of Liberty and Ellis Island are two celebrated symbols of American history. Millions of immigrants experienced America for the first time on Ellis Island. The centennial of the Statue of Liberty is an opportune occasion for a further examination of this subject. In both American and European literature on migrations, much has been written about immigrants on Ellis Island.[1] However, the most telling illustration of conditions on Ellis Island is to be found, perhaps, among the experiences of South Slav immigrants. These are particularly vivid because of the important role played by South Slav immigrant organizations and their immigrant press in the exposure of conditions prevailing on Ellis Island.

On March 24, 1900, the first Croatian daily in the United States, *Narodni list* of New York, printed an article that had been published by the *News* of New York. It concerned an investigation into staff corruption on Ellis Island and included some sensational facts that had been uncovered. Although names were not given, it was clear that several people would forfeit their jobs and that some might even end up in Sing Sing. An organized group of immigration personnel had systematically blackmailed immigrants. In return for a payment of $25.00 to $85.00, these staff members offered to relax immigration regulations. The paper also described cases of "girls and women who had no money, but were beautiful, and were often attacked and dishonored." In its commentary, *Narodni list* noted with pride that its associates had made the greatest contribution to fostering the investigation and anticipated the eventual improvement of the situation on Ellis Island.[2]

The investigation into the scandal ended in September 1901, and a report was sent to Washington. *Narodni list* wrote:

> The investigation disclosed some very interesting facts, which throw a very bad light on current immigration personnel, those people who receive and process aliens from Europe. It was revealed that travellers were forced to give $5 to those heartless persons to be allowed to disembark, because they were otherwise threatened with being returned to Europe. Everyone, including the lame, old, deaf and blind, were allowed to immigrate if the immigration officials were well paid. We hope that the new soldierly, militant President Roosevelt will know how to make these ten persons pay for their heartless acts, and especially, that the Commissioner of Immigration Fitchie will be removed from office and a new man appointed, a man more suitable to carry out the letter of the law.[3]

It was not by chance that *Narodni list* mentioned President Theodore Roosevelt. He had made a great effort to improve conditions on Ellis Island and to end the corruption that had flourished under Commissioner Thomas Fitchie, Powderly's successor. Roosevelt dismissed Fitchie and appointed a Spanish-American War commander, William Williams, to the post. Assuming office in April, 1902, Williams said: "Immigrants must be treated with kindness and consideration. Any government official violating the terms of this notice will be recommended for dismissal from the Service. Any other person so doing will be forthwith required to leave Ellis Island."[4]

South Slav immigrants were certainly among the groups who were the most discriminated against on Ellis Island. As early as October, 1899, *Narodni list* wrote that its pages often contained news about intrigues on Ellis Island

"...against our poor brothers, forced by sorrow, hunger and trouble to leave their dear homeland and find bread in America." The paper directed its primary accusations for these circumstances to John D. Lederkilger, a Hungarian by nationality, who was employed in an important position on the island. The paper indicated that it had already spent several months struggling with some success "...against this abuse of which we are sure the authorities in Washington know nothing, and neither do those in Vienna, although perhaps the latter prefer not to know; for several months now South Slavs have been persecuted, although the Hungarian should know that we are persistent and as hard as our rocks and mountains, and that he can bend us but never break us." The paper offered proof and described how the group associated with Lederkilger had quartered several South Slav immigrants on the premises of the Austrian Society and took their last dollars from them for that service. It made no difference that these immigrants already had paid for tickets for the trip from New York to Chicago in the offices of the immigrant Franjo Zotti.[5]

Narodni list began a persistent struggle for South Slav immigrants on Ellis Island to obtain their own interpreter, rather than the Hungarian Lederkilger.

> We ask now: Is it right and fair for all nationalities except ours to have their own interpreters? Is it right and fair for this Lederkilger, who has admitted he knows no Croatian and cannot understand the answers, nor do the poor immigrants know what he is asking them, to question South Slav immigrants on landing? It is this man who questioned all the Croats sent home as ineligible during the last several months.

The paper called for a petition to be sent to the Treasury Department in Washington demanding an interpreter of the Croatian language. It went even further, proposing bringing charges for unjust and inhuman treatment against the Hungarian Lederkilger.

> Among so many thousands of Croats there are quite a lot who are citizens of this free country, and it is our duty to care for our brothers. We hope the other Croatian papers will support us in this, and that we may work together to see justice done to our poor immigrants, who do not come here to satisfy a whim, but because hunger and despair make them leave their homes. *Narodni list* is conscious of its duty, so far and in the future, and will

fight for the rights of the Croatian people, for the rights of our oppressed and persecuted brothers; all the costs of this petition to the government we will take upon ourselves. Forms will be sent to all societies and private persons throughout America, on which they can sign their names if they wish. It would be the duty of every Croat who is a citizen of this great land to do at least so much for his brothers.[6]

The petition to the Treasury Department became unnecessary because a position for a Croatian interpreter was opened. Julius Westenock, a Slovenian by nationality, became interpreter. *Narodni list* expressed its satisfaction, stating that South Slavs would understand him better, and he them, than a German or Hungarian whose knowledge might be limited to a few words of Polish or Czech. The paper stopped collecting signatures for a petition, pleased that many Serbs and Slovenes had also answered its call.

American immigration officials found many a pretext for discrimination against and persecution of South Slavs on Ellis Island in vaguely written immigration laws which allowed wide latitude in their interpretation. In 1882, the first federal immigration act was enacted. It was later supplemented and amended. In 1903, Congress finally passed an act which prohibited the immigration of persons with physical or mental defects as well as those with a criminal record. Those convicted of political crimes were exempt, excepting anarchists, who were prohibited to enter the United States. Workers under contract as seasonal laborers were also banned from entrance to the United States.

The South Slav immigrant press condemned the strict and unjustified application of immigration restrictions. On February 17, 1900, *Narodni list* published an article in English entitled, "The Immigration Authorities and the Croats". The paper criticized some American newspapers for their repeated denunciations of Croatian immigration. It also criticized the *Evening Telegraph* for quoting the Commissioner General for Immigration Powderly to the effect that Croatian immigration should be discouraged.[7] On April 7, *Narodni list* continued to express its disapproval.

Everyone knows Powderly and how and why he treats immigrants harshly. As former head of the Labor Party, at the 1896 elections he joined the Republicans, who are aristocracy here and draw their might from great monopolies and trusts, and

> hate all aliens. To show himself as a protector and defender of the workers, he ordered strict treatment of immigrants, and sent back many of our poor Croats under the excuse of being 'contract laborers'.[8]

In the issue published on February 3, 1900, *Narodni list* wrote about fifteen South Slav immigrants in Galveston. They were initially allowed into the United States but were later charged with working as contract laborers. All the efforts made by the shipping company and *Narodni list* were in vain; they were returned to Europe.[9]

The Croatian Fraternal Union, then known as the National Croatian Society, worked diligently to obtain better treatment for Croats who came to Ellis Island. At its convention in Wheeling in 1900, delegates heatedly discussed the position of South Slavs on Ellis Island. The convention concluded that a memorandum should be sent to the President of the United States demanding that "...this illegal treatment end in the future, and that Croatian immigrants gain the same rights enjoyed by other nationalities immigrating into the USA... This refers not only to the landing point in New York but also to Baltimore and Phil- adelphia."[10]

The immigrant press, joined by prominent public figures in the immigrant community, turned to the South Slav public, demanding support for travellers on Ellis Island. In this effort, Father Martin Krmpotić, pastor of the Croatian church in Kansas City, wrote a letter to the Croatian Diet in Zagreb stating:

> All the nationalities immigrating here are better organized than the Croats, and their home governments take care of them through consulates. Immigrants are also supported on the other side, and help is given to them at once. Besides keeping consulates in Washington, home governments also often send special representatives to inquire into conditions among the immigrants. The Italian consul spends most of his time working on the colonization of his compatriots.

Krmpotić argued that immigrants from southern Europe were the most numerous but the least protected. This was particularly true of Austria-Hungary whose authorities showed little concern for Slav immigrants. According to Krmpotić, the Austro-Hungarian consul gave more attention to his banking business, the sale of transportation tickets, and other prohibited activities. Most of his time was spent in the compilation of reports concerning political speeches and movements against the Austro-Hungarian Monarchy among immigrants in America.[11]

The discrimination against South Slavs on Ellis Island disturbed the public at home. The feeling prevailed that something should be done for them. Juraj Biankini, editor of the Zadar newspaper *Narodni list*, national representative in the Diet in Zadar, and member of the Imperial Council in Vienna, articulated these sentiments most ardently. At a session of the Imperial Council on March 13th, Biankini submitted an interpolation to the Prime Minister pleading for the interests of South Slav immigrants on Ellis Island, and against the illegal behavior of the immigration authorities in the United States.[12] Biankini demanded that the Prime Minister intercede with the American government on behalf of South Slav workers. Other public figures also began to express their concern for immigrants. The question of immigration was the subject of heated discussions in the Croatian Diet. In 1902, Grga Tuškan spoke about it in the Diet, stating: "Some of us have different opinions about the sad emigration of our people. But I do not think anyone can say it is really in the interest of the people themselves, or that it would be desirable for emigration to continue in a greater measure that it has been to the present."[13] The representative A. Pinterović provided a more detailed survey of the question of immigration. He stated that the public, press, and various corporations in Croatia had studied the question extensively as had the Diet and many governments. "The immigration of our people into America," he said, "has been growing during recent years, from year to year more and more people are forced under various conditions to leave their homeland and escape into distant parts of the world. If this continues, the question of emigration can become a threat to our national survival itself." Emphasizing that there were one-half million immigrants from Croatia in America, Pinterović continued, "Many immigrants perish in America doing hard labor... some of them stay, and a minority return home. Taking all this into account, we can see the future in store for us if we do not try to put an end to this misery."[14]

Public discussion centered on ways to halt emigration. A widespread campaign was suggested to show people the advantages of working in their own country. Because much of the land in Croatia and Slavonia was unfarmed, it was thought that people could settle there rather than going abroad. There was also some discussion about the need to establish a patriotic society which could purchase peasant land and resell it to new owners at the cheapest installments and under the most favorable conditions. The perseverance and diligence that South Slavs demonstrated in American mines, factories, and railroad construction were also cited. If they worked with equal tenacity on their own land, it was said, they could become as wealthy at home as in America. Simultaneously, peasant land would be improved and its value increased. The peasants could work for themselves and not to enrich an already properous foreign land.

In America, the South Slav immigrant press reacted favorably to these currents among governmental representatives and the public at home but it did not have great faith in the success of any of these measures. Arguing that every man is master in his own house, *Narodni list* wrote that Austro-Hungarian intervention in Washington's policies would be dismissed. The paper censured Austria-Hungary for modernizing her consulates, citing rising costs for people under Austrian rule. South Slav immigrants had little use for those consulates in any case because no one spoke their language there and, as a rule, they received poor treatment.[15]

Expecting little help from home, and even less from official representatives of Austria-Hungary, some immigrant newspapers began a campaign among immigrants to accept American citizenship. The most active agents in this effort were *Chicago* from the city of the same name under its editor Nikola Polić, and *Narodni list* of New York. The latter recorded that Italians and South Slavs were the groups most persecuted by immigration authorities. However, the paper cited the ability of the Italians to organize. Thousands upon thousands of them had obtained American citizenship and became an important force in election campaigns. The paper recommended that South Slavs follow this course as well.

> Without any help from rotting Austria, which only knows too well how to milk us, we must help ourselves. When our people become part of this country even more, when we gain greater

> respect through our societies, when we make efforts to adopt the customs of this country as quickly as possible, we will also be able to take care of our immigrants, because a citizen has more rights and can do more in this land than all the consuls of Austria put together.[16]

Narodni list censured the press in the old country for its strong stance against emigration while simultaneously printing news stories such as "Hunger Here", "Trouble There", etc. It was quite evident that South Slavs were moving to America due to bad economic conditions; many wished to earn some money and send it home. Hungarians and Germans took that money away again through taxation. *Narodni list* suggested: "When our man comes here, let him build himself into this land, let him adopt her customs, let him move here permanently. It is well and good to think about the homeland, but at the end of the nineteenth century some sentimentalities must be put aside. Never forgetting in America our pride in our Croatian heritage, let us be Americans. This land offers us her citizenship, gives us our living, lets us enjoy freedom, treats us in the same way as she treats all her sons. Why then should we not move here permanently, when economic and political reasons make it impossible for us to live in our old country?"[17]

In 1905, however, *Napredak* of Hoboken published a critical review of writing by the South Slav immigrant press concerning discrimination against South Slavs on Ellis Island. Its author was Ivan Grgurević of Dubrovnik, a former medical student in Vienna. Grgurević immigrated to the United States in 1897 as a political émigré. In the following year, 1898, he took part in the Spanish-American War as an officer in the American army. In 1902, Grgurević was appointed as interpreter for Croatian and three other Slav languages on Ellis Island. Some time later, he was named to the high position of federal supervisor for immigration.

In *Napredak*, Grgurević wrote: "I must say openly that to me, the writer of these lines, the present immigration laws are known well, and in detail. I know their spirit, and as an official of several years standing at the Federal Immigration Bureau, I am also familiar with their official execution. On the basis of my own experience and of my official work, I openly say that the present laws are good and sufficient for the benefit of the country itself, and with regard to the fair treatment of the immigrant, they are honest and sufficiently mild." Grgurević denied the reports of the Croatian papers which stated that Croats were an "unwanted" people in the United States because all people are equal before the laws of the United States.

He said that officials had never been given either public or secret instructions about discrimination. Entry into the United States was not based on personal characteristics. If it was true that Croats and Serbs made up the majority of those returned to Europe, then the reasons for this should be analyzed and methods developed to prevent it, according to Grgurević. He suggested that advice be transmitted through the immigrant press in America. Furthermore, he proposed that people should become acquainted with American immigration laws prior to their departure to expedite their arrival. To the ignorant South Slav peasant, infected with "American fever", Grgurević stated that laws governing entry must be explained. These explanations would save many from financial ruin. He recognized that it was no small thing to sell part of one's land to obtain money for the trip and for other expenses in America, only to be returned home from Ellis Island.

Grgurević thought that the solution should not be sought on Ellis Island itself but primarily in the homeland where South Slavs could become familiar with American immigration regulations in an organized manner. He wrote that there were many colonies of Croats and Serbs in America which built expensive churches, halls, parish homes, and schools. They had large numbers of welfare, political, and cultural societies as well as their own printing firms, businesses and were even prominent members of American society. However, they had not yet thought to establish a society to protect their immigrants. Grgurević felt this would be the best way to assist South Slavs upon arrival. Society representatives could meet them, advise them, and direct them to those sections of America where it would be the easiest for them to start new lives. Grgurević stressed that there were few nationalities in New York, Baltimore, Philadelphia, Boston, etc. that did not have their own societies. The Germans had them as well as the Jews, Irish, Italians, Czechs, Poles and others. Such societies were supported by small membership fees from their many members throughout America and by contributions from wealthier compatriots who remembered that they had once been poor immigrants.[18]

Much of what Grgurević said was true. His critical review of the reports of the immigrant press must be respected. *Narodni list*, for instance, wrote the most extensively on the discrimination against South Slav immigrants on Ellis Island. The owner of this paper was Franjo Zotti who had founded an information bureau in New York in 1889 to serve South Slav immigrants immediately upon their arrival. Zotty probably overemphasized bad experiences on Ellis Island to gain the confidence of immigrants and promote his own business.[19] However, Grgurević's statements should also be viewed critically. He spoke as an official of the American administration and, perhaps, protected his professional interests to a certain degree. More importantly, he described the situation on Ellis Island in 1905 after many circumstances had already improved.

The journalist Hinko Sirovatka also described the great injury suffered by South Slavs due to their ignorance of American immigration regulations. He advised travellers to seek out sources in Zagreb who were knowledgeable on such matters prior to embarcation. Sirovatka emphasized that "... nothing is more perilous than to go so far in the dark. Therefore we must work on this problem, and I hope that all patriots will support the foundation of an 'Immigrant Information Centre' or office in Zagreb, which will give information to people who decide to travel to America." Sirovatka went even further, demanding the establishment of an "Immigrant Home" in America to aid South Slavs in that country.[20]

Some intellectuals of Yugoslav origin also described the difficulties encountered by immigrants on Ellis Island. Louis Adamič described his passage through Ellis Island in 1913 in his novel, *Laughing in the Jungle.* He painted a vivid picture of travellers on the ship, children in their arms, with eyes locked on the Statue of Liberty and the shore of their new homeland. The day he spent on Ellis Island was an eternity for Adamič.

> Rumors were current among immigrants of several nationalities that some of us would be refused admittance into the United States and sent back to Europe. For several hours I was in a cold

sweat on this account, although, so far as I knew, all my papers were in order, and sewed away in the lining of my jacket were twenty-five dollars in American currency —the minimum amount required by law to be in the possession of every immigrant before entering the country. Then, having rationalized away some of these fears, I gradually worked up a panicky feeling that I might develop measles or smallpox, or some other disease. I had heard that several hundred sick immigrants were quarantined on the island.

Adamič continued,

The first night in America I spent, with hundreds of other recently arrived immigrants, in an immense hall with tiers of narrow iron-and-canvas bunks, four deep. I was assigned a top bunk. Unlike most of the steerage immigrants, I had no bedding with me, and the blanket which someone threw at me was too thin to be effective against the blasts of cold air that rushed in through the open windows; so I shivered, sleepless, all night, listening to snores and dream-monologues in perhaps a dozen different languages.

Adamič also recalled the uncertainty that accompanied him while cold and bureaucratic officials asked him the usual questions. Their language was a "mixture of several Slav languages" and it was almost impossible to understand them.[21]

Mihajlo Pupin, later to become renowned as an inventor in electronics and a professor at Columbia University, also had problems upon his arrival. In his memoirs he wrote:

When my turn came, Immigration Bureau officials began to shake their heads in a displeased fashion. I admitted to them that I had only five cents in my pocket, that I have no relatives in America and that I know of no one except Benjamin Franklin, Abraham Lincoln, and the writer Beecher Stowe, the author of *Uncle Tom's Cabin,* whose translation I had read. This left a good impression on one of the officials. He looked at me kindly and said: 'you had good taste in your choice of American friends.'[22]

The need for a society to protect South Slav immigrants became increasingly evident and the suggestions of Sirovatka and Grgurević gained more and more adherents throughout the wider Slav community. For years, the Austrian Society had taken care of immigrants from Austria-Hungary on Ellis Island. However, by 1899, *Narodni list* had already criticized this society sharply for the exploitation of South

Slavs. The commissioner General of Immigration William Williams also investigated the operations of this society and found that it was primarily a commercial institution. It exploited immigrants, forcing them to live under difficult and unsanitary conditions on Ellis Island, and charging high fees. In 1909, the activities of the Austrian Society were prohibited.[23]

In 1907, the South Slav immigrant press published many proclamations and appeals for the foundation of the "Slavonic Immigrant Society". *Amerikanski Srbobran*, the newspaper of the Srbobran Alliance, printed the proclamation of the society's founders.

> Led by these views, we set to work and organized a society to represent all Slavs and to impartially and unselfishly care for all Slavs who are in America and who need help and advice. We come before you now, asking for your support in this great endeavor. This is the only work which we all be able to embrace harmoniously, regardless of our political and religious differences.[24]

The Slavonic Immigrant Society was founded on April 25, 1907. *Narodni list* published a detailed report on the inaugural meeting, stating that over one hundred prominent Slav immigrants had gathered in the Czech Hall and agreed to establish the Slavonic Immigrant Society "...which will have the noble task of caring for all Slav immigrants, receiving them in New York and giving them all the necessary instructions." Of the South Slavs present, *Narodni list* mentioned the banker Franjo Zotti and Professor Mihajlo Pupin. The paper referred to Pupin's speech on the difficulties faced by an individual upon his arrival in America, especially if the individual could not speak the American language. Pupin emphasized that the society would, among other aims, prevent the exploitation of immigrants by unscrupulous individuals who would prey on the new arrival's ignorance and naïveté.

Narodni list emphasized that Mihajlo Pupin was a friend of all Slavs and always protected Slav interests. As a professor at Columbia University, he served as the head of many Slav activities in America.[25] Although reluctant to serve, Pupin was elected president of the society. As noted by *Narodni list,* because "...of his work he did not want to take up his honor, but at the unanimous request of all members present, he nevertheless accepted. Since Professor Pupin is a respected and prominent person in American circles in New York, the society has achieved a lot in making him its president."[26]

The National Croatian Society heartily supported the establishment and activities of the Slavonic Immigrant Society. At its Tenth Convention, it decided to donate $500.00 to assist in the work of the Society, a considerable sum in those days. A donation from a wealthy American philantropist, Mrs. X. Jencinks, enabled the society to establish its headquarters. This hall served all Slav immigrants and was maintained with contributions from Czech, Serbian, Croatian, and Slovak benefit organizations. During their first days in America, immigrants could live there for sixty cents. Those who could not pay were given room and board without charge. The Society helped Slav immigrants greatly. The records of the Serbian Immigrant Society Sloga state:

> How much good was done by this Slavonic Immigrant Society for Slav immigrants can only be understood by one who had a chance to see with what care and great love its administration helped immigrants in everything. It is understandable that the Society had opponents in shiftcarders and private bankers, who thought it was taking away their business. Thousands of immigrants were helped by this Society right up to the World War, when the number of immigrants from Europe was reduced to almost nothing. A committee that supervised all institutions of this kind in the name of the Department of Labor, proclaimed the Slavonic Immigrant Hall in New York as the best."[27]

In spite of its merit, the Slavonic Immigrant Society was founded too late. Most Slavs had immigrated to the United States before 1907. Moreover, since Slav immigration to the U.S was reduced to a trickle following world war I, the Society no longer served a purpose.

Notes

1. See Harlan D. Unrau, *Statue of Liberty - Ellis Island*, Historic Resource Study (Historic Component), Volume II of III, U.S. Department of the Interior/National Park Service.

2. *Narodni list (The National Gazette)*, New York, March 24, 1900.

3. *Ibid.*, September 25, 1901.

4. Unrau, *op. cit.*, p.218

5. *Narodni list (The National Gazette)*, November 7, 1899.

6. *Ibid.*, November 14, 1899.

7. *Ibid.*, February 17, 1900.

8. *Ibid.*, April 7, 1900.

9. *Ibid.*, February 3, 1900.

10. *Records of the Croatian National Society*, Wheeling, West Virginia, p. 12.

11. *Arhiv Hrvatske, Spisi Sabora (Archives of Croatia, The Diet Reports*, No. 1069/1906-1911.

12. *Narodni list (The National Gazette)*, Zadar, March 17, 1900.

13. *Stenografski zapisnik Sabora (Stenographic records of the Croatian Diet)*, October 21, 1901, X, 19.

14. *Ibid.*, 1901-1906, 11, 463.

15. *Narodni list, (The National Gazette)*, New York, April 7, 1900.

16. *Ibid.* , April 7, 1900.

17. *Ibid.*,April 7, 1900.

18. *Napredak (Progress)*, Allegheny City, Pennsylvania, 1905.

19. Franjo Zotti, the owner of *Narodni list*, was one of the most interesting personalities as well as one of the most dubious characters to emerge in the history of South Slav immigration. From pauper, to New York street cleaner, to banker, shiftcarder and ship owner, he eventually became the richest Croatian immigrant of all. He died a poor man in America. For years, dozens of immigrant papers attacked him for fraud and corruption. Others praised him and emphasized his good work for immigrants in America. Zotti began his career among South Slav immigrants in 1889 when he opened a bureau in New York to instruct newly-arrived immigrants. After nine years of work, his business developed and he opened a large office at Whitehall and Bridge Streets, which became the centre for all South Slav immigrants for conducting financial transactions and other affairs. The properous business led to the establishment of branches in other towns and large immigrant colonies, notably in Pittsburgh and its surroundings where thousands of South Slavs already resided. In 1904, Zotti opened offices in Chicago. Most of his money came from the sale of tickets. During the first decade of this century, an average of 20,000 immigrants from the Balkans passed through Zotti's agencies. Zotti stated that at least half of the money sent home by South Slav immigrants passed through his banks, for a total of approximately eight million dollars. In 1898, Zotti founded *Narodni list (The National Gazette)*. This paper stated that its task was to serve the interests of Croats in the United States. The paper was "foreign in language only" and "American in spirit" and this attitude was regarded sympathetically in the United States. By 1907, South Slav immigrants had entrusted approximately $800,000 to Zotti. His personal wealth exceeded $500,000 and he owned up to one million dollars in land, houses, and bonds. However, during the American financial crisis of 1907, Zotti experienced his greatest financial setback; a defeat from which he never recovered. After that, he gave great attention to *Narodni list* in an attempt to strengthen

its position and disseminate it among immigrants. The paper was very successfully edited by Stjepko Brozović By 1914, it was a daily with 14,700 subscribers and, by the following year, the number of subscribers reached 24,000.

20. Hinko Sirovatka, editor of *Hrvatska zastava (The Croatian Banner)* of Chicago, described what awaited a traveller, especially a South Slav immigrant, when he arrived on Ellis Island. Sirovatka wrote:

"When the ship approaches any American port, she stops before reaching it, still at sea, and the pilot and a doctor board her from a small boat. All the third-class passengers are then examined by the doctor, to see if they are healthy. Eyes are examined especially closely, so we advise you not to cry on the way to America, because crying makes the eyes red and they may look ill. Cleanliness helps a lot towards making a good impression.

When the ship berths, first and second-class passengers disembark first, and then the ship is taken to a special island in New York, called Ellis Island, together with the third-class passengers. Here wait officials of the immigration department, who examine and interrogate the immigrants one by one. If you arrive against the law or give an answer that harms you, they will immediately place you aside and then you must be investigated.

Here then are some short instructions as to what you have to have and how you must behave there:

(1) You must say to what address (to whom and into which town) you are going;

(2) You must show that you have enough money to reach the person you are travelling to;

(3) You must not say that you have a job promised to you, buy say that you will look for work when you reach your destination;

(4) When you are asked your nationality and citizenship, say: I am from Croatia, or a Croat from Dalmatia, Istria or Bosnia —wherever you are from, or if your name is Serbian, it is not enough to say: I am a Serb, but you must also say the land you are from, because for immigration authorities it makes a great difference whether you are a Serb from Serbia, or from Montenegro, or from Croatian lands, which are in the Habsburg (Austro-Hungarian) Monarchy.

(5) If you are asked any questions about socialism or anarchism, and you do not understand well what that is, simply say that you know nothing about that."

Hinko Sirovatka, *Kaka ja u Americi i kome se isplati onamo putovati? (How It Is in America, and For Whom Does It Make Sense to Travel?)*, Zagreb, 1907, p. 15.

21. Louis Adamič, *Laughing in the Jungle: The Autobiography of an Immigrant in America,* New York, 1932, p.40.

22. Michael Pupin, *From Immigrant to Inventor*, New York/London, 1924.

23. Unrau, *op. cit.*, p. 255.

24. *Amerikanski Srbobran (American Srbobran)*, Pittsburgh, Pennsylvania, May 3, 1907.

25. *Narodni list (The National Gazette)*, April 25, 1907.

26. *Ibid.*, May 3, 1907.

27. *Izvjestaj glavnog odbora Saveza sjedinjenih Srba "Sloga" (Report of the National Committee of the League of United Serbs, "Sloga")*, Los Angeles, California, 1920, p. 8.

"For in America Poles Work Like Cattle": Polish Peasant Immigrants and Work in America, 1880-1921

Adam Walaszek

American historians dealing with social and labor history disagree on such issues as the development of class consciousness, the formation of worker culture, and the pace of proletarianization of European immigrants to the United States in the late nineteenth century. Discussions center on the problem of immigrant culture or ethnicity, which is understood, on the one hand, as a potential base for immigrant protest and, on the other, as a barrier preventing newly arrived immigrants of one ethnic grouping from recognizing the class experience they shared with immigrants of other ethnic backgrounds.

What was the character of the immigrants from Central and Eastern Europe? Were they docile and submissive, or did they play a significant role in the social struggles of the epoch of their arrival?[1] Or should the questions be put differently? Of course, answering these and similar questions is immensely difficult. One must attempt to reconstruct the modes of thought, the perceptions of reality, and the various experiences of people adapting themselves to a totally new environment.

One should begin with a reconstruction of their own subjective vision of things at different periods of time. The present remarks, which concern Polish immigrants from the Russian part of Poland and their opinions about industrial work in America towards the end of the nineteenth century, are a partial attempt at such a reconstruction It is hoped that they will help future historians shed light on the behavior of immigrants at work, their role in the union movement, and their activity or passivity in relation to radical movements.

Beginning in the 1880s, immigrants from Southern and Eastern Europe began to arrive in significant numbers. By 1910 they surpassed the numbers of immigrants from Northern and Western Europe. By the eve of World War I, the number of immigrants of Polish origin was estimated at between two and four million.[2] They arrived in America without skills or training for industrial work. About 85% were employed as common laborers in such industries as steel, furniture, textile, meat packing, and coal mining.[3]

To be sure, each immigrant had profound and complex motivations for coming. Fundamentally, however, the hope of work attracted these peasants to America: they crossed the Atlantic to earn money in order to buy land, build a house, or otherwise improve their lot.[4]

It is commonly assumed that American cities and factories overwhelmed the immigrants whith their complexity and immensity. But the realistic and often dramatic descriptions of living conditions in industrial cities and of working conditions in large factories on which this assumption is based have been left us in the form of notes and observations made by Americans and educated foreigners, i.e. by outside observers: they, not the immigrants, described the noise, the terrifying cries of animals behind the gigantic gates leading to the inferno of the slaughterhouse, they wrote the frightening accounts of the stench, dampness, and dirt of badly lit and stuffy rooms of the textile plants in New England and Illinois, where the roar of machines "hurt the ears so bad that cannon fire seemed a mere trifle compared with it;"[5] they argued that New York factories bore more resemblance to "penitentiaries, prisons, and barracks" than to workshops.[6] Did the immigrants themselves perceive their living and working environment in the same way during the first months or years after their arrival? How did they experience this brutal encounter with the most modern industrial organization in the world?

The rhythm of peasant labor in Europe had been set by nature. Work belonged to the ancient — however ruthless — order of seasonal change.[7] In industrial America, however, the order and organization of labor in industry were purely arbitrary. The worker, particularly the unskilled worker, was almost totally subjected to the supervision of the plant management. He had no part in the decisions which affected every facet of his work. Everything was new, from the job itself, the methods and organization of work, to the final products themselves. What then was the reaction of Polish peasants? Were they really as surprised and shocked as literate observers? In order to answer these questions, this study examines the reactions of immigrants from the villages near Rypin and Krosno.

Emigrants' letters seem the most appropriate material to shed light on these problems. Of course, one cannot rule out the possibility that emigrants falsified facts or described their experiences differently from their most profound feelings. Nevertheless, in these respects private letters are less problematic than memoirs, autobiographies, and other subsequent accounts.[8] These pose the problem of memory. The process of recalling past reality can be more or less conditioned by subsequent events. Writing subsequently, even the most intimate observers have difficulty in distinguishing between later knowledge about described events and awareness at the time the events actually occurred. Moreover, memoirs cannot be treated as representative if only because their authors are unusual in their love of writing. Every memoir should be evaluated and analyzed separately, as an individual source. The information, observations, and opinions it contains can perhaps throw more light on the author than on the realities he experienced. Thus drawing conclusions concerning the recurrence or universality of points raised in memoirs may be unwarranted or even erroneous.[9]

Letters are different, even if we do not dispose of as many as we would like. Witold, Nina, and Marcin Kula's edition of letters enables one to analyze emigrants' views during the first months or years after immigration. The volume contains 367 letters confiscated by tsarist censors in 1890 and

1891. Of these, 176 letters were written by Poles and sent from the United States to the "Old Country." The majority of them are private, sometimes intimate communications.[10]

Strangely, the authors of these letters devote little attention to the problem of work. To make use of these letters for an analysis of work a linguistic approach is required.[11] I have analyzed all the uses and contexts of the word *robota*, which meant work or job (hence here below *robota* is translated as "work," even where "job" would be more appropriate in English). What did these Polish peasants write about their work in the United States?

Hard Work

Most reported that work was hard. In factories it was almost unbearable. Mechanization did not shorten the working hours of common laborers: a twelve-hour day was usual. In steelworks, refineries, and distilleries, high temperatures added to the misery, especially since workers employed in the latter had to wear warm clothes. Work in mines, slaughterhouses, steelworks, or textile plants was qualified as "hard," not only by the immigrants in their letters, but also by outside observers.[12]

Writing to their families and friends in the "Old Country," the immigrants described their jobs in terms of the effort required: work was "hard," "slave-like," "everybody had to work very hard, as hard as a horse belonging to a Jew who burdened it excessively without giving it enough to eat." For some, work was particularly hard in the summer because of the heat.

For others, however, work was "light," "anybody could stand it." One author even wrote, "I have a good and easy job; I must say that I don't work at all but just stand in a steelplant."[13] Finally, others found their jobs both easy and hard. Hardship was defined in terms of the effort involved in doing similar work in Poland. Thus, one often comes across statements that "in America one has to sweat more during a day than during a whole week in Poland," or else that work is "American," "hard American work," or "peasant work." "Will he be able to do a peasant's work?" asks one author about his brother who is planning to leave for America. Why this emphasis on work's being "hard?" In

Poland peasants often did very strenuous physical labor. To quote Wladyslaw Orkan, a well-known Polish peasant writer, "working on the soil requires continuous effort, diligence, and thriftiness. For a farmer, an eight- or twelve-hour working day is a concept which he associates with foreign idleness... That is why, from a very early age, a farmer's bones and mind are permeated with the idea of permanent toil and exhaustion."[14]

Yet these immigrants thought that work in the United States was different. Skills and technologies they had known in Poland proved useless in their new surroundings. The new norms and principles, the new work discipline had to be learnt gradually. This required time. The recent immigrants were called "fresh" men, that is "stupid" men. At the beginning they had a hard time finding work. Then having found it they were unable to work in accordance with the new requirements they faced.

Unable to explain such experiential factors which made the work so hard, the immigrants resorted to quantifying the differences in terms of toil and exhaustion. Work in the United States required perseverance, strength, and stamina. Not all could manage it: "as long as one is healthy and can work hard everything is alright," wrote one immigrant, but another wrote, "because of hard work I became sick and my whole body swelled like a tree trunk."

Sometimes the letter writers contrasted work, which they associated with money and success, and inactivity, which they associated with lack of moral stature. Scoundrels, good-for-nothings, and lazy people simply cannot work in the "American fashion." To find work in the United States and gain from it, one had to fulfil certain conditions: only "hard-working," "thrifty," and enthusiastic people could succeed. The weak and the elderly would not survive. The letter writers agreed that in America a "poor" job, i.e. one involving "hard" work would destroy one, while a "good" job would render one happy.

"Work in America" was the antithesis of "freedom." In the New World the immigrants found no leisure time, no autonomy on the job, in short, no freedom. The foreman was always watching. Working hours were lengthened by artificial lighting and the traditional holidays did not exist: an immigrant's daughter wrote, "apart from Sundays, there are no other holidays."[15] In Poland, as Orkan suggests, holidays provided relief to the hardship of work: "The only bright moments in a succession of grey days, the only milestones of respite along an exhausting road of work, are Sundays; they are the only pauses in the continual toil; they are poetry in the midst of monotony."[16] In America there were no such "bright moments." Leisure time as understood in Poland did not exist in industrial America. "There is no freedom here at all," wrote more than one immigrant, though some found their condition improved: working, wrote one woman, "I have no other duties apart from taking the sewing home, and I can earn a ruble a day."

Language

Work was hard for another reason: the immigrants did not know the language. They were fully aware of their ignorance. Many letters oppose work as a culture to work in practice, "work" versus "foreign language," "not being able to understand," or "being Polish." A Polish girl who worked for a New York dressmaker did not understand any of the instructions given her: "God knows how many tears I shed in the evenings," she remembered in an interview.[17] Of 33,000 immigrants who reported for work in Detroit in 1915, 75% did not know English. Poles were apparently among the most likely not to know English, since they were one of the most illiterate ethnic groups among immigrants, with a literacy rate reportedly below 50%.[18]

Ignorance of English caused all kinds of difficulties. One immigrant presented the problem in a letter to the immigration Commission of the state of Massachusetts: "Better job to get is very hard for me, because I do not speak well English and I cannot understand what they say to me. The teacher teach me — but when I come home I must speak Polish."[19] Inability to communicate in English forced the immigrants to take simple, poorly paid jobs. In extreme cases employers fired those who did not know enough English to read instructions, regulations, and warning notices.[20] Without English it was impossible to get a miner's license.

Conversely, in the immigrants' letters "work" is often associated with "friends," "having a kindred spirit," "relatives," or "family." Friends and relatives helped "greenhorns" to find their first job and later to change it for a better one. They gave advice. Work itself was easier and more pleasant among one's own people. And to have Polish co-workers and a foreign foreman or supervisor was not unknown in the "Old Country," particularly among those who had already done industrial work. Thus paradoxically some Poles, especially those from Silesia, could accept a German foreman with relief.

Insecure Work

Work was not only hard. It was also insecure and unsafe. The irregular pace of production which characterized the American economy of the end of the nineteenth century led to irregular employment and, often, ultimately to unemployment. The immigrants were first fired and last to receive charity when there was any. In any case, they preferred not to accept help from any but their own ethnic group. They eschewed the soup lines.[21]

Unemployment and seasonal labor were totally unknown to the immigrants. They were accustomed, of course, to changing the nature of work with the seasons, but not to being laid off at the end of a season. They did not understand the workings of the American economy, but they could describe the insecurity of work in America. Thus one immigrant wrote to his friends, "there are no jobs in the winter time;" "the factories stop," "they cease working [perhaps a reference to economic cycles]." He went on to distinguish "permanent" work from "insecure", or "bad" work.[22]

The seasonal nature of work was a constant refrain. "This winter I had work but it was a poor one..., when it rained or snowed, we didn't work." "It is hard to get work in the winter." A "good" job was one which continued through the year: "I got a good work and I work all through the summer and winter." Like one of the Polish workers employed in a brickyard, most of the letter writers believed, "work can even be hard, as long as it is permanent."[23] Permanence is associated with "summer," "spring," "warmth," and "Easter."

"Work," conversely, is at least at times associated with the new organization of production and linked to words such as "foreman," "plant," "the burning of coke," and "different surroundings". The immigrants also noticed that fluctuations in the work force and mass immigration made it difficult to find work and keep it for any length of time. They wrote that there were too many people in America and that one "should look for work opportunities elsewhere."

Unsafe Work

Many factors rendered the immigrants particularly prone to accidents: haste, the desire for an increased income, the effort to save materials (as in using timbers to shore up mine shafts), frequent work changes, ignorance of the nature of the work, and ignorance of the language all increased the risks for immigrant workers in an already dangerous industrial system. Polish villagers still recount stories of dangers their relatives encountered in American mines. "One had to dig on and on, and seeing mice or rats, it was necessary to run away, as the walls could fall down," "a job in a mine was quite frightening, for there were many accidents," etc.[24] Obviously, an accident on the job was catastrophic for the immigrant worker since the loss of health and savings shattered the dream of succeeding and returning to Poland.

Work Compared

The immigrants compared work in America to work in Poland. In America work required a bigger or at least a different kind of effort. Many letters express a longing for stability and for a familiar and natural order.

The immigrants perceived that institutional and cultural differences interfered with their work. Yet, although they were aware of many individual elements of the new work environment, they did not understand the fundamental character of the forces behind the factory system and the labor market. Even those who were literate found it difficult to describe precisely the differences in the functioning of factories and in the essence of the jobs performed. Their descriptions lack adjectives, while they abound in metaphors: "one has to work like a horse or an ox, or even harder for horses and oxen in Poland are at least free on Sundays and church holidays."

The letter writers do not discuss the technology of their work. They simply "did the work." Writing to the "Old Country," they had to refer to experience known there. If they could not find a suitable comparison, they just stated that "the Drozdowskis have returned to Poland, so they will give a good account [of what I'm doing]." Nowhere do the workers name their jobs and only rarely do they name the companies or factories for which they work. The factory appears in their eyes as an impersonal institution which simply exists: it "slows down," "goes on," or "does not work at all." Does it have an owner? Only foremen are ever mentioned by name in the letters.

Wages

Work was identified above all with wages. A job meant "a few cents in the pocket," "work that pays one dollar, twenty-five cents," or "one dollar a day." Work was good or bad depending on the pay: "Emil does not have a good work; his wages barely cover his expenses." A "good work" was a better paid job which made it possible to amass some savings.

In Poland "all the efforts and all the toil of the whole family gained little more than something to eat and a few articles of clothing."[25] Recalling unremunerative "peasant work," immigrants wrote that whereas "sometimes in Poland there was nothing to eat and wear," in America, "what any farmer eats on a Saturday is fit to be eaten on a Sunday in Poland." Work in America was a better, "finer" life, measured by the kinds of clothes, food, and drink one could afford.[26] The immigrants perceived work in America in terms of financial gain, promotion, and "success" as defined by their peasant culture.[27]

If one perceives work in terms of gain, does it matter what kind of work one has to do? The nature of labor in the new society was neither interesting nor important enough for the letter writers to devote much attention to it. What was significant was that it could and often did help them in fulfilling their goals. Thus they did everything possible to get well-paid jobs. A difficult, indeed often painful present was to lead them towards a brighter future, even "happiness," as some of them put it.

The peasants came to a new idea of work. It became the work of the individual. It was supposed to serve him. Effort was defined not only by the hardship of the job itself but also by the expected benefits: wages in the short term, "success" in the long term. It would be some time before factory work became something to be proud of. This occurred during the first half of the twentieth century, whence numerous struggles for control on the shop floor. In the period immediately after their arrival, however, the immigrants faced "hard work," acceptable only because of the prospect of high wages and, far before them like a dream, "success."

Notes

1. On this controversy see J.J. Bukowczyk, "Polish Rural Culture and Immigrant Working Class Formation, 1880-1914", *Polish American Studies*, 41 (1984), no. 2, 23-25.

2. A. Brozek, *Polonia amerykanska*, Warszawa, 1977, 35.

3. J.J. Parot, "Ethnic versus Black Metropolis: The Origins of Polish-Black Housing Tensions in Chicago", *Polish American Studies*, 29 (1972), no. 1-2, 24-36; P. Panek, *Emigracja polska w Stanach Zjednozonych A.P.*, Lwów, 1898, 15; E. Morawska, "'T'was Hope Here': The Polish Immigrants in Johnstown, Pennsylvania 1890, 1930", in F. Renkiewicz (ed), *The Polish Presence in Canada and America*, Toronto, 1982, 33; A. Brozek, "Polish Ethnic Group in American Labor Movement", *Studia Historiae Œconomicae*, 13 (1978), 173; M.F. Byington, *Homestead: The House-holds of a Mill Town*, New York, 1910, 134, 138; G. Korman, *Industrialization, Immigrants, and Americanizers: The View from Milwaukee 1866-1921*, Madison, Wis., 1967, 35.

4. J. Kantor, "Czarny Dunajec", *Material y Antropologiczno-Archeologiczne i Etnograficzne*, 9 (1907), 57; E. Morawska, "For Bread With Butter: Life-Worlds of Peasant Immigrants from East Central Europe, 1880-1914", *Journal of Social History*, 17 (1984), 189-391.

5. H. Anielewski, "Z podrózy agitatora", *Robotnik*, no 1, Jan 2, 1902; L. Krzywicki, *Za Atlantykiem. Wrazenia z podrózy po Ameryce*, Warszawa, 1895, 111-113, 115-116.

6. G.M. Price, *The Modern Factory*, New York, 1914, 42, from A. Graziosi, "Common Laborers, Unskilled Workers: 1880-1915", *Labor History*, 22 (1981), 514.

7. J. Borkowski, "Z dziejów chlopów polskich. Rodzina chlopska po uwlaszczeniu", *Kultura i Spoleczenstwo*, 26 (1982), no. 3-4, 130; P. Rybicki, *Spoleczenstwo miejskie*, Warszawa, 1972, s. 288-290.

8. *Pamietniki emigrantów. Stany Zjednoczone*, Warszawa, 1977, Vol. 1, 2.

9. J. Szymanderski, "Znaczenie masowych matérialów pamietnikarskich w badaniach historycznych", *Dzieje Najnowsze*, 12 (1980), no. 2, 160.

10. W. Kula, N. Assorodobraj-Kula, M. Kula (ed), *Listy emigrantów z Brazylii i Stanów Zjednoczonych. 1890-1891*, Warszawa, 1973. When not

pointed differently all quotations from this volume. (translation: *Writing Home, Immigrants in Brazil and the United States, 1890-1891*, New York, Columbia University Press, 1986.

11. I am following the method described by R. Robin, "Approches des champs sémantiques: les expériences du Centre de lexicologie politique de Saint-Cloud", in: R. Robin, *Histoire et linguistique*, Paris, 1973.

12. Letters. Also M. Szawleski, *Wychodztwo polskie w Stanach Zjednoczonych Ameryki*, Lwów-Warszawa, 1924, 58, 61; S. Skylski, *Od Clebeland do Lipna*, Warszawa 1953, 27.

13. W.I. Thomas, F. Znaniecki, *Chlop polski w Europie i Ameryce*, Warszawa, 1976, Vol. 2, 304, letter from the year 1913.

14. W. Orkan, *Listy ze wsi i inne pisma spoleczne*, Warszawa, 1925, Vol. 2, 7; J. Borkowski, *op. cit.*, 129-130.

15. Interview with M.S., village of Ciche, Sept. 1983, in: Emigration from Podhale. Materials, research organized by M. Franci&ca., held in the Polonia Research Institute, Jagiellonian University, Cracow, hereafter PRI.

16. W. Orkan, *op. cit.*, Vol. 2, 7-8.

17. Interview with A.S., Witów, Sept. 1983, PRI.

18. Secretary of the Detroit Board of Education to the Mayor of the City of Detroit, July 15, 1915, Americanization Committee of Detroit Papers, Benthley Historical Collections, Ann Arbor; C.D. Wright, *The Slums of Baltimore, Chicago, New York, and Philadelphia, 7th Special Report of the Commissioner of Labor*, Washington, D.C., 1894, 50.

19. Massachusetts Commission of Immigration, *Report*, Boston, Ma, 1914, 134.

20. W. Kula, N. Assorodobraj-Kula, M. Kula (ed.), *op.cit*, 339; *Pamietniki emigrantów*, Vol. 1: 288. An example of firing workers for poor English is the Union Coal Co. in Shamokin, Pennsylvania, in 1887.

21. US Secretary of Labor, *8th Annual Report for the Fiscal Year Ended June 30*, 1920, Washington, D.C., 1920, 265-267; V.R. Greene, *The Slavic Community on Strike. Immigrant Labor in Pennsylvania Anthracite*, Notre Dame, 1968, 119; D. Brody, *Steelworkers in America. The Nonunion Era*, Cambridge, 1960, 100-101, 105-106, 137; M. Szawleski, *op.cit.*, 60; *Pamietniki emigrantów*, Vol. 1, 139, 197, Vol. 2: 227, 236, 432, 542-543; C. Golab, *Immigrant Destinations*, Philadelphia, 1977, 134-135.

22. W. Kula, N. Assorodobraj-Kula, M. Kula (ed.), *op. cit.*, 333; also ethnic press.

23. D.T. Rodgers, *The Work Ethic in Industrial America. 1850-1920*, Chicago-London, 1978, 170.

24. Interviews with J.F., Kojsówka, Sept. 1983 – R.O., Stare Bystre, Sept. 1983 – F.M., Mietustwo, Sept. 1983, PRI, UJ.

25. J. Slomka, *Pamietnik wloscianina. Od panszczyzny do dni dzisiejszych*, Kraków, 1929, 74.

26. W. Kula, N. Assorodobraj-Kula, M. Kula (ed.), *op. cit.*, 86-87.

27. E. Morawska, "For Bread...," passim.

Freedom in the Workplace? Immigrants at the Scovill Manufacturing Company, 1915-1921

Ferdinando Fasce

The scene of this article is a familiar one to the student of immigration. By 1915 the Scovill Manufacturing Company of Waterbury, Ct, was the single largest brass company in the United States. Like many other private and public institutions all over the country, during the war years Scovill discovered "the immigrant problem" and consequently addressed it for the first time in a systematic way. Equally important, despite its long standing open shop record, the firm could not escape the post-war strike epidemic and had to face two mass strikes carried out by its immigrant employees in 1919 and 1920.[1]

It is the aim of this paper to reconstruct the dynamics of control and adaptation that took place on Scovill's shopfloor between 1915 and 1921. These dynamics revolved, more or less explicitly, around the meaning to be attached to such words as "freedom" and "America". Thus the article will try to show how a company's discourse, centered on bureaucracy and nationalism, intersected and conflicted with one arising from the labor ranks and imbued with a complex blend of class, ethnicity and an embryonic American identity.

Scovill at War

"It would be interesting to have such [labor] figures [by nationality] for 1913 [and 1914]". These remarks, made by the Scovill employment manager in 1932, suggest the absence of any systematic concern on the part of the company about the nationality of its workforce prior to World War I. In fact, given the growing proportion of such foreign stock as Russians and Italians among the population of the city over the first decade of the century (Tab. 1), one might expect to find some detailed trace of this phenomenon among the records of the most important local industrial establishment as well. Yet all one can detect are pieces of scattered evidence showing quite a poor degree of accounting control, apparently common in the U.S. industrial concerns of the early twentieth century. Prior to 1914-15 no comprehensive statistical data was collected, comprising labor figures by nationalities. Such records came with the establishment of an employment department, that was set up to direct and rationalize the massive hiring operations prompted by the war.[2] (Tab.2)

In fact, during its first year of operation, the employment department performed largely an accounting function, while foremen retained most of their discretionary powers with regard to hiring and firing. Such prerogatives were deemed especially valuable by first line supervisors in that they formed the basis for a widespread set of clientage practices ranging from job selling to promotions, work assignments, etc. To be sure, some individuals or a small group of workers might occasionally benefit from the clash between the traditional "rule of thumb" and the new bureaucratic norms which tended to obstruct work organization. However, whatever small portions of "freedom" stemmed from individual maneuvers of informal clique action put workers at the mercy of their foremen in the long run. More importantly, they reinforced, in workers' eyes, the all too familiar patronage habits they were accustomed to within their ethnic communities, while hindering the potential for any collective inter-ethnic action.[3]

To those who resented foremen's clientage practices or, more simply, did not feel content with the average $3.20 wage for a 59 hour week and an unskilled job, the relatively favorable labor market conditions provided one last resort.

Those very people who had left previous jobs because work was "too hard", "too dirty", or "outdoor" could now leave Scovill, in search of better conditions. Hence management had one major concern: the labor turnover, averaging 176% annually between 1916 and 1917, which called for improvements in personnel policies. After America entered the war, the growing need for a wider recruitment, well beyond the usual foremen's reach, enabled the employment department to gain, at least temporarily, the upper hand and put most hiring operations under its direct supervision. Moreover, Scovill introduced an internal personnel transfer system which entrusted the accounting and employment departments with examining carefully any foremen's recommendation for discharge and, if possible, changing it to ensure the employee's transfer to another, more fitting job.[4]

Nevertheless, it would be misleading to isolate such measures from the overall picture of welfare, propaganda and rationalization initiatives carried out by the company during the war. A vantage point from which to look at the whole development seems to be the company *Bulletin*, issued monthly by the Scovill Foremen's Association (SFA) since May 1915 with a starting circulation of 250 copies. The early issues are dominated by one basic feature of "industrial betterment", i.e. safety. By late 1913, under pressures stemming from new state legislation for workmen's compensation, an industrial hospital had been installed within the plant to counter a health situation that was to become more and more serious as the number of workers increased on the payroll. Besides praising the results accomplished by the hospital, the *Bulletin* was also at the forefront of the "safety first" campaign. This was conducted through close cooperation with the National Safety Council, by posting signs printed in several languages throughout the plant.

Safety also provided management with one major channel through which to reach all employees. The issue resulted in the creation of safety committees and the launching of a system of boxes installed at various points in the main building to gather employees' "safety suggestions and any other ideas that will promote the welfare of workers and the efficiency of the shop". Given the dreadful safety record of the plant and the attractive prospects of some wage raises or promotions, it is no surprise that workers' messages filled boxes by the thousands. Nor was it unusual to find immigrant workers submitting their technical proposals.[5]

At the same time the severe housing problem plaguing Waterbury prompted the company to erect barracks, with large dormitories, for over 500 employees. Through close cooperation between the employment department and the local YMCA branch, dining and recreational facilities were provided as well. As regards recreation, a significant contribution also came from the SFA and the Scovill Girls Club (SGC). The latter had been established in 1916, at the time of the first "Get Together Day" open to all Scovill employees, in order to reach the growing numbers of women workers, who comprised nearly 21% of the workforce in 1914 (women employment reached a peak of 27% three years later). Soon to claim a membership of over 500, the SGC was instrumental in organizing various war propaganda activities that were of special importance in the fall of 1917, when some 500 former Scovill employees joined the ranks of the US Army in Europe. Writing or sending smokes to the "boys in khaki", organizing benefit balls and selling Liberty bonds were the main tasks performed by the SGC.[6]

"The army that stays at home"

Before long this patriotic propaganda was being integrated with a message more closely linked to the shopfloor and to the drive for efficiency which had occupied a significant portion of the *Bulletin* from the outset. From late spring 1918 onwards, Scovill discovered and extolled a new brood of patriot: "the army that stays home". Such an army was praised because it bought Liberty Bonds: by May 1918 some 83% of the Scovill workforce had bought one or more Liberty Bonds issued for the third campaign, totalling over $550,000. Praise was also directed at the seemingly unmistakable American patriotism of its foreign-born. At patriotic rallies held within the plant and featuring speeches in Russian, Italian and English, pictures revealed "(...) Thousands of uplifting hands repeating the pledge of *fidelity to the nation and the Scovill* (...) This pledge (...) promises the *speeding up of production for all materials*".[7]

This episode marks the culminating point in the company's campaign, as revealed in the *Bulletin*'s coverage of the immigrant problem over the years. Between May 1915 and September 1917 just two references to the subject appeared in the form of letters from immigrant workers. Then, in September 1917 the *Bulletin* featured an article on the second Liberty Bond campaign, and spoke highly of "our foreign-born employees" who "carried through nobly". Four months later, in recognition of the significant proportion of non-English speaking employees (14.6% of the whole workforce), the employment department started a program of English education classes. The program, based on Peter Roberts' method, included some fundamentals of arithmetic, basic knowledge of written English, plus such basic notions of both the US Constitution and history as would enable candidates to pass their court examinations for citizenship. Classes were originally provided for some 112 male workers. They were carefully selected by room foremen among "the most intelligent and faithful of our foreign-born employees."[8]

In a few months the educational program was enlarged and extended to female workers. Thus, when all these initiatives, together with soaring sales and profits, are viewed in the light of workers' response, that is the "thousands of uplifting hands" and "the pledge of fidelity", managerial efforts seem to have reaped rewards. Moreover, workers' response mirrored the strong interpenetration between the company and the national cause that went well beyond the factory gates, as any employee could testify. It was quite common to find the names of various members of the Goss family, Scovill's owners and managers, on patriotic posters, printed in different languages by the local section of the Connecticut Council of Defense, which were circulated throughout the city. No less common was the sight of the Scovill employment manager jumping on the stage of a local burlesque or movie theater and interrupting the show, in order to make a short, inflamatory speech as a leading member of the local "Four Minute Men" committee.[9]

Individual efficiency and loyalty to Scovill were the best way to show one's allegiance to the new country, as well as to lay the foundations for a better future, both as a Scovill employee and as an American citizen: this was the message conveyed at Americanization classes and propagated by the *Bulletin* among its 8,000 readers. On the other hand, the magazine also stated no less clearly what illicit and un-American behavior was. Sponsored by the Committee on Public Information, pages featured warnings against "spies and lies" (i.e. labor organizers) and urged "every citizen (...) to be a detective." Indeed, for people like Mario De Ciampis, a Scovill employee, but also a radical organizer for the Italian Socialist Federation, there was no need to read the *Bulletin* in order to realize that the shopfloor was increasingly filled with company informers. By 1918 this danger prompted him to leave the city, where he had come a couple of years before to join his brother, "because they (the Scovill management) were looking for me."[10]

This case calls for further investigation of the active, but largely underground presence of the "radical persuasion" in Waterbury between 1917 and 1918. At the same time it testifies to the complex reality of competing cultures and interests workers were exposed to daily. For example, Goss sent a notice to his overseers on the eve of patriotic rallies urging them to "impress upon the employees that the factory is closed simply for the purpose of allowing them to attend the Rally and not to go elsewhere". Other examples raise similar questions. It would be interesting to know to what extent such practices as the zealous canvassing for military censuses or selling of Liberty Bonds by 109 Italian Scovill employees, who had served in the Army, were influenced by their ethnic middle class search for legitimation. Relative to Liberty Bonds, we need to assess whether the "pride" with which an eighteen year old Albanian told of his $100 certificate during an oral English lesson reflected an economic or an emotional investment, or both.

The same question concerning the balance of psychological and utilitarian motives arises when one looks at teachers' and foremen's reports on education. For some workers the incentive to attend classes came from informal promises of wage raises and promotions made by foremen, or from the conviction that learning the language would prove a good asset, especially in the changing labor market of the reconversion era. On the other hand, some married women were urged to learn English by the desire to "keep up to the standard which their children (...) were setting for them". These women resented "being called 'Wops', 'Dagoes', and 'Polacks' by children, sometimes their own". The case of Joe Persio, an Italian worker, provides one crucial clue to our understanding of the often covert interests and energies the company was able to mobilize. Persio felt stimulated by English classes to bring his first citizenship paper to his teacher the very day before the seven year limit to apply for the second. He wanted her help before it was too late.[11]

All in all, Scovill was moving beyond the boundaries of a mere economic actor. Rather it was establishing itself as a paternalistic institution with a "broadened conception of its *duty* towards them (the employees)", as one local newspaper put it. In exchange for their allegiance to a set of commonly shared values, Scovill seemed able to furnish its employees with at least some of the material and cultural resources they needed in order to solve the dilemmas and conflicts posed by their immigrant status. It was the company that during the war helped immigrant workers to get in touch with their families residing in belligerent countries. After the war, it was again the company that proved instrumental in personalizing the abstract American outside world, by taking workers to visit the local public institutions, "even the police station", so that they might "become real to them". Thus "America... seemed a little nearer" to one class of girls who, during a visit to the local park, "had finally realized that it belonged to them for recreational purposes." Nor did management overlook the importance of finding such ways to mediate between native and ethnic cultures as distributing paycheck forms printed in Italian or Russian, promoting and largely publicizing, through the SFA, dances and music performed by employees from different ethnic groups, and using Italian and Lithuanian instructors for education classes.[12]

Scovill teachers also recognized the difficulties immigrants found in trying to reconcile new interests with more traditional, but no less demanding ones that stemmed from family or ethnic ties. Class attendance often dropped according to seasonal events. Teachers could easily ascribe this to workers' desire to devote some time to their own small gardens or to recreational and religious celebrations held within their ethnic communities. No less important, according to teachers' reports, were the objective contradictions between education classes or safety committees, on one side, and, on the other, foremen's persistent practices which undermined the inner logic of paternalistic bureaucracy. In some cases, it was the harshness and seasonal nature of particular jobs that exposed workers most easily to the risk of layoffs and prevented them from taking full advantage of company's welfare measures.[13]

The eternal law of supply and demand

After the armistice the payroll was more than halved during four months (December 1918-April 1919) of massive layoffs. By July 1919 Scovill management could point to what seemed to be the unquestionable benefit of its educational plan. During a three weeks strike that had just ended, "fifty-three per cent of all foreign employees left the plant, whereas only three and one-half per cent of those attending the Scovill Manufacturing Company's school were out." Prompted by a significant increase in the cost of living (15.2% between 1918 and 1919), the strike, the first to hit the "brass valley" in almost twenty years, was conducted by immigrant workers at Scovill and other major brass concerns through an *ad hoc* local organization, the Waterbury Workmen's Association (WWA). Not a union in the strictest sense of the word, the WWA was rather a cluster of ethnic societies that received assistance from the conservative North American Civic League for Immigrants. After one week, the strikers were joined by the native skilled workers, some 15% of the whole workforce, wage increases of 25% for the skilled workers and 10% for the unskilled settled the strike.[14]

Such wage raises, however, were soon nullified by another 15.75% jump in the cost of living, which was compounded by the company's decision to abolish bonuses that had been granted to immigrant workers since the war. As a result, it was now almost impossible for the average family to live on a $22.50 weekly wage. Against this re-emergence of the "eternal law of supply and demand", as the company termed its tough reconversion policy, a new immigrants' strike ensued in April 1920. And this time the participation was so massive that there was no cause for speculation as to whether education classes were a deterrent against conflict. With no national or local official union behind them and almost no support from native skilled workers, immigrants replaced the WWA, which had been disbanded shortly after the end of the 1919 strike, with the New England Workmen's Association (NEWA), an organization quite similar to the previous one.

It is hard to establish the role played by such individual union men as Carlo Cappoza in conducting the strike and shifting the self-proclaimed "conservative" NEWA towards an increasingly militant position. A former AFL organizer at Scovill, Cappoza, after being discharged for possessing a union card, joined the NEWA. It is even harder to assess the influence exerted by a few IWW members who, having survived the Palmer raids, though officially banned from the NEWA, took part in strikers' meetings. What is clear is the quite accurate knowledge of the factory problems revealed by the strikers' committee, a knowledge that only people who had passed though patriotic parades, safety boxes or Americanization classes could possess. Thus it is no wonder to find at the core of the strike, workers with one to six years' service with the company.[15]

Besides asking for wage increases, for abolition of all piece-work and for recognition of independent shop committees as a bulwark against foremen's abuses, such workers did not fail to point out that "welfare work in the shops is nothing short of a joke [...] but a mask to camouflage the shortcomings of foremen". Similarly they gave their own interpretation of the "eternal law of supply and demand" by "bombarding [...] managerial representatives with scores of questions of an intricate economic nature, asking the why and wherefore of demand and supply, of fluctuating prices, of profiteering, of low prices." And when Goss stated in one local newspaper that strikers were like children who "go into tantrums", workers immediately replied that "we don't go into the shops to sing any 'ring-around-the-rosies'. We produce, and we have a right to demand our *price*". Accordingly they rejected any proposal to settle the conflict by enlarging such welfare measures as the company store that Scovill had opened a few months before to counter the recession. Time and again Italians and Lithuanians stated that what they wanted was no company gift, but a decent "American" wage, that would also cover them during the slack seasons and provide them with some recreation in their leisure time.[16]

Behind the firm opposition to the company store there also lay the strong solidarity between workers and their ethnic shopkeepers who, along with bankers and merchants, supported strikers by donating large sums, opening special forms of credit and refusing to accept rents. That same ethnic community was penetrated, in turn, by the solidarity arising at the point of production. Many Lithuanians and Russians, who were mostly single, donated money to Italians, who had to support large families. Nothing better illustrates this point, however, than the sympathy and support Italians received from other ethnic groups when Libero Tiso, a young Italian striker, was killed during a dramatic clash with the police at the Scovill gates. The impressive funeral, with floral tributes valued at close to $400, as well as the big wreath bearing the inscription "Deepest sympathy from the people of Waterbury" struck a defiant response to Yankee middle class claims that unions and strikes were just the offspring of the "excitable type of Italians" and that the only legitimate union was that established in 1776.

On the other hand, the circular which was found on Tiso's body well summarizes the full awareness of their own rights that workers had repeatedly expressed during both 1919 and 1920 strikes. On such occasions strikers paraded in their veterans' uniforms, wore Liberty buttons, carried American flags, defined their foremen as "kaisers", and charged the police and employers were violating American laws by denying workers their fair share. The circular read: "Where is the word of honor of our manufacturers who promised everything and gave nothing? Where is the democracy that our boys gave their lives for? Wake up, American workers; can't you see that we have another kaiser, another von Hindenburg, another czar who is conspirating to destroy humanity?" Yet, it was probably Tiso's father, an absolutely unpoliticized immigrant worker, who best captured the collective quest for dignity and freedom that so many observers, even the least sympathetic, would notice when describing strikers' meetings: "What's American respect of the people? What's America doing? What are we doing in this country?"[17]

Several weeks later this quest was smashed, when Scovill immigrants, after a three months' strike, had to give up. When John Sampino, just a few months after his arrival from Montepagano (Campobasso, Italy), entered Scovill's buff department in the early 1920s, he soon understood that the limits of freedom within a workplace increasingly dominated by time and motion studies were clearly set: "La fattoria era grande: se io ero in una room non potevo andare nelle altre. Se ti pescavano, ti dicevano: You don't belong over here (...) Non dovevi parlare di unioni."[18]

Conclusions

This inquiry into Scovill's shopfloor life over the years 1915-21 has emphasized, along with deep structural changes, the complex process through which immigrant workers, who comprised most of the company's workforce, formed a distinctive if temporary, collective identity. Thanks to several propaganda and welfare activities, Scovill had emerged out of the war as a paternalistic *institution*, an institution that, through rituals and symbols, seemed able to personalize, in workers' eyes, the model of the "employee-citizen". This meant, on the one hand, a stronger vision of the state and the nation intruding upon workers' lives, and, on the other, the emergence of the company as a state within the state, that might successfully compete in winning over workers' loyalty with more traditional sources of allegiance such as kinship and ethnicity.

After the war no less dramatic changes occurred, and ones which look familiar to the student of labor relations in that era.[19] Scovill management did not live up to its "new duty" towards its employees and, under economic pressures, turned swiftly to massive layoffs and heavy wage cuts. As a result, in 1919 and 1920 this long standing open shop city witnessed two major spontaneous immigrants' strikes.

What surfaces, especially in the 1920 strike, appears to be consistent with other scholars' findings on the relations between class and ethnic cohesiveness in nineteenth and twentieth century America.[20] Far from conflicting, these two facets of consciousness mutually reinforced each other. By rejecting paternalistic managerial proposals to settle the dispute, Scovill employees identified themselves primarily as workers, with an instrumental attitude toward the company. But, in order to do so they had to draw largely on the organizational and emotional resources offered by traditional ethnic ties. However, class and ethnicity needed one common (and legitimating) language to express themselves. This was provided, to some extent, by the word "America" and the whole symbolic system it evoked. When taken away from its most conservative arenas — be it Scovill's Americanization classes or the North American Civic League for Immigrants' halls — and transferred into the heat of strikers' meetings, the rhetoric of "American democracy" proved to be quite a well-suited tool for workers' needs. Besides functioning as a legitimizing weapon towards the public, it probably worked as an emotional, anti-anxiety valve for immigrants who had been undergoing a critical phase of individual and collective stress and uprooting because of the war. For all its ambiguities, workers found in the "American" idiom a way to turn upside down the "employee-citizen" model purported by the company on its very ground, and a better means to articulate many different and not always easily reconcilable levels of discontent. This discontent ranged from radical appeals against the employers, labeled as "new kaisers", to individual expressions of one's life-time disillusionment with the new country.

The sudden disappearance of such a fragile collective stand from Waterbury's public discourse, after the strike's failure, does not seem a good reason to dismiss it on the basis of some abstract notion of hegemony or structural exceptionalism. Rather it is a challenge to dig further into the intricate mixture of collective aspirations expressed during the strike and to examine what happened to that mixture on an individual and family basis within the pacified ethnic quarters of the "lean years".[21]

Notes

I wish to thank Jeremy Brecher, David Brody, Leon Fink, A.M. Martellone, Richard Oestreicher, Linda Schneider, and Loretta Valtz Manucci for their helpful comments on an earlier draft of this paper.

1. John Bodnar, *Immigration and Industrialization* (Pittsburgh, Univ. of Pittsburgh Press, 1977), 119-126; John F. McClymer, "The Americanization Movement and the Education of the Foreign-Born Adult, 1914-25" in Bernard J. Weiss (ed.), *American Education and the European Immigrant, 1840-1940* (Urbana, Ill., Univ. of Illinois Press, 1982), 96-116.

2. Scovill Collection II (hereafter cited as SCII), vol. 240-42 and cases 28, 33, and 59, Baker Lib., Harvard Business School, Boston, Mass.;

Sanford Jacoby, *Employing Bureaucracies* (New York and Oxford. Oxford Univ. Press, 1985), *passim.*

3. SCII, cases 34 and 65, vol. 257-58, box 33a; Jeremy Brecher, Jerry Lombardi, Jan Stackhouse, *Brass Valley* (Philadelphia, Pa., Temple Univ. Press, 1982).

4. SCII, vol. 54-55, 57, 76, 328 and case 34.

5. SCII, case 28.

6. Cecelia Bucki, *Metals, Minds, and Machines* (Waterbury, Mattatuck Historical Society, 1980), 76-77; Jim Cusack, interview by Jeremy Brecher, Brass Workers' History Project, Mattatuck Museum, Waterbury (hereafter cited as BWHP,MM); SCII, cases 28 and 33-34 and vol. 313a.

7. SCII, vol. 313a. Emphasis mine.

8. SCII, vol. 313a.

9. Connecticut Council of Defence (hereafter cited as CCD), RG 29, box 24, RG 30, boxes 166 and 312, Connecticut State Library (hereafter cited as CSL), Hartford, Ct. On the Council see Bruce Fraser, "Yankees at War: Social Mobilization and Connecticut Homefront, 1917-18", Ph.D. Dissert., Columbia Univ., 1976.

10. SCII, vol. 313a; Mario De Ciampis, interview by Jeremy Brecher, courtesy Jeremy Brecher.

11. SCII, cases 28, 33 and 34; B.B. Schubert, "The Palmer Raids in Connecticut", *Connecticut Review* (October 1971), 65 ff.; R. Oestreicher, *Solidarity and Fragmentation* (Urbana, Ill., Univ. of Illinois Press, 1986).

12. SCII, case 33; CCD, CSL, RG 30, box 169. Emphasis mine. On paternalism see Tamara K. Hareven, *Family Time and Industrial Time* (Cambridge, Mass., Cambridge Univ. Press, 1982).

13. SCII, cases 28 and 33.

14. SCII, case 33, box 33a and vol. 243-45.

15. SCII, vol. 243-48; box 33a; case 33.

16. SCII, vol. 244-45; case 58. Emphasis mine.

17. SCII, vol. 244-45; Department of Justice File, RG 65, Roll 799, M-1085, National Archives, Washington, D.C.; James Tiso, interview by Jeremy Brecher, BWHP,MM.

18. SCII, vol. 246-47; John Zampino, interview by Ferdinando Fasce, Waterbury, Oct. 8, 1985; *Brass Valley*, 118.

19. David Brody, *Steelworkers in America: The Non-Union Era* (New York, Harper, 1969), 180-198; David Montgomery, "New Tendencies in Union Struggles and Strategies in Europe and the U.S., 1916-22" in James Cronin and Carmen Sirianni (eds.), *Work, Community, and Power* (Philadelphia, Pa., Temple Univ. Press, 1983) and "Nationalism, American Patriotism, and Class Consciousness among Immigrant Workers in the U.S. in the Epoch of WWI" in Dirk Hoerder (ed.); *Struggle a Hard Battle*, (DeKalb, Ill, Northern Illinois Univ. Press, 1986); Rudolph J. Vecoli, "Anthony Capraro and the Lawrence Strike of 1919" in George E. Pozzetta (ed.), *Pane e Lavoro* (Toronto, Multicultural History Society of Ontario, 1980); Linda Schneider, "American Nationality and Workers'

Consciousness in Industrial Conflict: 1870-1920", Ph.D. Dissert., Columbia Univ. 1975.

20. Eric Foner, *Politics and Ideology in the Age of the Civil War* (New York and Oxford, Oxford Univ. Press, 1980); Hoerder (ed.), *op. cit.*, *passim*; Jonathan Gillette, "Italian Workers in New Haven" in Joseph L. Tropea, James E. Miller, Cheryl Beattie-Repetti (eds.), *Support and Struggle* (Staten Island, N.Y., The American Italian Historical Association, 1986); Gary R. Mormino, George E. Pozzetta, *The Immigrant World of Ybor City* (Urbana, Ill., Univ. of Illinois Press, 1987).

21. John J. Bukowkzyk, "The Transformation of Working Class Ethnicity", *Labor History* (Winter 1984).

Table 1. Waterbury Population by Country of Birth, 1890-1920

Country of birth	1890	1900	1910	1920
Native-born				
Native parents	19,068	30,941	47,643	61,821
Foreign-born				
Canada	1,362	2,266	1,901	1,521
England & Wales	724	982	1,243	1,086
Germany	887	1,195	1,433	1,010
Ireland	5,402	5,866	5,838	4,507
Italy	308	2,007	6,567	9,232
Lithuania	*	*	*	3,674
Poland	102	*	*	1,629
Russia	123	1,265	5,600	3,209

* In designated years Lithuanians were enumerated as Russians and Poles were enumerated as Russians, Germans or Austrians.

Source: U.S. Census, designated years, Washington, D.C., 1891, 1901, 1913, 1922.

Table 2. Scovill Workforce by Nationality, 1914-21

Year	Total	Amer.	Fren.	Ger.	Rus.	Irish	Ital.	Lith.	Pol.	Alb.	Port.
1914	3,509	-	-	-	-	-	-	-	-	-	-
1915	6,379	38.2%	5%	1.8%	1.1%	11.6%	18.8%	7%	4.7%	-	-
1916	11,000	36%	3.8%	1.1%	8.9%	9.7%	19.5%	6.3%	9.6%	-	-
1917	12,808	40%	3.4%	0.93%	9%	8.5%	19.3%	5.8%	8.3%	-	-
1918	12,900	45%	1.41	0.50%	9.8%	5.9%	18.4%	3.6%	12.7%	-	-
1919	7,242	45.9%	-	-	7.5%	6.6%	18.8%	4%	3.1%	1.9%	3.1%
1920	6,816	50.2%	-	-	5.2%	7.3%	17.8%	3.4%	2.8%	0.9%	2.5%
1921	4,704	57,3%	-	-	2.5%	7.6%	17.1%	2.8%	1.5%	0.8%	0.9%

Source: SCII, cases 34-35-36.

III

The Transatlantic Perspective

Part III underlines the necessity of adopting a transatlantic perspective in order to grasp the meaning of immigrant experience and radicalism which can be understood only if one examines the interaction between social events and social movements on both sides of the Atlantic and the continuous exchange of political ideas and symbols between the old and the new worlds.

1 Immigrant radicalism: the European connection

The papers by Bruno Cartosio, Julianna Puskas and Ronald Creagh enable us to take a new look at three immigrant groups — the Sicilians, the Hungarians and the French — all of whom were connected in one way or another with radicalism in the U.S.

As mentioned in the Introduction, the term "immigrant" has been criticized for its imprecision, and for the confusion to which its indiscriminate usage gives rise. The inadequacy of the term "illiterate" is even more striking. Until recently, immigration historians have lumped together illiterate immigrants in a kind of undifferentiated mass. Bruno Cartosio and Julianna Puskas invite us to pay more attention to what lies below the term. Cartosio's description of Sicilian radical peasants and workers challenge the commonly held assumption there was a necessary relationship between illiteracy and inability to organize. Some of these illiterate peasants were highly articulate and had a well-defined political culture. He reminds us that ideas are not spread exclusively by writings and by books but also orally. Radical ideas were not brought into the U.S. by "educated" people only but by these "illiterate" peasants as well. Cartosio thus brings into new focus the cultural profile of the politicized immigrant.

Nor were Hungarian immigrants the primitive brutes Terence Powderly and others claimed them to be. According to Julianna Puskas the rate of literacy among them was extremely high at the end of the nineteenth century. The living and eating habits for which they were so despised should be linked to their life strategies. Mass migration of Hungarians was based on the premise of a quick return home. Hungarian immigrants constituted a highly diversified group, socially, nationally and politically. A number of them were Socialists, who organized associations, published newspapers and played an active role both in the Socialist Labor Party and the Socialist Party of America. Divided as they were as to how they should relate to the American labor movement and to American political organizations, they nevertheless significantly enriched the radical culture of the American working class.

Contrary to the widespread opinion that French immigrants were so few as to be insignificant and that they were mostly middle class, Ronald Creagh has uncovered the presence of French workers in Pennsylvania coal mines in the 1880s and 90s and studied their role in spreading radical ideas through newspaper publication and militant action during the last quarter of the nineteenth century.

These papers raise several questions about radical ideas and forces in the U.S.: what happened to them when they were transplanted from Europe? What conditions ensured their permanence? Of course, many variables were involved: local conditions, vitality of the radical movement in the homeland, role of militants, reception of the immigrant groups in the U.S. But essential was the interaction between events taking place on both sides of the Atlantic, interaction between immigrants and social movements in their native land. For instance, close contact existed between the young Swedish labor movement and socialist immigrants in the U.S. (Tedebrand in Part I). Sicilians and Italians were "part of the Italian labor movement" (Cartosio). Connections between immigrants and political groups in the old country, networks of correspondents for the labor and socialist press were extensive and lasting. The link between immigrants and their native land was not just nostalgia that fed on idealized memories, it could be militancy. Several of the papers in this volume are an invitation to investigate further the continuity of radicalism across national borders and the fact that ideas travel in more than one direction.

The study of European radicalism in the U.S. also implies that one looks at how it takes to the new soil and strikes roots in its new environment. The papers by Julianna Puskas, Bruno Cartosio, and Ronald Creagh give us an insight into the ways in which European socialist and anarchist groups developed a dynamics of their own and attempted to build a strategy in relation to the American social movement.

This movement in turn had its impact on Europe. American struggles and conflicts fueled labor unrest in various places – in Italy, for instance (Vecoli) and struggles in the old country caused agitation among radical circles in the States (e.g. the general strike of 1909 in Sweden; Tedebrand). More than once, events were turned into symbols that gave new meaning to the lives of militants on both sides of the Atlantic. Exchanges took place on a symbolic level. The Commune was a living symbol that precipitated action: It was an inspiration to militants in the more faraway corners of Pennsylvania in the 1880s and 90s. Meanwhile Haymarket aroused and mobilized socialist and labor militants in Europe.

2. The Impact of Haymarket on European social movements

Not only was Haymarket crucial in reshaping the representation of America among European radicals but it also influenced the socialist and labor movements (Hubert Perrier and Michel Cordillot).

To understand how this influence worked and through what instrumentalities, Hubert Perrier and Michel Cordillot investigate the origins of May Day and its relationship both to the AFL eight-hour campaign and the Haymarket Tragedy. First they attempt to unravel the complex interactions between the American and the European socialist and labor organizations that may account for the choice of that symbolic date. Then they examine very closely the processes which led to the original decision taken by the International Socialist Congress in Paris in July 1889 to select the First of May as an international workers' holiday and a day of struggle. The founding of international May Day cannot be separated from "labor's debates and experiments in the field of social legislation and in that of political or economic tactics." Finally, the authors make clear the fact that the decision was related to the impact of Haymarket upon the European socialist and labor movements. At the time the "Great Upheaval," the trial and judicial murder received considerable attention in Europe. The radical and labor press drew its conclusions from the Haymarket trial: the "model republic" was a sham, the United States a "blood-thirsty" Republic. And the anarchists proposed that the Statue of Liberty be renamed "The Goddess of Murder." The Haymarket affair inspired an unprecedented solidarity campaign throughout Europe. It was the most important demonstration of internationalism during the period between the First and Second Internationsl. Here again, recent research has uncovered extensive and intricate networks of correspondents and contacts which kept militants up to date on recent developments and played a part in the launching of numerous initiatives. These are paths which need to be explored. Besides, the Haymarket affair became a symbol whose legacy was diverse. Its commemoration was observed quasi religiously in Italy (Vecoli). It caused the "conversion" of some outstanding personalities to anarchism and socialism. It was the starting point of the formation of political groups.

No doubt, from what Perrier and Cordillot demonstrate, it was instrumental in bringing together – in spite of noticeable tactical differences and ideological divergences – American and European labor and socialist organizations at one moment in time, around 1889-90, when some convergence regarding May Day took shape. Things changed in the years that followed. On the one hand, the relationships between the AFL and the Socialist Labor Party deteriorated and, on the other, the mainstream of American trade-unionism became estranged from the Second International. Then, early in the 1900s the AFL lost interest in the First of May, marking its preference for Labor Day. While in Europe the influence of the Haymarket Tragedy remained very much alive, especially in Spain, the "link between 1886, the U.S.A. and May Day" was "considered as seminal by the anarchists who dominated the labor movement." In France, its import was self-evident in the growth of revolutionary syndicalism whose advocate, Emile Pouget, vice general secretary of the Confédération Générale du Travail (CGT), "raised the American example to the status of a doctrine, the idea of direct and simultaneous mass action conceived as a preparation for the general strike."

Sicilian Radicals in Two Worlds

Bruno Cartosio

At the beginning of the twentieth century, Italy was still a predominantly rural country. Its economy was based on agriculture and the majority of its active population was working in the fields.[1] Even so, unionism was fairly widespread. Peasants' unions contributed to this. In fact, the unionization of agricultural workers was a distinctive feature of the Italian political and social scene. In no other European country were socialism and unionism so widespread among non-industrial workers as in Italy. In 1901, the members of Italian unions and "Camere del Lavoro" were 661,478. Among them, 152,122, or 23%, were agricultural workers members of the National Federation of agricultural wage workers, the *Federterra*.[2]

Many Italian immigrants to the United States came from this kind of background. American anti-immigrationists were opposed to Italians because, in their opinion, they were nothing more than illiterate southern peasants. The same viewpoint was common within the labor movement. To Samuel Gompers Italians overwhelmingly belonged to "that class which by reason of its lack of intelligence, is slowest to appreciate the value of organization."[3] A class that depressed wages and the standard of living as well as increased unemployment, maintained Terence Powderly.[4]

It is true that the majority of them were peasants and illiterate. In 1901, 44.47% of all emigrants from Italy were small landowners and tenant farmers, and 26% were laborers.[5] In the period 1900-1914, 52% of all southern Italians of 10 years of age and over entering the United States were illiterate.[6] What cannot be held is that they did not and that they could not understand the principles and practice of workers' organization. Illiteracy did not prevent either southern or northern Italian peasants from organizing themselves. Word of mouth, collective reading of newspapers, political materials, and of general literature was extremely common. Poems written by radical poets were often known by heart. Moreover, propaganda tours, lectures, and speeches by local and national leaders were the usual ways whereby the obstacle of illiteracy was overcome and organization was attained. In turn, becoming a unionist or a socialist was in itself an enormous spur towards learning. And very often the organizations supplied their militants with evening school education, conducted by other militants.

Emigrants quickly learned the importance of literacy and attended evening schools or learned how to read in other ways while abroad. Both emigrants and returned emigrants put pressure on their families to make sure that children would be sent to school. Actually, after emigration started to increase in the 1890s, a demand for schools grew in the Italian South. It should not be overlooked "that it was exactly in the period of maximum growth of foreign emigration that literacy increased rapidly in certain Italian regions, particularly in the South."[7]

Of course, radicals and unionized workers were a minority, both in Italy and among Italian emigrants. But it was even more so among "American" workers before the "new immigration" took place. Trade and industrial unionism, socialism, and radicalism in general grew considerably in the United States after Southern and Eastern Europeans immigrated. That growth brought into contact different ideas and practices of organization. Gompers's hostility against the new immigrants was also due to their being "revolutionists" more often than "pure and simple" trade unionists. But even within the field of revolutionary radicalism there is no doubt that being an anarchist or a socialist, a Sicilian socialist or an American socialist, or a German socialist in America meant quite different things. These differences, among other factors, accounted then for the exclusionary policies of the trade union movement and subsequently for the biased perspectives of those labor historians who assumed Gompers's ideology as their own.[8]

I have written elsewhere about Italian immigrants attracted by the Industrial Workers of the World.[9] In the same essay I analyzed the hostility of American trade unionists and socialists, and pointed out the reasons why the IWW attracted them for as long as it did. In this paper I shall not go into this again, but prefer to concentrate on the experience of Sicilians, who were probably the largest and the most maligned group of Italians to emigrate to the United States around the turn of the century. I only intend to describe very briefly Sicilian radicalism, while giving a few examples to support the thesis that a continuity existed in the militancy of Sicilian radicals on both sides of the Ocean, that the continuity was possible because radical groups existed in the United States, and that close ties were often maintained between radicals abroad and their comrades in Sicily.

In 1897, the American Federation of Labor, still a small national organization with 265,000 members, for the first time endorsed the proposed Literacy Test to restrict immigration. In the year, 12,400 Sicilians emigrated to the United States.[10] They exceeded the 10,000 mark for the first time. Fears of the Literacy Test, the end of the depression in the USA, and the persistent agricultural crisis at home accounted for the increase to a great extent. Foreign emigration was also part of a more general movement of population that, in the last part of the nineteenth century, was taking many Sicilians from inland areas to the coast, and from small towns and villages to larger towns and cities.[11] Only recently have historians taken into adequate account this background of Sicilian emigration. The same can be said of other political events that were peculiarly related to emigration. Actually, quite a few of those who left Sicily in 1897 had recently come out of jail, where they had been put for having been members of the *Fasci*.

The *Fasci siciliani* was a socialistic movement that developed among farm workers, tenant farmers, and small holders as well as artisans, intellectuals, and industrial workers in more than 170 centers between 1889 and 1893. It had a membership of more than 300,000 by the end of 1893.[12] In the second half of 1893 it led a three-month long, massive strike against landowners and against state taxes in Western Sicily.[13] That great and successful struggle convinced the government that the "upheaval" had to be stopped. On January 3, 1894 a state of siege was declared all over Sicily and the Fasci were outlawed. Scores of protesters were killed, hundreds wounded by the army and the police, and thousands of militants, including all the leaders, were put in jail.

In 1896 a new liberal national government recognized the excessive brutality of the repression, pardoned the jailed *fascianti*, and released them. At the same time, though, Prime minister Di Rudini made it clear that a reorganization of the *Fasci* under any form would not be tolerated. Many soon had confirmation that Di Rudini meant every word he said. Bernardino Verro, one of the most dynamic among the leaders of the *Fasci*, returned to his hometown of Corleone and started to reorganize tenant farmers. The prefect dissolved the organization immediately and Verro was put on trial and again sentenced to a term in jail. Subsequently, in 1897, Verro left for the United States.

As we have seen, many others left Sicily at about the same time. Very seemingly, for countless among them life had grown hard and employment difficult to find because of their involvement with the *Fasci*. Thus they left Italy as soon as it became possible. And yet they were far from defeated people. Ten years later, Giuseppe De Felice Giuffrida, himself one of the leaders, wrote of those who left:

> when the *Fasci* developed, Sicilian landowners did not accept workers' requests. Instead they asked [Prime minister] Gripsi to use use a heavy hand. But the workers did not bow in front of the owners...they left the sunny land where they were born, and ran away to find elsewhere that higher form of society so many of them dreamt of, paying for their dream with their freedom or their life. Rebellion, which was latent in Sicilian fields,...took up the active form of emigration."[14]

De Felice, who remained a socialist and remembered well how things were after 1894, emphasized the continuity of militancy, the persistence of the dream. For others, who were more distant from the *Fasci* both chronologically and politically, rebellion and emigration were not part of the same process, but alternative choices. The young conservative economist Epicarmo Corbino, referring to Sicilian emigration, wrote in 1914: "The worker who wanted to change his own life could only do one of two things: rebel or emigrate. Rebellion was a hard choice — a harsh lesson had been handed down from the *Fasci*. Only emigration remained available."[15] The "safety valve" theory of emigration was there: let them go, the more they emigrate, the less trouble they cause here. Of course, there was some truth in Corbino's words. After all, the *Fasci* had been harshly repressed, and Sicilians had resorted to emigration. But the political message behind his words was that rebellion was futile, and that the desire to change things was a personal problem which could be solved through emigration. Corbino was trying to remove from political reality and from the historical record the fact that the struggle for change had been a mass struggle wich was not brought to an end by emigration.

In fact, if the 1890s and the early years of this century are considered, it is apparent that Sicilians both rebelled and emigrated. This is true not only in the strict sense that the two phenomena were simultaneous, as it is very clearly the case for the years 1901-1904, but also in the wider sense that they were undivided parts of the same political experience, as we shall see.[16]

American historian Donna Gabaccia has demonstrated that Sicilian "emigrants came from precisely those towns and those backgrounds where labor militance enjoyed its greatest appeal," and also that "the most militant towns" in Western Sicily "had the highest average migration rates."[17] Emigration did not make these towns less militant. In many cases these towns that were "red" at the turn of the century remain "red" to this day.

In Western Sicily, where emigration was higher after the turn of the century, socialist agitation and organization had its major successes. Historian Giuliano Procacci shows that "the organized peasant movement that grew in Sicily after the formation of the Zanardelli-Giolitti government [in 1901] had considerable proportions," and that the participation of Sicily "to the general peasants' agitations was much greater than we would assume on the basis of available statistics."[18] The movement reorganized itself around the refusal to accept the existing property, work, and social relations. The protagonists of the 1901-1904 struggles were again tenant farmers tilling the lands of the *latifondi* of the inland. And the fundamental document of the *Fasci*, the "Carta de Corleone" of 1893, was still the basis upon which the sharecropping system was to be reorganized.

In those years, socialist producer cooperatives were also organized to obtain, among other things, the collective tenancies of large estates. Their immediate goal was the dividing up of the *latifondi*. For a part of the cooperators the ultimate goal was probably the individual property of a piece of land. But for many others it remained the socialization of land. Among this second group were the organizers and leaders of the movement, who had in most cases led the *Fasci* in the same areas ten years earlier.

Many of these leaders experienced emigration at one time or another over the period 1897-1910. Bernardino Verro, released from jail in 1896, had left for the United States in 1897. He settled in Buffalo, where a small group of Sicilian socialists lived already. In fact, his presence, among fellow *fascianti*, most probably contributed to give the Sicilians as a group the leadership among Italian socialists in Buffalo.[19] He was in the USA when, in 1898, the Italian army bloodily repressed strikers in Milan and other cities. He returned to Sicily soon after, probably in 1899. Less than one year later he started a newspaper — *Lu viddanu*, The Peasant, in Sicilian dialect — and reorganized the *contadini* of the Corleone region into a federation, "La Terra sicula", Sicilian Land. In 1901, 485 of the federated farmers obtained the "feudo Zuccarone", a very large estate, on a collective tenancy. But cooperation was not the only activity. Unequal forms of sharecropping remained a major problem in the region. Before 1901 was over, Verro was leading a new strike involving more workers than the one he led in 1893. The man Verro may have been exceptional, but only as far as his personal qualities as an organizer were concerned. He was far from alone in taking an active part in the struggle for socialism on two continents.[20]

Another organization, similar to Verro's in Corleone, was started in the Trapani province, also in Western Sicily. In the summer of 1901, it led a successful, two-month long strike in all the major centers of the province. In the following months, many workers' leagues and cooperatives were formed in the area. And on April 20, 1902, a Federation among all the leagues and cooperatives of the Trapani province was founded in Monte S. Giuliano (now Erice). Within two years the Federation had 12,000 members, divided in 50 leagues and 7 cooperatives. The cooperatives, which also practiced collective tenancy, had 3,000 associates. Among the organizers were "old" *fascianti* like Sebastiano Cammareri Scurti and Giacomo Montalto, and young socialists like Sebastiano Bonfiglio. Bonfiglio emigrated to the United States in 1906. Though very little is known of his life there, we do know that he settled in the New York area, where he was active in the socialist movement. He wrote for *Il Proletario*, the organ of the Italian Socialist Federation that had espoused IWW syndicalism in 1906. He took an active role in the protest following the ban on the use of mails by the anarchist newspaper *L'Era Nuova* in 1909. After his return to Italy in January 1913, Bonfiglio again took his place in the Sicilian socialist movement. Later on he became a member of the National Executive Board of the Socialist Party at the Livorno Congress of 1921. One year later he was assassinated by the mafia.

Another league was formed in S. Stefano Quisquina, also in Western Sicily, by Lorenzo Panepinto, who had organized the *Fascio* there in 1893.[21] After the *Fasci* had been crushed, many Stefanesi had emigrated to the United States, particularly to Tampa, Florida, where they entered the cigar-making trade. They were radicals when they left Sicily and were to remain radicals in Tampa. They also maintained close and relevant contacts with their comrades back home. Telling evidence of this relationship are the 101 shares of the "Unione agricola" cooperative that the Stefanesi living in Tampa bought on its inauguration day in 1902. The Sicilians in Tampa also invited Panepinto to the United States in 1907 for a trip that lasted eight months, during which he visited his own comrades in Tampa and radical Italian groups elsewhere. When he returned home he was welcomed by all the leagues of the S. Stefano region. He too was assassinated in 1911. After his death, his comrades in Tampa dedicated to his name what was to soon become the most popular socialist group of the city. This group, as Mormino and Pozzetta write, pledged a yearly stipend of 1,200 lire to the socialist section of S. Stefano Quisquina to help in its work among the peasantry.

The examples given above are representative of a general trend. Even when emigration increased, after 1904, local and regional organization did not subside. Leagues, cooperatives, socialist sections, and Camere del Lavoro were organized in those years all over Sicily. In 1910, the leagues numbered 117, with 32,580 members.[22] And a more detailed analysis of the personal histories of the leaders — particularly in the more militant and socialist oriented western section of Sicily — would also confirm that emigration and organization coexisted during the fifteen or more years that followed the repression of the *Fasci*. At the same time, though, such an analysis would reveal how little is known about the period spent abroad by these people — that is, those who returned home, like the ones mentioned above.

The clearer example of both international militancy and of lack of information is provided by the experience of Nicolò Barbato, who with Verro, De Felice Giuffrida, Rosario Garibaldi Bosco, and Nicola Petrina, was one of the main leaders of the *Fasci*. When he was released from jail in early 1896, his return to his home town Piana dei Greci (now Piana degli Albanesi) was greeted by 5,000 people, more than half the population of Piana. At that point he was probably the most popular class leader in Sicily. In the subsequent years, he also attained national prominence in the Italian Socialist Party. He was elected to Parliament in 1900 and was a member of the National Executive Board of the Party until 1902. In 1903, Barbato travelled through Europe on a long propaganda tour among Italian emigrants, and in 1904 left for the United States, where he was to remain until 1909. Those five years in America remain slightly less than a void in his biographies, notwithstanding his political prominence. He was active in the Italian Socialist Federation and within the Italian communities on the East coast. In 1905 he gave speeches in New York and Philadelphia in support of the Russian revolution. He spoke "as a man of action," and in the same spirit, he wrote, "together with a few others, I offered to engage in an expedition of volunteers to Russia."[23] After 1906, he seems to have favored the association of Italian socialists with the IWW.[24] He returned to Sicily in 1909. He was again elected to Parliament in 1919, and died in 1923.[25]

Again, the names and fragments of the lives of many leaders and militants could be quoted to give quantitative support to the thesis of the continuity of radicalism across national borders.[26] But on the other side, generally speaking, too little is known of the American experience of these people to make other generalizations possible.

Historians of two continents have neglected them for decades. And that past neglect means lack of sources today. The majority of Italian historians considered the emigrants the lost sons of the Italian proletariat. Labor historians, focusing on the institutional, national history of the Socialist Party, ignored Italian socialism abroad. Thus, Italian emigrants have become part of the history of the Italian labor movement only in the 1960s.[27] Since then much has been done, but far from enough. And only in the very last years a new perpective has been developing within the studies of Italian society, that follows the emigrants from their native land to the New World – and back. The same attitude is very well exemplified in the United States by the research of Donna Gabaccia, Mormino and Pozzetta, and others.[28] Their work is establishing new criteria for the study of American society at the time of the new immigration. Among other aspects, one is particulary relevant in their work – the emphasis upon the need to start studying the emigrants in their country of origin, before they leave. And since that implies the acknowledgement that cultural and political collective identities formed in those countries are relevant, it also requires the adoption of a comparative and relativistic approach to the study of both societies, the one of origin and the one of destination. If such a perspective was adopted by earlier Italian and American historians, the American experience of the militants mentioned above – and of countless others – would not be so little documented and known as it is to this day.

Notes

1. According to the Census of 1901, industrial workers were 15% and agricultural workers 37% of the population of working age (over 9 years of age). Statisticians and historians agree that the number of industrial workers (3,989,000) was incorrect. They bring it down to 2,592,000, or about 10% of the population of working age. See S. Merli, *Proletariato di fabbrica e capitalismo industriale,* La Nuova Italia, Firenze, 1972, pp.94-8; I. Barbadoro, *Storia del sindacalismo italiano,* Vol.II: *La CGdL,* La Nuova Italia, Firenze, 1973, pp.21-3

2. Barbadoro, *Storia del sindacalismo italiano,* Vol.I: *La Federterra,* p. 139; Vol.II: *La CGdL,* p.118.

3. S.Gompers, *Labor and the Common Welfare,* compiled and edited by Hayes Robbins, E.P. Dutton & Co., New York, 1919, p.82.

4. See: 57th Congress, 1st Session, House of Representatives, doc.n.184, *Reports of the Industrial Commission on Immigration and Education,* Vol.XV, Government Printing Office, Washington, 1901, p.LXXVII, 170. These arguments, commonly used by anti-immigrationists and particularly by trade unionists, were effectively countered within the Industrial Commission by various people. Especially effective on the question of wages and immigration was the secretary of the Immigration Protective League, Senner; *Ibid.*, pp.170-84. See also I.Hourwich, *Immigration and Labor: The Economic Aspects of European Immigration to the United States,* B.W.Huebsch, New York, 1922 [1912].

5. E.Sori, *L'emigrazione italiana dall'Unità alla seconda guerra mondiale,* Il Mulino, Bologna, 1979, p.38.

6. *Ibid.*, p.206.

7. *Ibid.*, p.207

8. The reference is to historians of the "Wisconsin school", and particularly to its founder John R.Commons. Commons's gompersianism biased his attitude towards the new immigrants and seriously marred his historical work. It is to be asked to what extent the immigrants' experience in the United States must have gone unrecorded simply because immigrants did not fit in the political-historiographical criteria of the founders of American labor history.

9. B.Cartosio, *Gli emigrati italiani e l'Industrial Workers of the World.* in B.Bezza, ed., *Gli italiani fuori d'Italia,* F.Angeli Editore, Milano, 1983, pp.359-95.

10. Ministero di Agricoltura, Industria e Commercio, Direzione generale della statistica. *Statistica della emigrazione italiana,* Roma, 1896.

11. See: F.Renda, *L'emigrazione in Sicilia,* Tip. La Cartografica, Palermo, 1963, pp.54-5; Id., *Storia della Sicilia,* Vol.II, Sellerio Ed., Palermo, 1986, p. 278.

12. S.F.Romano, *Storia dei Fasci Siciliani,* Laterza, Bari, 1959; F.Renda, *I Fasci siciliani, 1892-1894,* Einaudi, Torino, 1977.

13. Between August and November 1893, F.Renda writes, the strike "involved the populations of scores of towns, and...the work stoppages were such that they created serious economic and political problems. National statistics of agricultural strikes for 1893 did not include the participants...on the basis of the fact that it had been a political strike, not an economic one. The press estimated that...50,000 peasants went on strike. But the number of those who participated in the three-month long struggle was two or three times higher. By the end of October, over 800 strikers had been arrested. Renda, *Fasci siciliani, op. cit.*, pp.170, 257.

14. Quoted in Renda, *L'emigrazione italiana..., op. cit.*, pp.64-5.

15. Quoted in Sori, *L'emigrazione italiana..., op. cit.*, pp.221-22.

16. Sicilian emigrants were 200,666 in the four years 1901-1904. According to official statistics, strikes in the fields and in the sulphur mines were 157, with 65,130 participants in the same period. Actually, the number of strikes and of strikers were much higher than recorded. Strikes that had "political" motivations very often went unrecorded, as we have seen already. Strikes or protests that took place out of the harvest season, or that did not create serious disturbances to public order were often ignored. Participation in recorded strikes was frequently underestimated. Enormous discrepancies between official data have been detected. See: G.Procacci, "Movimenti sociali e partiti politici in Sicilia dal 1900 al 1904." in *Annuario dell'Istituto storico italiano per l'età moderna e contemporanea*, Vol.XI (1959), pp.109-216.

17. D.Gabaccia, "Neither Padrone Slaves nor Primitive Rebels: Sicilians on two Continents", in D.Hoerder (ed.), *"Struggle a Hard Battle" – Essays on Working-Class Immigrants*, Northern Illinois University Press, DeKalb, 1986, pp.104-5. Gabaccia's work is very important; see her *From Sicily to Elizabeth Street*, State University of New York Press, Albany, 1984; *Id.*, "Migration and Militance: A Case Study", Paper presented at the 98th Meeting of the American Historical Association, December 27-30, 1983, Session # 155 (typescript).

18. G.Procacci, *La lotta di classe in Italia agli inizi del secolo XX*, Editori Riuniti, Roma, 1972, pp.148-49.

19. On the presence of *fascianti* in Buffalo, see: N.Mastrorilli, "Il movimento dei socialisti italiani di Buffalo, N.Y.," in *La Parola del Popolo*. 50th Anniversary 1908-1958, December 1958-January 1959, pp. 32-3. Verro's presence and the militancy of old *fascianti* in Buffalo seems to have been overlooked by V. Yans-McLaughlin in her *Family and Community: Italian Immigrants in Buffalo, 1880-1930*, University of Illinois Press, Urbana, 1982.

20. Actually, in his case, on three continents. In 1903, facing jail again for political reasons, Verro left Sicily for Marseilles. One year later he went to Tunis, where a Sicilian community existed. There, he started *Il Socialista*, as the organ of the Federation of Socialist Sicilian Workers. He finally returned to Sicily in 1906. In 1914, Verro became the socialist mayor of Corleone. He was assassinated in 1915.

21. The following account is based on the writings of Gary R.Mormino and George E.Pozzetta. Their work on Tampa is of enormous importance. See: G.Pozzetta, *Italians and the Tampa General Strike of 1910*, in G.Pozzetta, ed., *Pane e Lavoro: The Italian-American Working Class*,

The Multicultural History Society of Ontario, Toronto, 1980; G.Mormino, "'We Worked and Took Care of Our Own': Oral History and Italians in Tampa," in *Labor History*, Vol. 23, n.3 (Summer 1982); G.R.Mormino, G.E.Pozzetta, *Spanish Anarchists in Tampa, Florida, 1886-1931*, in Hoerder, ed., "*Struggle a Hard Battle..., op. cit.*
Id., *The immigrant World of Ybor City, 1885-1985*, University of Illinois Press, Urbana, 1987.

22. Barbadoro, *Storia del sindacalismo italiano*, cit.; Vol.I: p.1181; Vol.II: p.120.

23. N.Barbato, *Scienza e Fede*, Social Printing Co., Philadelphia, 1908, pp.232-33. The expedition was never organized. In 1897, after his release from jail, Barbato had gone to Crete, that had insurrected against Turkey, to make his contribution to Greek independence.

24. See: M.De Ciampis, "Storia del Movimento Socialista Rivoluzionario Italiano," in *La Parola del Popolo, op. cit.*, pp.144, 151; A.Argentieri, "Prefazione," to N.Barbato, *Scienza e Fede, op. cit.*, p. X.

25. I have no evidence that Barbato was ever in Chicago. In any case, socialist Chicagoans from Piana dei Greci kept in contact with their comrades in Sicily. They also sent them an embroidered banner in 1920, which is today in the custody of Piana's "Casa del Popolo". I owe this information to Elisabetta Burba, who is writing a thesis on Sicilians from Piana in Madison, Wisconsin.

26. Significant pieces of new biographical-political information can be found in: Elisabetta Vezzosi, "Immigrati socialisti italiani negli Stati Uniti: la federazione Italiana del Socialist Party of America, 1910-1921," unpublished Ph.D. dissert., Firenze, 1987; S.Garroni, "Serrati negli Stati Uniti: giornalista socialista e organizzatore degli emigrati Italiani," in *Movimento operaio e socialista*, n.3, anno VIII (1984), pp. 321-44; A.Molinari, "Luigi Galleani: Un anarchico italiano negli Stati Uniti," in *Miscellanea storica ligure*, nn.1-2, anno VI (1974), pp.259-86. See also B. Cartosio, *Gli emigrati italiani..., op. cit.*, and *Id.*, "Italian Workers and Their Press in the United States, 1900-1920," in C.Harzig-D.Hoerder, eds., *The Press of Labor Migrants in Europe and North America, 1880s to 1930s*, Publications of the Labor Newspaper Preservation Project, Bremen, 1985, pp.423-42.

27. First among Italian historians, Ernesto Ragionieri focused his attention on the problem. His long essay "Italiani all'estero ed emigrazione di lavoratori italiani: un tema di storia del movimento operaio," in *Belfagor*, XVII (1962), pp.640-69, has been correctly defined "a seminal article" by Rudolph Vecoli

28. In recent years, no historian has done more than Rudolf Vecoli to open up new paths in the study of Italian immigration to the United States and to put Italian immigrant workers within the broader context of the multinational working class of America.

Hungarian Immigration and Socialism

Julianna Puskas

What was the relationship between the "new immigrants" and the political movements of the age? Were the "new immigrants" sources of radicalism and violence or of stability and compromise? Were they supporters or oppents of unions? Did they refuse to flock to the red banner of socialism in America only because the Socialist Party, imbued with nativism and racism, was unable to attract Eastern and South-Eastern European immigrants, or did other factors also play a role?

These questions have been widely debated in studies of working class history in America in recent years.[1] They are also being discussed in studies of international migration, which have been reconstructing the movements of individuals, beginning with their departure from their old communities and ending with their integration into their new environments.[2] These studies have also examined how the different social strata of migrants adjusted to work in mines and factories, how the different ethnic cultures clashed, and how these clashes affected working-class solidarity.[3] At the present stage of research it is impossible to answer these questions adequately. The aim of this paper is simply to shed light on them by outlining some characteristics of Hungarian migration.

The Process of Migration and the Participants[4]

During the period between the 1880s and World War I, the industrial revolution reached Hungary. Although it gained impetus from the elimination of the feudal social relationships (the liberation of the serfs), the process of industrialization was slow in Hungary. Even at the turn of the century, the agricultural population still accounted for approximately 75% of the inhabitants. The characteristic strata of agricultural society were big landowners with extensive land, masses of poor peasants working on their small plots, and millions of landless agricultural laborers.

The period of mass migration coincided with the beginning of the modernization of the Hungarian economy and society. Mass migration began in the 1880s, but emigration became a striking social phenomenon only in the first decade of this century. Then it was abruptly cut short by the introduction of the quota system in 1924, by which the United States closed the gates before the masses of "new immigrants," deemed "undesirable."

Between 1871 and 1913, more than two million people from Hungary were registered boarding ships at European ports, while about 1,800,000 immigrants from Hungary were recorded by the authorities in America. The population loss, i.e. the migration balance between 1880 and 1910, was close to 900,000 according to the Hungarian censuses, but the American census of 1910 registered only 495,600 immigrants from Hungary. There are thus great differences between the migration traffic, the migrating population, and the migration balance. These can be ascribed at least in part to the two-way movements of the migrants, despite a relatively large proportion of final settlement in America.

Prior to 1914, the population of Hungary was multi-"national," that is, composed of a number of ethnic groups as we should say today. The migrants too came from all the different "nations" of the Hungarian state, but in different proportions from their percentage of the population. In 1900, Hungarians composed 45.4% of the population of Hungary but, between 1900 and 1913, they furnished only

26.2% of the migrants. At the other extreme, Slovaks accounted for 10.3% of the population but made up a comparatively massive 26.5% of the migrants. The proportions of other non-Hungarian "nations" among the migrants were also higher than their proportion of the population. Thus the migrating mass of approximately two million people was constituted by many different ethnic groups. In the new environment this division widened and conflicts within and between ethnic groups arose.

The overwhelming majority of the migrants – even more than in the population – were peasants and agricultural laborers. In the peak period of their migrations such a high proportion of peasants and agricultural proletarians was not to be found among the migrants from the countries of Western and Northern Europe. There were few skilled workers among the migrants from Hungary during this period and almost no intellectuals or other members of the middle classes.

The migration movement was influenced by one major characteristic: most people who left Hungary, with few exceptions, did not intend to leave their homes for good and settle in the United States. They wanted to find work, make money, and return home. Not only did many re-migrate, but also many others bought land in Hungary even though they remained in the United States for good.

Because these aims characterized most migration, the majority of migrants during the period 1901-1913 were men (66.9%) and the proportion of the young age group was conspicuously high. Rarely did whole families set off together: married men usually left alone. The members of their family followed them only years later, if at all: most married men returned home. It was rather the unmarried men (28.7% of the male migrants above 14) and the unmarried girls (35% of the female migrants above 14) who founded families in the new world.

Hungary established compulsory four-year elementary schools in 1868, which should have enabled everybody to acquire the basics of reading, writing, and arithmetic. In reality, however, elementary education spread only slowly. The proportion of illiterates in Hungary was still high even at the turn of the century, but a remarkable 86% of Hungarian immigrants could read and write. How many of the peasant migrants were regular readers of books and newspapers is unknown. Although the circulation of "popular papers" increased from the beginning of the 1880s, reading newspapers was not characteristic among peasants for decades to come. Around this time, however, reading circles and amateur theater groups began to work in the villages. Thus, in addition to school, potential migrants disposed of several avenues of basic education.

In the last decade of the nineteenth century, the "agro-socialists," harvesters' strikes, and other movements articulated the radicalism of the agricultural laborers and poor peasants in certain areas, but not usually in the areas which provided the main sources of migration. All the peasants and agricultural laborers were strongly oriented towards the land. At the center of their lives stood the activities required by nature and the village community, in an order conditioned for generations. In this world, land and work gave man his honor and people would not participate in any political movement unless it accepted these values.

Migration and assimilation played an important role in forming the working class within Hungary.[5] The first skilled workers in Hungary were migrants from abroad or from the economically developed territories of the Austro-Hungarian monarchy. Subsequently, to acquire experience abroad was part of the training of skilled workers, artisans, and tradesmen. During their travels they picked up other languages, most often German, the language of their technical terms. They brought the idea of socialism back with them and, under their influence, workers' organizations were established at a relatively early stage. The labor movement quickly caught up with that of the more highly developed European countries.

The number of workers' leagues and associations increased rapidly from the 1860s. The first workers' party was formed in 1890. It modelled itself on the German and Austrian social democratic parties. The party and the unions were closely linked. All party members were obliged to belong to a union and each union member was expected to support the party's political objectives.

The predominant strata among the migrants, however, were not these workers, but peasant-workers who were forced to do manual labor in the United States. The migrants also included some people from other strata of society, but they too usually had to do manual labor once in the United States. The cases of career-migration were still rare, but not unknown: some artists, engineers, and other professionals did migrate, seeking the opportunities offered by the American dream, but they generally remained outside the migrant communities in the United States. Priests, teachers, and journalists, on the other hand, joined these communities, which were their reason for being in the New World and the sources of their existence. But in most cases, at least at the beginning, those professionals who had been induced to find refuge in America by broken careers and reduced social status sank to the level of manual workers.

The migrating masses looked grey from the outside but varied sharply when viewed from the inside. Their culture, values, and traditions varied according to their social position. How were these variations manifested in their reactions to the new environment?

On the Land in America: Experiences and Conflicts[6]

The masses migrating from Hungary to America settled primarily in the Eastern industrial states. There were jobs for them in the mines of West Virginia and Pennsylvania, in the iron and steel factories of Ohio and Illinois, in the iron, brick and tobacco factories as well as in road and railway construction of New Jersey. Most, including the peasants, began to work in the mines and factories. Artisans, tradesmen, and members of the middle class, however, hoped to make a living in New York City.

Relatives and people from the same village or the same region tried to stay together in the new environment. They were aided in this by chain-migration: people migrating from one place tended to settle together in the same area. Conversely, however, the establishment of new workplaces, the opening of new factories and mines, and the pursuit of higher wages transformed the migrants into American industrial workers, moving about in search of better jobs. Thus we find not only "resettled communities" but also dispersed migrants. This is shown both in American censuses and in local studies.

What looked from Hungary like high wages turned out in America to be low wages in dangerous workplaces. Worse, the immigrants were not always welcome. Contemporary Americans were outraged by the "primitiveness" of the immigrants' way of life. They were said to undertake all kinds of jobs with servility and to lend themselves to strike-breaking. When they did go on strike (more and more frequently from 1904 on), their strikes were called "disturbances of aliens."[7]

American opinion reflected not only unfounded prejudices (although there were many of these), but also real differences between native and immigrant ways of life. That of the immigrants was influenced by strategies and objectives set in their previous environment, requiring them to reduce their living standards and obtain jobs at any price, whatever the conditions.

At the time of migrating, the Hungarian peasant did not yet plan to live his life out in America doing jobs different from those to which he had been accustomed. Although it was common for people in Hungary to move around in search of work, their society was nevertheless fairly traditional. Migration was possible only if envisaged as a temporary measure. This vision gave migrants the strength to put up with the vicissitudes of life in the new environment. Subsquently, to be sure, a great many changed their minds and remained in the United States, as a result of the attractions of the new environment, of inertia, or (paradoxically) of inability to achieve their goals.

Through the 1920s the fact of immigration left marks on the communities and institutions the migrants founded in the United States. These communities were usually established by groups of ten to fifteen persons and fluctuated a great deal after their establishment. They multiplied with immigration and, mainly after the turn of the century, were often linked by fraternal organizations in "a nation-wide network"[8]

Such national groupings were hindered, however, by the different backgrounds and cultures imported from the mother country. Socialists organized their small communities for themselves and so did workers of peasant background from the same region or the same religious denomination. Village artisans and tradesmen organized their own associations as well. All tried to keep away from the "gentlemen" who came from Hungary. The statutes of several associations stipulated that only those who had been manual workers in Hungary could hold office.

Migrant communities and organizations were pulled in two directions ideologically: on the one hand, by socialist ideas emanating from workers or militants linked to the Socialist International and, on the other hand, by nationalist ideas articulated by religious or secular middle-class intellectuals.

The Socialists[9]

Immigrant Hungarian socialists began their organizing campaigns in the 1890s. At the beginning they called their groups "trade unions" although they could not actually protect economic interests and instead sought to satisfy social and cultural needs. By 1892, however, a Hungarian branch of the Socialist Labor Party was already operating in New York. In 1894 the socialists established a fraternal association in Cleveland. In 1896 they began to organize in Newark, Bridgeport, and New Haven.

The first Hungarian language workers' paper published in the United States appeared in 1894: it continued up to 1897 under the title *Amerikai Népszava (American People's Voice* — the title of the Hungarian social-democratic newspaper was *Népszava* also). The purpose of publishing a newspaper was to educate workers, to propagate socialist ideas, and to limit the patriotism emphasized by the "bourgeois" associations.

The knowledge of several languages, especially German, facilitated the communication of skilled workers and tradesmen originating from different language groups in Hungary. In the United States they received information about the American labor movement, the trade unions and political parties, from other German-speaking immigrants. This helped them establish links to the Socialist Labor Party relatively quickly. Under its auspices they formed "language associations," which were really Hungarian branches of the party.

At the turn of the century these sporadic local groupings established a central organization in New York and on May 1, 1903, began publishing a new workers' paper, *Népakarat* (People's Will – another title originating from Hungary). At this time socialists of Hungarian origin still sought to remain neutral in the debates which were increasingly straining the American labor movement, but their neutrality was of short duration. In 1904 they split over two problems: on the one hand, how they should connect economic and political struggles; on the other hand, how they should relate to the American unions and the American political organizations.

Thus from 1905 socialists of Hungarian origin in America were split into two parties, two parallel associations,[10] and two newspapers *(Elöre ran Népakarat)*. From articles in these newspapers and from letters, studies, and other information sent to Hungary by the party leaders, it is clear that the conflicts stemmed from the confrontation between ideological positions developed in Hungary and the experiences of the new environment.

In particular, the experience of the labor movement in Hungary made it difficult for these socialists to understand that in America unions and parties were going their separate ways and were even in conflict. The Hungarians looked askance at the "pragmatism" and the "lack of theory" of the American labor movement.[11]

The social composition of the Socialist Party (as distinct from the Socialist Labor Party) seemed suspect even to those Hungarian socialists who accepted it as the necessary reality in America. They looked on it as a "conglomeration of people of different theories and trends, from the Christian Socialists up to the Radical Bourgeois scientists."[12] Similarly, they criticized not only the Socialist Party but also American trade unions for shrinking away from newly-arrived immigrant workers and for adopting a nativist and racist stance in general.

Thus, up to 1910, the majority of Hungarian socialists were still attracted to the declining Socialist Labor Party. As they often repeated, "its theoretical standpoint is closer to that of the Hungarian workers and the immigrant workers in general."[13] "The Socialist Party devotes all its efforts to the election campaign," from which most immigrants were excluded: few of them were citizens. The Socialist Labor Party "on the other hand considers as its most important task the establishment of trade organizations based on the class struggle ... and in this activity all the immigrant workers would be able to participate. Through the trade organizations the aliens may really become an integral part of the American labor movement."[14]

Hungarian members of the Socialist Party defended themselves against these arguments on the basis of the specificity of conditions in America. In particular, they replied that the Socialist Labor Party's European ideological position, though attractive, was not suitable to America; only the Socialist Party and the American Federation of Labor were social realities, even if they did not represent directly the interests of immigrants. Furthermore, they argued, the immigrants had to accept that they could take their place in the American labor movement only if they became Americanized and assimilated as soon as possible. Those who took this position had to find excuses for the behavior of unions affilliated to the AFL. These unions, they argued, were becoming more positive towards the new immigrants and were increasingly moving towards the correct views on the class struggle.[15]

The policy of the Socialist Party concerning "language associations" also posed a problem for the Hungarians. Hungarian branches were not allowed to pursue any national policy. They were subject to the discipline of the Socialist Party in all matters, so that the "Socialist Federation" was a front whose only tasks were agitation and proselytization among Hungarian workers. Under such circumstances, wrote the editor of *Elöre*, "belonging to the Socialist Party had in the strictest sense of the word a paralyzing effect on propaganda among Hungarians."[16] In the face of such problems, the Hungarians began to affirm their independence. Most of them broke with the Socialist Party at the Hungarian Workers' Federation convention of 1910, at which they proclaimed the independence of their organization and newspaper. Only a minority remained in the

Socialist Labor Party after 1910. They founded the newspaper *Munkàs* (worker).

The "independence" of the Hungarian Socialist Workers' Federation paved the way for those who sought the reunification of the fragmented groups of Hungarian socialists. Arguing for the need for unity, they called for the establishment of the Independent Hungarian Workers' Alliance to organize Hungarian workers on an economic basis and to educate them in socialist ideas. "The revolutionary trade organization could give strength and unity to the Hungarian immigrants exposed to American capitalist exploitation. The Hungarians do not need the Socialist Party." They put their argument in terms to which migrant workers were likely to respond: "Why should we join the American party if we cannot obtain citizens' rights and liberty anyway, as our stay here is only temporary?"[17]

In 1911, after several attempts, the various groups were unified and the United Hungarian Socialist Federation was founded. The newspapers *Népakarat* and *Elöre* merged into a new journal called *Testvériség* (Fraternity).[18]

Basic differences could not, however, be masked for long. Unity lasted only until 1912, when a new split occurred. In this schism the majority supported the Socialist Party. From this time on, however, small groups of Hungarian supporters of the Industrial Workers of the World (IWW) began to form around the newspaper *Bérmunkàs* (Wage Worker).

At the same time, the associations sought increasingly to exclude political arguments. They hoped that by avoiding theoretical arguments, they could achieve cohesion on the basis of acceptance of class consciousness and socialist ideas.

The different trends of the labor movement manifested themselves in great fluctuations among the Hungarian socialists, who fluttered from group to group. But though uncertainties and personal factors such as friends or other workers on the job influenced their choices, these also reflected in a general way their adjustment to the new environment: supporters of the Socialist Party were more American, supporters of the Socialist Labor Party more Hungarian.

The class-conscious Hungarian workers proclaiming socialist ideas were more numerous (if all their groups and community organizations are considered) than the number of those who appear to have been part of the mainstream American labor movement. Thus among the Hungarians (and probably among other ethnic groups of the "new immigrants") there existed a radical trend which their isolation rendered invisible.

This does not mean that large masses of Hungarian immigrants were deeply imbued with socialist ideas. The total number of socialists cannot have been more than a few thousand even if we take into account the large-scale fluctuations caused by re-migration.

Several signs indicate that among the Hungarian immigrants the socialists were not only the most highly trained and most intelligent but also the best paid workers. Their serious and regular work in promoting education made their cultural influence greater than their number would indicate. They organized lectures, assemblies, entertainment, free shools (New York), workers' schools (Chicago), debates, and regular courses (Pittsburgh, Cleveland). Since they were not citizens and only a few could participate in political movements, they concentrated their activities on propaganda and education.

However, because their cultural level was so different from that of immigrant workers of peasant origin, they had too little empathy with those who remained rooted in Hungarian culture to offer them appropriate programs and activities. Instead, they urged melting into the American working class as quickly as possible, which was neither an effective slogan nor a viable option for the masses of immigrant workers of peasant origin. Similarly, they refused to debate trade union problems on a theoretical level, seeking instead to solve them "in practice." The socialists did not study the specific strikes of the "new immigrants" and analyze their causes, their spontaneity, and their bitterness. Their ideology was so imbued with internationalism that they refused to differentiate among Hungarian, other ethnic, or native American workers even when it was apparent that each group differed enormously from other sections of the working class.

Geographical mobility and seasonal jobs were not alien to the population of pre-industrial villages. What was alien to these villagers, however, was the strategy of improving their lives by settling permanently in another country. The peasants and agricultural laborers migrating to America worked in mines and factories to improve their economic position in their original community in Hungary. Since until they gave up hope of returning home they expected to live the "American way of life" only temporarily, the bonds that linked them to their original communities remained strong even if slightly loosened over time.

Since they perceived their stay in America as a temporary effort which they sought to pass through as quickly as possible, they reacted strongly to reductions in wages. Their strikes were spontaneous and usually free from external influence; they were bitter protests against the reduction of wages or against wages so low that they jeopardized the goal of amassing wealth and returning home. In their embittered state of mind, strikers occasionally listened to socialist agitators and union organizers. But they were still unable to integrate their individual aim of returning to Hungary with the collective struggle for the realization of long-term goals in America. Their protests ended, they soon slipped back into behavior dictated by the values brought from the "Old Country." They were primarily susceptible to religious and ethnic ideas, i.e. nationalist ideas, which were reinforced not only by their traditions but also by their continual confrontation with the native American community, for in most cases they could connect the grievances of their working lives with their treatment as aliens, as despised "Hunkies."

Thus, for the Hungarian migrants, social and political attitudes were conditioned by their slowly shifting perception of their long-term prospects. The radical or conservative nature of their actions depended on the compatibility of the American labor movement's objectives with these prospects.

Notes

1. See Charles Leinenweber, "Socialism and Ethnicity" and Rudolph J. Vecoli: "Comment," in *Failure of a Dream*, ed. John H.M. Laslett and Seymour Martin Lipset (University of California Press. Revised Edition, 1984), pp. 245-283.

2. See John Bodnar, *The Transplanted. A History of Immigrants in Urban America.* (Indiana University Press, 1985)

3. See Milton Cantor: *American Working Class Culture* (Westport, Conn. 1979)

4. Julianna Puskas: *From Hungary to the United States, 1880-1914.* (Studia Historica, 1982, Budapest.) pp. 15-63.

5. In the 1880s 14% of the skilled workers came from abroad; 52% of the skilled workers' mothertongue was Hungarian at that time. P. Hanák-F. Mucsi, *Magyarország története (History of Hungary) VII/1.* (Budapest, 1978) pp. 508-509.

See also K.H. Kende-P.Sipos "Industrial Workers and Assimilation in Hungary, 1870-1910" (Paper delivered at the U.S.-Hungarian Conference, Budapest, 23-25 August, 1980).

6. Puskás, *From Hungary to the United States, 1880-1914*, pp. 126-154.

7. *Reports of the Immigration Commission*, Vol.41. 305-424. "Statements and Recommendations" (Second Ed. New York, 1970).

See also the chapter on strikes in G. Hoffmann, *Csonka munkásosztály Amerikai magyarság (The Truncated Working Class. American Hungarians)* (Budapest, 1911) pp. 98-122.

8. In 1911, 1339 "Magyar" associations existed in the USA. See Puskás, *From Hungary to the United States, 1880-1914*, p.160.

9. See in more detail, *ibid.*, pp. 156-169.

10. In 1911, the Socialist Party supported the "Workmen's Sick Benevolent and Educational Society". It had 33 branches and 990 members. The Socialist Labor Party backed the "Hungarian Workers' Benefit Society" which had 55 branches and 1170 members.

11. Imre Bárd's Letter to Ervin Szabó, Budapest, Febr. 26, 1909, in *Szabó Ervin Levelezése /The Correspondence of Ervin Szabó/ 1905-1918.* (Budapest, 1978). J. Jemnitz, "The relations of the American-Hungarians' Labor Movement as revealed in the correspondence of Ervin Szabó", *Acta Historica*, (Budapest, 1963)

12. *Ibid.*

13. Ferenc Paál, "Magyar Szocialisták Amerikában" / Hungarian Socialists in America/, *Szocializmus*, (1911), pp. 117-126.

14. *Ibid.*

15. Imre Bárd, "Magyarok az amerikai munkásmozgalomban" /Hungarian in the American Labor Movement/, *Szocializmus*, (1911), pp. 357-361.

16. *Ibid.*

17. *Népakarat*, (November 1, 1910)

18. See J. Puskás, "The Differentiation of the Hungarian Newspapers, *Reflecting Some Aspects of Acculturation, 1853-1914," in The Press of Labor Migrants in Europe and North America, 1880s to1930s*, ed. C. Harzig and D. Hoerder (Bremen, 1985). pp. 385-402.

Socialism in America: The French-speaking Coal Miners in the Late Nineteenth Century

Ronald Creagh

The history of the French in the United States is "a scholarly *terra incognita.*" With the exception of Louisiana, two centuries of French presence throughout the American Republic have been the object of less than a handful of important books. Historians have always presented the French influence as if it came directly from Europe and bypassed French immigrants. Social history has not dealt with the French presence because historians have assumed that French migrants to the United States have been "middle class, urban, antitraditionalist and incapable of sustaining their ethnic identity."[1]

In spite of the accepted idea that French-Americans were middle-class, there has been a steady flux of French workingmen ever since the colonial period: we find French miners as early as the 1720s.[2] Ever since then this laboring class has been continually replenished with French-Americans of three kinds. First there were, of course, French speakers from France. Second, there were non French-speaking French (e.g. Alsatians, the Basques and the Bretons). Third, there were French speakers from colonies and former colonies (e.g. West Indies, Canada, Haiti, French Africa...) and from French-speaking countries (e.g. Switzerland, Belgium).

The "French connection" with early American socialism starts with the doctrines of Fourier in the 1840s; it continues through the social ramifications created by the thousand or so followers of Victor Considérant who settled near Dallas, Texas, and by half a century of arrivals and experiences of so-called "Icarians", disciples of Etienne Cabet. Later, Proudhonism, Blanquism, and anarchism found an outlet in the International Workingmen's Association (1868-1876), in which French groups emulated or rivalled the German ones from New York to the Pacific and from New Orleans and Saint Louis to Chicago.[3]

Did these varieties of socialist currents disappear after the demise of the International? How were they linked with France? It is the purpose of this paper to answer this question through the study of a particular group, the French-speaking miners in the coal industry during the last quarter of the nineteenth century.

The Aftermath of the International Workingmen's Association

New York has always been one of the most important centers of the French in America and it is not surprising that the city was one of the sources of the socialist movement in Pennsylvania. In both New York and New Jersey, French-speaking socialists had been active since the late 1840s, although the movement was momentarily interrupted during the Civil War. In New York the French house-painter Joseph Déjacque invented the word "libertaire" and published utopian essays depicting an ideal anarchist society. In that city the Proudhonian Claude Pelletier wrote a play, *The Hussites*, which sought to present the problems of a post-revolutionary situation. New York was also a refuge for some of the Communards; its presses printed for the first time "L'Internationale". Its halls were the meeting-places of the advisers of the working class movement, such as Victor Drury.[4]

The French militants of the International remained active even after it collapsed. Their organization endured several mutations in names and personnel, and finally gave birth to the "Société communiste-révolutionnaire de New York" (c. 1874) which probably drew its inspiration from Blanquism, although the French were very divided in their opinions. The press was considered by socialists and anarchists alike as a major propaganda outlet.[5]

In 1885 the first known French socialist newspaper appeared in the Pennsylvania "anthracite valley". It was founded with the help of the above-mentioned "Société communiste-révolutionnaire de New York", and more particularly though the action of a social-revolutionary named Edouard (or Edward) David, who assumed the editorial work. The Revolutionary-Communist society paid fifty dollars for the purchase of the printing press and Arsène Sauva, an obscure French tailor, added the fifteen dollars to reach the required sum. To celebrate the fifteenth anniversary of the Commune, the publishers intended to put out a special issue with a print run of 10,000 copies. The newspaper was given out free. We do not know what the real circulation was. The new monthly, published in Pennsylvania, chose a provocative title: *La Torpille* (The Torpedo).

The Coal Industry

France exercised an influence which, on the whole, was much more important than French leaders were aware of. People like Jean Grave and papers like *Le Père Peinard* had an impressive readership in America. Thus one of the most powerful links was provided by the periodicals.[6]

Nevertheless the emergence of the French-speaking socialist and anarchist movements in the Pennsylvania mines was a product of the social structures of the region. The immigrant miner could not anticipate any improvement of his standard of living. Nor could he anticipate the creation of any organization articulating his aspirations. Furthermore, ethnic disparity among the miners encouraged hostility and even hatred between the old miners and the "newcomers". The French did not generally like their American coworkers.[7] The French capacity for theoretical expression found an outlet in French-American associations which, in spite of their weaknesses, provided the initial impetus for French workers' movements.

It is difficult to establish an accurate map of the implantation of French-speaking coal-miners and still more difficult to determine the number of socialist and anarchist activists. Many of the French-speaking miners worked in the anthracite region, in northeastern Pennsylvania. However, at the end of the 1880s and at the beginning of the 1890s, some of the most active groups could be found elsewhere in the state: in Monongahela, Calamity, Hastings, Houtzdale, Ashcroft, Willow Grove, Carbon (Wyoming county) and in Spring Valley, Illinois. There was also a sprinkling of militants in Drill, Federal, Jeannette, McDonald, Noblestown, Pennsylvania, as well as in Pittsburgh, Kansas and in other places. We do not know either when those groups really came into existence or when they disappeared. Most of the records are gone. However, the newspapers that succeded one another during a quarter of a century provide the historian with a unique source of information on the life, organization and fate of French socialism in the United States. French periodicals related to socialist and anarchist movements mention at least a hundred correspondents by name. Most were concentrated in Pennsylvania, but there were also writers, readers and press distributors in Illinois, Iowa, Kansas, New Jersey, Wyoming and Arkansas.

The anarchist newspapers lasted for almost a quarter of a century. Obviously, they were geared toward a wide audience. In spite of their explicit commitment to anarchism, they often insisted that they were not hostile to socialism, but only to some of its practices. Differences in opinion between anarchists and socialists were irrelevant by and large because all grass-roots militants agreed about the ideal society and for a French miner in that period there were hardly any choices in the means.

Portrait of the Miner Waving a Red Flag

The harshness of the living conditions in coal mines was used to persuade the French-speaking miners to join in the struggle. Every issue of the French workingmen's papers reminded the reader of the endemic misery of the mining population. In the mines the men often worked only a few days a week and more than once the management found reasons to reduce their salary. On one occasion, a Walloon miner named H. Haubry attempted to dissuade miners from going to Rocky Hollow, near Johnson:

> You are cheated with a vengeance on the weight of the vehicles, water leaks in all the mine chambers... With a comrade I have moved forward 18 meters in a heading. The boss had promised us a dollar per meter, and on pay-day we received fifty cents. He cheated us of nine dollars. From there I went to Millwood Shaft. We get thirty-eight cents a ton, and the coal is as hard as the coal by the river. Then I came to Lilly; no sooner did I arrive than a strike started. If at least it were the last one! For how long will we have to travel from one place to another, going without food, looking for a tiny bit of bread?[8]

In 1889, the management closed the Spring Hill mine for an indefinite period. The French population, which included twenty-five families and eight bachelors, a total of one hundred and eleven individuals, was in great distress: "We are condemned to die of hunger if no one comes to our help. Every week, we receive from the aid committee some flour and salted meat, hardly the tenth of what is necessary to satisfy the hunger of our wives and children."[9] These lines accompanied the information that a miner's two children had literally starved to death.

Every issue of the paper annouced new victims. Death often struck in the mines, caused by the insecurity of the labor conditions but also by fights with the police. The two following letters, printed in the same issue, are typical:

> (At Fayette County) the police... succeeded with great difficulty in operating two evictions in Adelaide. The strikers finally got the advantage and chased the policemen. Not long after, the latter returned with hangman Mc Cormick and a new gang of assasins. Men and women, about hundred in number, rivalled with eagerness against the policemen. A tall Hungarian and a young woman were going to overcome a gang of policemen. Sheriff Mc Cormick went to the help of the latter; revolver shots roared; a good number of policemen had wounds, the hangman's thumb was torn off. Suddenly the young woman falls dead, a bullet having crossed her chest. This brought to a climax the strikers'rage, and not a policeman would have escaped alive if a regiment of soldiers had not arrived.
>
> Alexander Jonas and Ungest Delaher[10] spoke before 4000 strikers at Scottsdale, on Wednesday April 22. The red flag waved. A worker who suggested resuming work was strongly applauded with kicks and thrown out of the hall.

> ... On Thursday the battles were more numerous than ever. The sheriff of Fayette and his policemen were chased from Monarch. The hangman received a bullet in his hand and terrible strokes of an ax from a woman. He wanted to evict Thomas Farr; a party of 400 men and women encircled him. Farr was on his doorstep with an ax in his hand. A woman who was staying in the other part of the house, and who had given birth to a child two days before, hearing the uproar, got up and seized a revolver which she directed to the sheriff's chest.[11]

The portrait of the socialist miner would not be complete without the utopian traits that characterized his vision. The world of the future would be free and money would be abolished but it would only come through violent revolution. This coming society was heralded by the militant press; it also was to be anticipated and, as far as possible, put into practice in the present. The socialist press strove to give freedom: every reader could express himself in its columns. The coming society would abolish monetary relations; in the meantime copies would be given free to all workers in need.

Alarms, Torpedoes and Red Roosters: The French Socialist and Anarchist Papers

La Torpille adopted a violent tone that would be continued by its successors. There was no doubt in David's mind that America was waging a class war and that revolution was at hand. What was needed, he wrote, was a herald of revolution, a publication that would detect in the succession of economic crises and of bloody conflicts those "premonitory sounds that announce that the hour of the first battles is to be tolled simultaneously across North America and through Europe."[12] On the eve of the Haymarket affair, the tone of the paper was indeed threatening: "STRENGTH in the workers' hands will be the auxiliary of RIGHT and the safeguard of socialism." He argued that if the workers made a legal revolution

> The privileged and their henchmen would rise up against the popular will and one would need to resort to brutal force to overcome the resistance. It is an idle dream to think that the bourgeoisie would submit gracefully, when, at all times, for much less important reasons, we may see it using the most violent and the most ferocious means. And it is an idle dream to expect that, for humanitarian reasons, they would spontaneously renounce such means; they joke about this, bragging in a

way that should destroy all illusions of those who dream of reconciliation.

If persuasion had some effect, it should have produced its effect on the privileged class a long time ago.[13]

The paper, manifestly inspired by Blanquism, was also in the line of the notorious German anarchist, Johann Most, who had recently settled in the United States.

David did not hide his sympathy for anarchism. The editor would signal to his readers the publication of the Chicago *Alarm*[14] and mention Benjamin R. Tucker's arch individualist *Liberty* but he rejected individualists of all kinds, "disguised more or less under the names of cooperativists, communalists, autonomists, possibilists etc."; for him such groups were but "cocoons in which the bourgeoisie enters or will enter as a caterpillar and exit as a butterfly."[15]

As early as June 1886, David understood perfectly what was at stake in the Haymarket trial. While he saw the bomb as a "striking riposte", justified on the grounds of the unqualifable violence of police and private militia, he predicted that one should be prepared for those acts of repression that "will recall ... the hanging of John Brown".[16]

In the heat of the social tension caused by the affair, the paper probably ceased its publication; it could not be traced after that date. However, its successors would also seek to inflame the American working class.

David's next paper, *Le Réveil des Mineurs (The Miners' Alarm)*, started in Hastings, Pennsylvania, in 1890. It first presented itself as a working class periodical and later called itself communist-anarchist. The paper complained that it had given free more than 5,000 copies but that about fifty correspondents had received the newspaper for several months without paying. It was decided that only those who paid for their subscription would receive the number of free copies that they desired. This was an anarchist practice, based on the ideal of abolishing money as much as it was possible at the present time.

The publisher moved to New York where he kept publishing the paper until 1893. He then engaged in another venture; the title of the new publication, *La Crise sociale (The Social crisis)* indicated that his ideas had not greatly changed.

A new publisher was to succeed Edouard David in Pennsylvania, the Belgian Louis Goaziou who is undoubtedly the most important figure of the French anarchist and socialist press. The quality of his publications, which were open to all currents, reveal the evolution of the French working class in those years.

In 1885, while in Sturgeon, Pennsylvania, Goaziou joined the Anarchist International Association, known as "the Black International". For almost twenty years, from 1890 to 1909, he published several successive miners' newspapers. His style was flamboyant: "The day the red rooster starts crowing, many a joyfully beating heart and the true anarchist will be ready to fit the gun to their shoulders and will march to conquer liberty, with the red flag heading them."[17]

This quotation shows clearly that the legend of the revolutionary red rooster also appears in the United States. Louis Goaziou, who was later to rally parliamentary socialism, did write these lines after the Haymarket affair had induced many American anarchists to give up the use of violence. Fifteen years later, when that publisher strove for the triumph of the socialist party, he would still say: "It is possible, and even very likely, that the social question will only be solved with the help of a violent revolution, when the present owners of the capital will refuse to obey the legal mandates of the majority."[18]

L'Ami des Ouvriers (The Workers' Friend), published in Hastings, Pennsylvania, succeeded *The Miners' Revenge* in 1894. It was to appear as often as possible and to be given free to strikers and unemployed, but the little number of its subscribers made it very difficult to continue publication. It lasted two years only, but would soon be succeeded by a paper with another title. This new periodical called itself *La Tribune Libre (The Free Tribune)*. It too was edited by Louis Goaziou, from 1896 to 1899. As usual, most of the articles were unsigned, written by miners. There were some poems and a serial entitled "Souvenirs of a Communard." The paper accepted advertisements, which was very rare in anarchist publications. It also published two booklets and songs.

In April 1900, Goaziou bought the paper, wrote and printed it with the help of his wife and daughter. He had to abandon the publication, however, because less than a hundred readers had paid their subscription.

He was not a man to give up. In March 1901, Goaziou was again editing a periodical, this time in Charleroi, Pennsylvania. *L'Union des Travailleurs (The Workers' Union)* was open to all the varieties of socialism: Marxists, De Leonites, Social-Democrats expressed themselves as well as anarchists. In 1915, the paper was superseded by *The Union Worker*, which was the official organ of the Monongahela Valley Trades Council. And again, Louis Goaziou was the editor. He was now more and more interested in politics. French miners were turning to socialism.

As early as 1899, there had already been a French socialist paper, *Le Bourdon (The Drone)* published in Jeannette, Pennsylvania. This four-page weekly gave information about France, Belgium as well as about Europe in general. It contained articles by some of the leading figures of the movement, such as Jean Jaurès and August Bebel. It was interested in the various English-speaking form of socialism in the United States. It does not seem to have lasted for a very long time.

The Emergence of Anarchist Groups

Emma Goldman gives a colorful description of the strong anarchist group of Spring Valley, Illinois, which at the time of her tour (1899) consisted mostly of Belgians and Italians.[19] Informal groups with varied life-spans met in Kiokotte, Kansas or in Calamity, Monongahela City and Willow Grove, Pennsylvania. A formal association appeared at Hastings (Cambria county), giving birth in 1890 to *The Miners' Alarm* (see above). That circle seems to have vanished almost immediately afterwards. In the same place, in September 1893, however, a group named "Les Gueux" (The Beggars) held bi-monthly meetings at the editor's house. French and Belgian miners also had weekly meetings in Ashcroft (Clearfield county); their wives and companions complained and demanded to participate in these gatherings.

It is very likely that the birth of many of these groups was due to the efforts of a leader who came from France: Joseph Tortelier, a cabinet-maker who was well-known as one of the first advocates of the general strike. It had long been rumored that he travelled at some time in his life in the U.S.A. We can now confirm this, having found an account of his voyage in the *Réveil des Mineurs* of May 1891, under the title "L'Anarchie aux États-Unis".[20] The report was so precise that the information deserves to be presented.

Tortelier's lecture tour began at Hastings, Pennsylvania on a Tuesday in the spring of 1891[21] when he spoke before a group of about twenty Frenchmen, recently impoverished by a strike that had lasted for a month. He was the next day at Houtzdale where, to the dismay of the narrator, only twenty people showed up, perhaps on account of the bad weather. On Thursday, however, although the speaker and his host got lost in the mud, they finally reached Ashcroft and succeeded in mobilizing the French community, which immedialely assembled in their meeting place: about forty miners were present. After a second lecture at Houtzdale on Saturday evening, more lectures took place the following week in places like Lilly, Federal, Hope Church and Calamity, with an audience varying between ten and sixty people; at Jeannette, the anarchist Tortelier was confronted with the socialist window glass workers; in MacDonald he spoke to his largest audienee, about two hundred and fifty people.

After this lecture tour free associations emerged among miners. One of the more lively circles was "group No I" of "La Revanche des Mineurs" ("The Miners' Revenge") in Spring Valley, Illinois. Founded in 1891, probably by Jean Brault, it met twice a month in the German saloon of the town. The group gave theater performances, a practice common among anarchists. The following year it commemorated the Paris Commune with a play and songs and staged several performances in some mining neighborhoods in order to recruit new members. The group performed at Hope Church, Calamity, Monongahela City, Noblestown, Willow Grove, MacDonald and Primerose, all located in Pennsylvania. In 1893, the Commune celebration reunited some fifty to sixty men and women of French and Belgian origin and, for the first time, some Italians; a German group was also present. In May of the same year, according to *Le Réveil des Mineurs*: "The anarchist comrades of Spring Valley, numbering three hundred to four hundred, marched through the streets of the city, headed by a band and red flags, shouting

'Long Live Anarchy!', 'Down with capitalists!'. The bourgeois must have pulled a long face."[22]

The year after this feat, the group was dispersed and Jean Brault wrote, from Mystic, Iowa:

> "I had to run away from Spring Valley and here as everywhere people are destitute. Over there we have worked well during the strike. When we have been short of food we have looted the company store. What we could not eat we broke. The next day five or six hundred of us headed for Ladd. But the Englishmen were worse than the crawfish: they prefer to die of hunger while working for those who exploit them rather than die in fighting for their rights. We have had several Frenchmen, Belgians, Italians and Poles arrested and that was the fault of the Englishmen and their respect for the law."[23]

Other French settlements were also very active. In March 1889, the anniversary of the Paris Commune was celebrated by the Houtzdale group with a farce entitled "An Enormous Heritage", designed to bring some money to the cause.[24] At Weir City, in 1895, there was a weekly discussion group named "the antipatriots".[25] A ball was also organized by the French and Italian groups so as to help six anarchist periodicals.[26]

Strikes and the Unions

Perhaps it was thanks to Tortelier that anarcho-syndicalist ideas started making their way as early as 1891 among the French-speaking miners of Pennsylvania. Until then, activists recognized the usefulness of unionism, although they complained that it did not cope with the roots of the workingmen's troubles with capitalism. The attitude of the Knights of Labor in the Haymarket affair disenchanted them, but it took several years before they split from the Order, probably because there was no alternative.

However, dissatisfaction grew with the United Mine Workers of America, founded in 1890.[27] Their president, John Rae, was particulary disliked. The French miners nicknamed him "King John". They said he could have made a good senator "with his demure look, his big belly and his white waistcoat."[28] They criticized him, for instance, because he had called for a strike on May Day (1891) for the eight-hour day and then had reversed his decision a week later.[29] The *Réveil des Mineurs* wondered if "the ardor of the leaders had been calmed down at the last minute by a shower of icy water or of banknotes".[30] A letter signed "The Black Bellows" accused the union leaders of exploiting the workingmen: "They have truly fleeced us like sheep. Besides, that was easy. The majority of miners did not even know that a representative was being sent to Pittsburgh. The Belgians and the Frenchmen have not accepted the report of the representative who went to sell us like sheep in the capitalist chapel. Good heavens! they could neither accept nor reject it since their very existence was not even acknowledged."[31]

The press underlined the contrast between the leaders' wages and those of workers. The leaders' wages increased at the very time when they abolished the defense fund so necessary during strikes.

Thus in the early 1890s the French miners were in the avant-garde of the defense of ethnic minorities in Pennsylvania. They demanded that English-speaking union leaders employ interpreters so as to enlighten the workers about their goals and that they receive explicit mandates. Whenever these proposals were rejected, they broke with the leaders and kept the union money; they then built "free unions" and fought against the leadership in the national conventions.[32]

Repression and the economic crisis combined to weaken the movement. In June 1892, the Belgian miners of Spring Valley were arrested and expelled from the country. When, after the coming of Italian and Slavic miners to the area, the French-speaking workingmen lost their influence, it was up to the newcomers to pursue their action. Furthermore, at the end of the century, a number of French militants joined the American socialist party (often not for long), in spite of their proclaimed anarchism. This meant that their anarchism and socialism, which up to that time had been rooted more in the struggles they were waging than in ideology, were now being assimilated. Eventually, the anarchists found their place inside the Industrial Workers of the World. Their monthly, *Germinal*, now appeared in Paterson, New Jersey, a sign of their decline within the mines of Pennsylvania.

Notes

For publication Ronald Creagh has sent us a different text from the one delivered at the colloquium.

1. Higonnet (1980).

2. Garraghan (1945); Thwaites (1968 and 1903).

3. Creagh (1986) and (1987); Perrier (1984).

4. Drury was one of the leading spirits of the International Association, and later, in 1876, of the New York *Socialist* weekly. He was a frequent orator of the Socialistic Labor Party, and also an organizer of the Knights of Labor, a participant of the National Suffrage Convention in Washington in 1891, and even a friend of Samuel Gompers. Drury also published the *Easton Labor Journal*; see Creagh (1986) passim.

5. For a bibliography of anarchist papers quoted here see Blanco, Creagh et Riffaut-Perrot, 1986.

6. See Archives nationales, Paris, F7 12506 and F7 12507, Jean Grave (1854-1939) was a leading figure of the French anarchist movement. He was in charge of the paper *Le Révolté* founded in 1879. It became *La Révolte* in 1887. *Le Père Peinard* founded and edited by Emile Pouget (1860-1931) was published from 1889 to 1894.

7. "Observations générales", *Réveil des Masses*, oct.1889, p.1. The articles have been translated from the French by the author.

8. *Le Réveil des Mineurs*, janv.31, 1891, 2.

9. *Le Réveil des Masses*, août 1889, 1-2.

10. Speakers and journalists of the Socialist Labor Party.

11. *Le Réveil des Mineurs* 2 mai 1891, 2.

12. *La Torpille*, janv.1886, 5.

13. *La Torpille*, janv.1886, 6.

14. *La Torpille*, janv.1886, 11.

15. *L'Ami des Ouvriers*, I Nov. 1894:2.

16. *La Torpille*, juin-juil. 1886, 8.

17. *Le Réveil des Masses*, août 1889.

18. *L'Union des Travailleurs*, III, 13 août 1903, 3.

19. Goldman 1931.

20. *Le Réveil des Mineurs*, I, 2 mai 1891 9, 1.

21. It was on March 31.

22. *Le Réveil des Mineurs* III, avr. 1893, 2. This issue was probably published later than its date indicates.

23. *L'Ami des Ouvriers*, I, sept. 1894, 3.

24. *Le Réveil des Masses*, ser.A,7 mars 1889.

25. *L'Ami des Ouvriers*, I,6: 1 févr. 1895.

26. *ibid.*

27. Founded in 1890.

28. *Le Réveil des Mineurs*, II, 30 janv. 1892, 3.

29. "To the Miners and Mine Laborers of the United States and Territories," Columbus, Ohio, Apr. 17, 1891, in Evans (n.d), vol. II, pp. 114-117.

30. *Le Réveil des Mineurs*, I, 2 mai 1891, 2. One would be tempted to choose the second hypothesis. J.B. Rae's arguments are poor and uncon-

vincing. For instance, he declares that the Hocking Valley is demoralized because the New Straitsville (Ohio) miners have accepted the proposals made by the management; yet, a few days later, on May 1, these miners are striking. See *Le Réveil des Mineurs*, I, 16 mai 1891, 1.

31. *Le Réveil des Mineurs*, II, 20 févr. 1892, 4.

32. These "free unions" were founded in many settlements. Unfortunately, the growing irregularity of anarchist papers does not allow us to follow the evolution of this interesting enterprise. On Joseph Tortellier, see Brécy (1969).

Bibliography

L'Ami des Ouvriers (1894-1896), Paterson, New Jersey.

BIANCO, René, Ronald CREAGH et Nicole RIFFAUT-PERROT (n.d.). *Quand le Coq rouge chantera. Bibliographie. Anarchistes français et italiens aux États-Unis d'Amérique*, Marseille: Editions Culture et Liberté (B.P.40, 13382 Marseille Cedex, France).

BRECY, Robert (1969). *La Grève générale en France*, préf.Jean Maitron, Paris: Etudes et documentation internationale.

CREAGH, Ronald (1986) *L'Anarchisme aux États-Unis*. Paris: Didier Erudition, 2 vol.

CREAGH, Ronald *Nos Cousins d'Amérique. Histoire des Français aux Etats-Unis*. Paris: Payot, à paraître.

Easton Labor Journal (1886-1887) Easton, Pennsylvania.

EVANS, Chris (n.d.) *History of the United Mine Workers of America.*

GARRAGHAN, Gilbert J. (1945) "The French in the Valley", *Missouri Historical Review* XL (Oct.).

GOLDMAN, Emma (1931). *Living My Life*, AMS Press repr. chap. xx, p.245

HIGONNET, P. L. R. (1980) "French", in *Harvard Encvclopedia of American Ethnic Groups*. Cambridge, Mass.: Harvard University Press, pp.379, 380.

KNIGHTS OF LABOR (1896) *Proceedings 1896 General Assembly.*

KNIGHTS OF LABOR (1897) *Proceedings 1897 General Assembly.*

PERRIER, Hubert (1984). "Idées et Mouvement Socialistes aux États-Unis 1864-1890". Thèse Doct. d'État, Université de Paris VIII.

Le Réveil des Masses (1888-1890), New York, N.Y.; Newfoundland, Pennsylvania.

Le Réveil des Mineurs (1890-1893), Hastings, Pennsylvania.

THWAITES, Reuben Gold (1968 and 1903) "Early Lead Mining on the Upper Mississipi," in R.G. Thwaites, *George Rogers Clark and other Essays in Western History*. Freeport, N.Y.: Book for Libraries Press.

La Torpille (1885-1887), Newfoundland, Pennsylvania.

*L'Union des Travailleurs. Organe d'Emancipation Ouvrière (1901-*1916), Charleroi, Pennsylvania.

WARE, Norman J. (1959 and 1929). *The Labor Movement in the United States 1860-1895*, Gloucester, Mass.: Peter Smith.

The Origins of May Day: The American Connection

Hubert Perrier and Michel Cordillot

A recent trend among labor historians has been to examine the symbolic contents of socio-political demonstrations. May Day, for instance, has been and still is fruitfully studied from this angle in various national, regional, or local contexts. Such a trend, however, should not deter us from revisiting the *political* history of May Day, especially that of its origins and early stages, for at least two reasons. First, the original decision to select the First of May as an international workers' holiday and day of struggle came from above, and therefore calls for an investigation of the roles played by various labor leaders and organizations. Second, it is impossible to separate the founding of international May Day from labor's debates and experiments in the field of social legislation and in that of political or economic tactics at the end of the nineteenth century.[1]

As is well known, the decisive step was taken when the participants at the International Socialist Congress held in Paris in July 1889 – the so-called Marxist congress now associated with the founding of the Second International, as opposed to the rival "Possibilist" one – adopted the following resolution:

> A great international demonstration shall be organized for a fixed date in such a manner that the workers in all countries and and in all cities shall on a specified day simultaneously address to the public authorities a demand to fix the workday at eight hours and to put into effect the other resolutions of the International Congress of Paris.
>
> In view of the fact that such a demonstration has already been resolved upon by the American Federation of Labor at its convention of December 1888 in St. Louis for May 1, 1890, that day is accepted as the day for the international demonstration. The workers of the various nations shall organize the demonstration in a manner suited to conditions in their country.[2]

Up to a point, this text merely synthesized a number of themes that for some years had been agitated in various countries and in all international labor gatherings, namely the indispensable entente among workers of all countries, the necessity of an international social legislation, the emphasis on the eight-hour workday, and, last but not least, the concept of large-scale simultaneous demonstrations by the workers of one or several countries. But it also contained crucially innovative elements since, by recommending a practical method for "putting into effect" the demands for social legislation that had been at the center of the debates of the congress, it not only gave definitive form to the idea of "a great international demonstration" aiming at achieving the eight-hour day and other social demands, but also designated May 1, 1890, as the date for the said demonstration.[3]

The circumstances under which the resolution came to be proposed and adopted have been clearly established, except as regards the second paragraph, the one that provided for an international demonstration on May 1, 1890, in connection with the precedent set by the American Federation of Labor (AFL).[4] The resolution was submitted by delegate Raymond Lavigne in the name of the Guesdists (i.e., the French Marxists).[5] According to a reliable first-hand account, the original draft, which had been penned at the Bordeaux congress of the *Fédération nationale des syndicats et groupes corporatifs ouvriers de France* in October–November 1888, contained only the first paragraph of the text that was finally adopted, and the third paragraph was added at the suggestion of Liebknecht and Bebel.[6]

Concerning the second paragraph, it has been established that the choice of May 1, 1890, was made in order to have the international demonstration coincide with the day already chosen by the AFL for the culminating point of its own ongoing eight-hour campaign. But one encounters difficulties when trying to ascertain through what influences and instrumentalities it was decided by the Paris congress to refer to the precedent set by the AFL, and what such a reference meant in terms of the relations between European socialists and U.S. trade unionists.

A first series of questions pertains to the attitude of the diverse American labor organizations concerning the congresses held in Paris in July 1889. What stance did they adopt towards the attempts to set up a new workers' International, what was their perception of the Paris congresses, and what were their specific contributions to these? As regards the AFL, did it only provide the date – May 1 – of the international demonstration in favor of the eight-hour workday, or did it also help to impose the idea of such an action? And on what measure of genuine knowledge and understanding did the European socialists' reference to the AFL's ongoing campaign rest?

A second set of questions has to do with the way in which not only the 1888-91 AFL campaign, but also the wealth of the Americans' experience in the field of the struggle for the eight-hour workday and in that of the general strike (or at least of large-scale simultaneous strikes and demonstrations), especially during the "Great Upheaval" of the mid-80s, were perceived in Europe. As is well known, when the AFL embarked on its campaign for the general inauguration of the eight-hour day on May 1, 1890, it resumed the struggle initiated by its predecessor, the Federation of Organized Trades and Labor Unions, in 1884, a struggle which aimed at achieving the eight-hour day on May 1, 1886, and which, although it was ultimately defeated, did nevertheless reach an impressive climax on that date and the following days with giant strikes and demonstrations, and even outbursts of violence – especially in Chicago, the seat of the Haymarket tragedy and of the resounding trial of anarchists that resulted from it.[7] It has been shown that those struggles, as well as the trial and the ensuing "judicial murder," received considerable attention in Europe.[8] That they were virtually ignored during the 1889 congresses (according to the official as well as unofficial reports available) does not mean that they were irrelevant, either to the setting up of international May Day, or to its subsequent history. In order to try and analyse their relevance (which will be the object of the second part of this paper), it is necessary to look beyond the July 1889 congresses for signs of the interest shown for the "American example" and for some hint of a possible U.S. influence on the labor theoreticians and organizers of May Day.

Before examining the Americans' contribution to the birth of international May Day, it will be useful to review the international policies of U.S. working-class organizations in the 1880s, especially those of the Socialist Labor party (then the foremost socialist organization in North America) and the two leading organizations in the economic field, the Knights of Labor and the American Federation of Labor.[9]

The Socialist Labor Party (SLP), a tiny but active grouping with an overwhelmingly German membership, professed working-class internationalism. It paid considerable attention to the struggles of European workers and to the plans of international labor congresses. In 1881, it was represented at the international congress at Coire (Chur), Switzerland, by Peter J. McGuire, one of its leading English-speaking members.[10] From late 1888 onwards, its leaders were at some pains to form a clear opinion on the successive moves made in Europe in order to promote international labor legislation and, hopefully, set up a new International.[11] The SLP at that time was prey to a fierce internal fight between the leadership, notably W. L. Rosenberg and T. F. Busche, who denigrated trade unionism and advocated shifting the fulcrum of party activity to electoral campaiging, and a faction favoring conciliation with non-socialist economic labor organizations, especially the American Federation of Labor.[12] Busche was the one finally sent to Paris as the SLP's official delegate after several other socialists (including Thomas Morgan of Chicago, Philip Rappaport of Indianapolis, and Meurguet of Philadelphia) had declined the nomination. On leaving for Europe Busche apparently shared his comrades' hope that the two congresses might fuse into one. Once in Paris he chose the Marxist gathering rather than the Possibilist one, but during the prolonged debate over the possibility of unity between the two factions he sided with the advocates of unconditional fusion.[13]

Concerning the Knights of Labor, it must be recalled that the years 1885 to 1889 witnessed first the Order's meteoric rise and then its rapid decline.[14] Although not easy to establish, the causes of this decline included fierce opposition from employers and public authorities, bitter internal factionalism, and rivalry with the AFL. By the end of the decade the Order, while still influential and prestigious, saw its room for manoeuvre severely restricted, both at home and in the international field, by its shrunken membership as well as its leadership's insistence on cultivating an image of moderation and respectability.

In 1887, the Knights' leadership became interested in the *Exposition universelle* (World Fair) due to take place in Paris in 1889 for the Centennial of the French Revolution. During the next year they showed increasing interest in the idea that the Order send a delegation to the *Exposition* and make an exhibit in its department of Social Economy. This idea was first suggested and then pushed vigorously by French admirers of the Knights, notably Abel Davaud and F. Veyssier, both connected with the Paris *Moniteur des Syndicats ouvriers*. These men not only hailed the Order's doctrine and formula of organization but also wished to set up French branches of the Order.[15]

In November 1888, the Knights' General Assembly accepted the formal invitation sent by the commissioner in charge of the *Exposition* both to send a representative and to exhibit there. The elected representative was Grand Master Workman Terence Powderly.[16] During the following weeks the Order's leadership set about gathering the best of its literature for distribution in Paris and to persuade the local assemblies to collect "flags, banners, and insignia" in order to exhibit them "in the capital of our sister republic."[17] By the middle of March, the Order's official organ was thoroughly pleased with the preparations, and in May it started covering the *Exposition* in friendly and laudatory terms.[18]

It is unclear why Powderly, who had warmly supported the plan to send a delegate to Paris, finally decided not to go. We have the testimony of Paul T. Bowen, himself a delegate from District Assembly 66 of Washington, D.C., who attended the Possiblist congress, that "Brother Powderly was expected" and "his absence was a great disappointment."[19]

Powderly's subsequent efforts to explain his change of mind were rather muddled: he simultaneously referred to personal health problems, to his changed evaluation of the pros and cons of his visit to Paris,[20] and to the suggestion, apparently made by critics of his turnabout, that he had been afraid to become somehow entangled in the undertakings of the socialists convening in Paris.[21]

Despite the Grand Master Workman's denegrations, there, in all probability, lay the main factor in his decision to default upon his mandate to attend the French Centennial. While in favor of the Knights' participation in the official *Exposition*, which would have boosted the Order and hopefully stimulated its development in Europe, Powderly was anxious to avoid any association in the public eye of the Order with socialism. It would seem that his decision (while possibly also linked to the notion that it would be inexpedient for him to travel abroad at a time when internal problems required his full attention) was, above all, one aspect of his concern to wed the Knights of Labor to an image of respectable and constructive policies, as opposed to those of "Anarchists or Communists" of all kinds.[22]

Contrary to the Knights of Labor, U.S. trade unions gained strength and self-confidence during the second half of the 1880s. In December 1886, the rather ineffective Federation of Organized Trades and Labor Unions (FOTLU), created in 1881, merged into the newly formed American Federation of Labor. By the end of the decade the AFL, in comparison with the Knights, was definitely the more dynamic organization.[23]

Throughout its brief career the FOTLU, mainly through the agency of those of its founding members who came from a socialist (e.g., P. J. McGuire) or quasi-socialist (e.g., Samuel Gompers) background, paid considerable attention to the theme of international working-class unity. Thus in 1882, McGuire (even though he had now broken with the SLP and was proclaiming the superiority of economic over political unity), in a letter of greetings to the FOTLU convention, hailed the recent advance of the labor movement in several European countries, and expressed confidence that the development of friendly relations between the workmen of all countries would lead to "an era of peace and good-will among nations" as well as check the importation of laborers from one country to another at the behest of capital in order to lower wages.[24] Likewise, in 1884, Frank Foster, in his secretary's report to the FOTLU convention, dealt at length with the friendly correspondence that had been started with the (Possibilist) *Fédération des travailleurs socialistes de France* following the visit of a delegation of fourteen French trade unionists in the fall of 1883, and recommended that the FOTLU lend a hand in the building of a "federation of the workers of the world."[25]

The American Federation of Labor's spokesmen continued in the same vein. For instance, at the very outset of his President's report to the second AFL convention (1887), Samuel Gompers, pointing to the fact that the founding of his organization had been "hailed with the heartiest expressions of joy and hope on the part of many trade unionists in other lands," urged his fellow-unionists to feel "comforted and inspired by the knowledge that [the AFL did] not stand alone and unsupported in the struggle to secure better conditions for the working classes."[26]

In practice, however, it proved difficult to pass from proclamations of solidarity to concrete steps toward unified action. Thus in 1884 the FOTLU's convention, allegedly for lack of funds, declined the French Possibilists' call to support their project of "a Workingmen's International Exposition in Paris, independent of official protection."[27] Again, in 1887 the AFL's convention voted down President Gompers' recommendation to honor the invitation tended by the British Trades Union Congress to take part in the international congress scheduled for the following year in London on the grounds that it was "wiser to first unite the labor organizations of America, before trying to unite with the workingmen of Europe."[28] The convention contented itself with adopting a resolution recommending that "the present friendly relations, through correspondence with European Trades Unions, be encouraged and continued."[29] At the next convention, held in December 1888, Gompers himself pronounced it unreasonable to send delegates to the two international gatherings which at that time had been announced for 1889, one in Paris by the French Possibilists and the other in Switzerland by the German Social Democrats. He argued that the recent London congress could not "be considered as having been highly successful," owing to the insufficient development of "the Trades Unions of continental Europe," and that the AFL would have to wait until the former had "more opportunity to develop" before "anything like harmonious or successful results" could be expected from another international meeting.[30] The convention, while declaring itself "in favor of extending the cordial sympathy of this Federation to all legitimate efforts of the wage earners of other lands to secure industrial emancipation," approved Gompers' argument and so it happened that the AFL was not officially represented at either of the congresses that were finally convened in Paris in July 1889.[31]

It is doubtful, however, whether Gompers' argument before the 1888 convention explains away the AFL's refusal to send delegates to Europe. Interestingly, Gompers himself justified this refusal in different ways, depending on his interlocutors. Speaking to Europeans, he stressed the weakness not of *their* trade unions (as he had done before the AFL convention), but of the *American* labor movement.[32] Later on, he was to invoke the AFL's preoccupation with the ongoing eight-hour campaign in the United States.[33]

In fact, behind this variety of official statements lurked deep misgivings about the ideological orientation of the European movement. By the late 1880s, Gompers was already drawing a distinction between strictly trade-unionist conferences, which he favored strongly, and those more politically minded labor gatherings where a socialist orientation was likely to predominate, to which he was hostile. The international labor federation he had in mind would be modeled along AFL lines and eschew a socialist ideology.[34] In January 1889, in a letter to Auguste Keufer, general secretary of the *Fédération française des travailleurs du livre*, Gompers stressed the vanity of political, radically minded international labor congresses, arguing that they were premature in the light of working-class organizations' present stage of development. The rest of his letter was tantamount to a manifesto for "pure and simple" trade unionism.[35]

On the other hand, Gompers was eager to obtain support from the Paris congresses for the eight-hour day campaign launched by the AFL at its annual convention in December 1888. In his President's report to that convention Gompers recommended "that some day be set apart . . . not later than 1890, when the working people of the entire country" should "be called upon to simultaneously demand the enforcement of eight hours as a day's work."[36] The proposal was endorsed by the convention, which "amid tumultuous cheers and enthusiastic applause," voted to fix the date for the inauguration of the Eight-Hour work-day at May, 1, 1890."[37] It should be emphasized that the convention rejected suggestions that the movement be confined to the best prepared trades, with the others offering whatever support they could.[38] However, after a few weeks had elapsed, the leadership realized that most of the affiliates were not strong enough to enforce the eight-hour demand by May 1, 1890. At the AFL's next national convention, held in December 1889, it was decided, upon Gompers' proposal, that the Federation's executive council would select one or two trades to demand eight hours on May 1, 1890, the strikers receiving financial aid from the trades that remained at work.[39] Accordingly, on March 17, 1890, the executive council selected the Carpenters and Joiners to spearhead the movement. Thus it was only on the eve of the decisive date of May Day, 1890, that the AFL leadership reached its final decision as to what precise tactics should be followed, and even though Gompers by the middle of 1889 had clearly rejected a general strike approach, there are signs that as late as October he was not certain what course the eight-hour campaign would exactly take.[40]

In any case, the leaders of the AFL were determined to lead as energetic a struggle as possible, and were therefore interested in obtaining support from European labor organizations. Although the AFL's convention had refused to send delegates to Europe, it had instructed Gompers to send a "letter of fraternal good will" to the international labor congress to be held in Paris.[41] He selected Hugh McGregor as a personal envoy, without an official mandate, to deliver his message[42] and also, though this was not made explicit, to observe the proceedings and possibly act behind the scenes: for Gompers and his associates were clearly determined to play a significant role in international labor relations in order to promote their own organizational and ideological preferences.[43]

All these reasons may account for the fact that neither the Knights of Labor nor the AFL had official delegates at the Paris congresses of July 1889. At the Marxist congress, the five American delegates were, besides Busche from the Socialistic Labor party, F. E. Kirchner from the United German Trades of New York, Louis E. Miller and Yisroel Barsky from the United Hebrew Trades of New York, and Carl (John?) Ahles from the Brotherhood of United Labor.[44] At the Possibilist gathering, the Americans numbered four: Paul T. Bowen, William S. Waudby, from the Washington Federation of Labor and the International Typographical Union, Thomas Crowley, also from the ITU, and Max Georgii (or Georgei), from the *Arbeiter Verein* of Washington.[45]

At the Marxist congress the Americans, although none of them played a prominent role, reported on labor conditions in the United States and may therefore have helped to draw the Europeans' attention to the American scene. Kirchner, in particular, spoke about the AFL and referred, if only vaguely, to the eight-hour movement it had initiated.[46] On the last day Busche and Miller had a resolution passed to the effect that economic struggle alone was insufficient, and that wherever possible the people should turn to independent political action within the fold of their country's socialist party. This was in keeping with the Rosenberg-Busche leitmotif in the U.S. intra-socialist debate, and they subsequently made much of the fact that their "program and tactics" had "thus received the approbation of the representatives of the world's socialists,"[47]

At the Possibilist congress, the Americans seem to have played a somewhat more significant part. Bowen explained that in its struggle to achieve the eight-hour day, the U.S. labor movement encountered two kinds of difficulty. One, the regulation of the conditions of labor depended on the state legislatures, and these were so numerous that anything like simultaneous and uniform parliamentary legislative action was well-nigh impossible. Two, the action of labor organizations was crippled by the constant arrival of immigrants from Europe. He therefore submitted a resolution – which was unanimously adopted – condemning "immigration as a remedy for industrial evils," approving "the law of the United States of America prohibiting the importation of labor under contract," and asking that every government pass "a law to prevent the inducement of immigration by false promises and representations."[48] The American delegates also participated actively in the discussion about the new phenomenon of trusts, and they submitted, via Bowen, a radical-sounding motion – also adopted without dissent – according to which the major resolutions adopted by the congress (for the reduction of the hours of labor, the limitation of woman and child labor, and kindred measures), were "not to be considered as expressing its full program of industrial reform," but were "demanded to secure the present mitigation of the hardships of labor and to promote the leisure, education, and organization necessary to secure the ultimate ownership and control of all the means of production by the workers themselves, which . . . is the only measure that will secure to labor its complete rights."[49]

As for McGregor, once in Paris he apparently visited both congresses. At the Marxist gathering, he read Gompers' letter during the third session, held on the evening of July 15.[50] And he apparently did the same in front of the Possibilist body during the evening session of July 16.[51]

Gompers' letter, which has not been preserved, cannot be reconstructed with any degree of accuracy.[52] According to the minutes of the Marxist congress, "Hugh McGregor read an address of sympathy from the American Federation of Labor, signed by his president Samuel Gompers, explaining why, engrossed in the eight-hour movement, the Federation had been unable to send a representative to the congress, and recommending union with the Possibilist congress and the greatest caution with the resolutions to be taken."[53]

With regard to the Possibilist congress, the minutes are silent about the contents of the letter, but relate that on July 20 evening the following resolution was voted by acclamation:

> The secretary of the International Labor Congress has been delegated to send acknowledgement of receipt of his letter to citizen Samuel Gompers, of New York, President of the American Federation of Labor, and express the debt that the Congress owes him for the most useful information he supplied it with.
>
> The secretary will, in addition, acquaint citizen Gompers with its deep desire for the success of the eight-hour campaign that the American Federation of Labor is to pursue effectively as of May 1890.[54]

Gompers and other AFL spokesmen later claimed that the letter suggested mass meetings and demonstrations in other nations to lend support to the AFL's eight-hour campaign. Gompers also stated that he proposed that May 1 be celebrated "as an International Labor Day," and that this inspired the historic move by the international congress.[55] As far as we know no report by direct participants in this congress corroborates the latter assertion. It is beyond doubt that in his address Gompers mentioned the AFL's plan to secure the eight-hour day on May 1, 1890, and more than likely that he called for international solidarity in that respect. Moreover it is not impossible that he might have suggested international mass meetings or demonstrations to express such solidarity.[56] It is safe to conclude that whatever its precise wording, Gompers' letter, combined as it was with the American delegates' reports on the U.S. labor scene, did draw the attention of both congresses to the ongoing struggle for the eight-hour day, and, in the case of the Marxist gathering, did lead to the choice of May 1, 1890, as the date for the projected international demonstration.[57]

Yet there remains the problem of the clear discrepancy that existed between the type of action undertaken by the AFL and that suggested by the European Marxists (notably the Guesdists, who had shown most initiative) concerning at least two points.

First, whereas Lavigne, in his historic resolution, referred to a "demonstration" resolved upon by the AFL for May 1, 1890, and implied that it was similar to that which he himself proposed, the AFL had not in fact decided to organize any such demonstration for that date. True, its St. Louis convention in December 1888 had made provision for "simultaneous mass meetings" throughout the country, but these had been called not for May 1, 1890, but for February 22 (Washington's birthday), July 4 (Independence Day), and September 1889 (on Labor Day), as well as February 22, 1890, in order to propagandize the cause.[58] As to May 1, 1890, it was the date on which the *inauguration* of the eight-hour day system had been fixed. As already noted, the tactics through which this goal was to be achieved had not been clearly determined by the St. Louis convention. Apparently, the common understanding at first was that some kind of general mobilization would be effected, but the AFL leadership subsequently lowered their expectations.

That leads us to consider a second, and more crucial, discrepancy between the AFL's approach and that of the Guesdists. U.S. trade-unionists believed in workers confronting employers directly with the shorter-workday demand. In other words, their *simultaneous demand* was to be made in the industrial field, with the backing of the combined economic power of the unions. Such an approach was in keeping with U.S. trade-unionists' disillusionment with eight-hour legislation. As the organ of the Brotherhood of Carpenters and Joiners put it, eight-hour "laws made by politicians will never be observed by employers," and the "only eight-hour law that will have any binding force in this country will be made and enforced by the workingmen."[59]

In contrast with such a view, the Guesdists believed in mass demonstrations on a fixed date in order to make a formal demand to the "public authorities" – i,e., the state at its various levels – that social reforms be enforced, the eight-hour day foremost among them. The Guesdists, in other words, "were anxious above all to channel the energies of the working class towards the State, to give the movement a political . . . thrust."[60]

Not only are such discrepancies – regarding both the use to be made of the First of May and the general approach to the eight-hour issue – easily identified by the modern historian, but they were acknowledged by the Guesdists themselves in their retrospective surveys of the historic decisions of 1889. Deville, for instance, discussed these differences with the utmost clarity of mind in 1896.[61] But that does not answer the question whether *in July 1889* the European delegates at the international Marxist congress (and, for that matter, at the Possibilist one) fully understood the AFL's plans, as well as the differences between them and the Guesdists' program of action. For want of a systematic review of the Europeans' perception of American trade-unions at that time, we cannot answer this question with any precision. One has, however, many reasons to believe that the AFL's decision to "fix the date for the inauguration of the Eight-Hour work day at May 1, 1890" may have been all the more easily interpreted as a call for a general demonstration (or strike) since not only were the words of the original resolution, which was perhaps included in the letter read by McGregor, extremely vague, but, as already noted, as of July 1889 the AFL had not decided on its definitive plan.[62]

Besides, whatever differences the Europeans may have perceived were probably of less moment to them *at that time* than the opportunity which was offered them, in adopting the date already chosen by the AFL in order to win the eight-hour day, to demonstrate the strength of the international labor movement by enabling it to act simultaneously around a common objective in both the Old and the New Worlds.

On the other hand, when Deville wrote his *Historique du Premier Mai* in 1896, the Guesdists had become inclined to minimize the AFL's contribution, both because they scorned the Federation's more and more explicitly pure and simple unionism and because they were trying to get as much credit as possible for the genesis of May Day. As Michelle Perrot reminds us, working-class memory "is a constructed phenomenon," the focus of controversies and struggles,[63] and clearly, by the end of the 1890s the Guesdists were satisfied to give "the Americans" credit for the *date* of May 1 while assigning the main role to French workers (and, most of all, the Guesdists themselves) as regards the idea of a simultaneous international demonstration at a fixed date.[64]

But this was in 1896 and does not apply to the time of the Paris international congresses – nor even to the period that immediately followed them. Indeed for at least twelve and maybe eighteen months after those congresses, diverse European labor leaders expressed their high regard for the U.S. labor movement's contribution to the international struggle for the eight-hour day. For instance Friedrich Engels, in the preface he wrote on May 1, 1890, to the fourth German edition of the *Communist Manifesto*, expressed his enthusiasm in seeing "the proletariat of Europe and America . . . holding a review of its forces" and "mobilized for the first time as one army."[65] Again, late in 1890, at a gathering in London on the occasion of Engels's 70th birthday, such eminent socialist and labor leaders as Liebknecht, Bebel, and Tom Mann praised the AFL for its active role in the common struggle. And when, early in 1891, many of the same figures took steps to establish a series of international bodies to prevent the export of strikebreakers from one country to another, the AFL was chosen to represent the United States, and its leader was appointed one of the International Secretaries of Labor.[66] Meanwhile Gompers hailed the mighty celebration of the First of May 1890 in Europe, which, he asserted, "proves the universality of our movement and is a ray of hope for the attainment of the poet's dream, The Parliament of Man, The Federation of the World."[67] He accepted the offer to become an International Secretary of Labor on behalf of the AFL, expressing his hopes to see "the closer international Alliance to crystalize and attain the fondest hopes of laborers; their amelioration and final emancipation."[68] And, on the eve of the 1891 May Day celebration, while crediting "the agitation of the American Federation of Labor" for the fact that the First of May was becoming an annual celebration for the working class, he declared: "May 1st of each year is now looked upon by the organized wage-workers and the observing public as a sort of new Independence Day upon which they will every year strike a blow for emancipation and steadily weaken the shackles of wage slavery."[69]

At the same time, however, the bone of contention between the AFL and the Socialists grew increasingly weightier, both at home and abroad. In fact, beyond the declarations of mutual esteem and superficial convergences, the ever more noticeable strategic and tactical differences were themselves pointing to distinct ideological orientations, which were in fact more and more antagonistic. It has already been said that Gompers was in no way ready to involve himself in a socialist international workmen's organization. The evolution of events, both in the United States and on an international level, was to add seriously to his reservations, and, in the end, turn them into outright hostility.

The deterioration of the relationships between the AFL and the American socialists (the SLP) materialized in the controversy that followed Gompers' refusal to return to the Central Labor Federation of New York, a SLP-controlled body, the charter it had formerly held, on the grounds that the CLF had formally admitted SLP delegates. After SLP leader Lucien Sanial, who claimed admission to the AFL convention in Detroit (December 1890) lost the battle on the convention floor, the tensions between the AFL and the SLP rapidly came to a head. In the early 1890s the SLP (now led by Daniel DeLeon) pronounced the AFL leadership the main stumbling-block in the march of American workers towards socialism, while Gompers not only fought staunchly to prevent his organization from adopting a collectivist platform, but also heaped abuse and invective on his left-wing opponents while at the same time striving to allay the suspicions of the European socialists.[70]

The now open hostility between the followers of Gompers and DeLeonite socialists was soon to have spectacular consequences in the international field. Contrary to Gompers' wish the AFL did not send a delegate to the Brussels international congress in 1891. On the other hand Gompers, more eager than ever to promote the trade-union idea internationally, devised the plan to convene an international labor congress at the same time as the Chicago World Fair of 1893. But it was in vain: the Brussels Congress declined the offer, preferring Switzerland as the place for the next international gathering. Gompers claimed that such a decision had been made "owing to our nonrepresentation at Brussels on the one hand, and, on the other, the misrepresentation of the character of the American Federation of Labor by one who was excluded from our last Convention." (i.e., Sanial).[71] As a matter of fact Sanial urged the Europeans to go to Chicago, but the Internationals preferred Zurich.[72]

Those events resulted in estranging the mainstream of American trade unionism from the Second International, so that the delegates from North America to its subsequent congresses were virtually all socialists.[73] At the same time Gompers did not succeed in getting any European country to join in his scheme of international organization on a purely trade-union basis. The best he could do was to tighten the AFL's bond with the British Trades Union Congress by means of fraternal exchanges of delegates. Thus John Burns of the TUC attended the AFL convention in 1894, and the following year Gompers and P. J. McGuire visited that of the TUC.[74] But it was not until the late 1900s [?] that Gompers began to achieve practical results in his plan to set up an international federation of trade unions.[75]

Meanwhile, in the United States the AFL had given up interest in the First of May, preferring to adopt Labor Day as an American workers' holiday. Labor Day grew out of a parade and picnic of the Central Labor Federation of New York on September 5, 1882, and evolved into a national celebration over the next twelve years. By 1884, several leading working-class organizations had declared they would observe the first Monday in September of each year as a holiday, and by the end of 1887 New York State and several other states had adopted legislation recognizing the said date as Labor Day. Finally, in 1894, President Grover Cleveland signed the measure making the first Monday in September a "legal public holiday."[76]

The AFL, which had agitated for federal law to recognize Labor Day, greeted the event. Yet for some time it resisted the pressure of the commercial press to ignore the "Red" European First of May and observe only the American Labor Day holiday.[77] In 1897, the AFL's official organ still called for workers' mass mobilization on the following First of May: "May 1, 1898 – Prepare for it. This date has been set for the general enforcement of the eight-hour work day among all labor in the United States."[78] But May 1, 1898, passed uneventfully, and by 1901 the AFL no longer recommended May Day strikes, but only "discussion and commendation" of eight-hour efforts.[79] Moreover, the AFL leadership "disowned May Day as a workers' holiday, claiming that it belonged to Europe and the socialists rather than to the United States and U.S. trade unions. They ceased to mention the origin of May Day in the United States and threw all of their support behind Labor Day."[80] The double retreat of the AFL – from large-scale, nationally coordinated eight-hour campaigns and from the celebration of the First of May as an international worker's holiday – should be viewed as part of the triumph of craft unionism, class collaboration, and an openly anti-socialist orientation within the mainstream of U.S. Labor. As a result of such policies the cause of international working-class solidarity suffered a serious blow. In early twentieth-century America, it remained for the left wing of the movement, i.e., for important but definitely minority organizations, the Socialist Party of America and the Industrial Workers of the World, to go on celebrating the First of May as the principal workers' holiday and day of struggle.

But one should also keep in mind that, originally, the date of May 1 had been associated not only with the campaign launched by the AFL in 1886, but also with its tragic outcome in Chicago.

It is safe to say that there was no explicit link between the Haymarket affair and the decision to institute an international First of May. In the course of the confused debate that led to the choice of that particular date by the Marxist congress, no reference whatsoever was apparently made either to the Haymarket affair or to the Chicago anarchists tried and condemned for their alleged responsibility in it. Yet in 1886 and 1887, the affair had caused considerable concern in the European labor movement. Indeed numerous expressions of sympathy and solidarity for the accused had come from diverse European quarters, especially at the time of their indictment and trial (May–August 1886) and on the eve of their execution (November 11, 1887). But, by July 1889, the Chicago anarchists' ordeal was certainly *not* the aspect of the American social scene that the delegates assembled at the Marxist congress in Paris had most clearly in mind, or, at least, were prepared publicly to throw into relief, let alone identify with.

With respect to memory and symbolism, in the early 1890s the most direct legacy of the Haymarket tragedy was to be found in the celebration of November 11 by labor militants in many countries.[81] Another form of legacy lay in the fact that the Chicagoans were often placed side by side in the Pantheon of labor martyrs with the victims of the mass executions which had followed the demise of the Paris Commune. The Possibilist international congress of 1889 itself witnessed a striking example of such an association: a delegate from Dublin having laid "on the desk weeds that had been picked on the Chicago grave," Strassart, a framemaker by trade and member of the French delegation, contributed a frame in which the "weeds were laid in such manner as to depict an axe, the axe with which the old world will be struck down in order to usher in the world of justice and equality." It was then resolved to march in procession to the Père Lachaise cemetery in order to carry the picture over to the grave of the Commune martyrs.[82]

Moreover many prominent participants in the Marxist congress had played too great a part in organizing the solidarity movement with the anarchists on trial not to be aware of the symbolic significance of the date of May 1 and its association with the events that had led to their tragic death. For example, as regards French participants, Charles Longuet, at a meeting of the Paris municipal council, had submitted a plea for mercy to be presented to the United States legation; Z. Camélinat and E. Vaillant had spoken at public meetings in defense of the defendants; and Jules Guesde had written scathing articles in *Le Cri du Peuple* and *Le Socialist*. In England, Eleanor Marx-Aveling and her husband had been very active on behalf of Parsons and his comrades. In Germany, A. Bebel had denounced the *Justizmord* and signed, together with Liebknecht, Singer, and Grillenberger, a telegram sent on the eve of the execution to the Governor of Illinois to beg for his clemency.[83] In the same connection, special mention should be made of the Belgian socialist Anseele, who had explicitly referred to the American example when at the International Trade Union Congress held in London in October 1888 he proposed that the first Sunday of May be celebrated as an international day of action, and who was the following year one of the members of the committee in charge of drawing up the preliminary platform for the (Marxist) Paris congress, which contained a plank on the shortening of the hours of labor.[84] As to Ferdinand Domela Nieuwenhuis, he later explained in his autobiography how deeply affected he had been by be Chicaco events, whose outcome eventually led him to "be converted" to anarchism.[85] What was true for the luminaries must also have been true for the more obscure militants, given the fact that the protest movement against the Chicago frameup in 1886 and 1887 was the most significant manifestation of concrete internationalism throughout Europe in the period between the demise af the First and the birth of the Second International.

More generally speaking, the link between the American labor struggles of 1884-87 and the international May Day should be examined against the background of the developing socialist and labor movement in each national context, as the main points raised by U.S. workers (the eight-hour workday as their central objective and simultaneous mass action as their tactic) were also crucial issues on the agenda of most European labor organizations. A brief overview of what happened in France on the one hand and in Spain on the other will offer both an illustration of this and a glimpse of how different the situation could be from one country to another.

As regards France, the extent to which the American eight-hour struggles of the mid-1880s influenced the contemporary debates on the general strike remains a moot point. It was in October 1887 that, for the first time, the principle of the general strike was adopted by the *Fédération nationale des Syndicats*. The motion was submitted by three Parisian anarchist delegates, Berger, Tortelier, and Combomoreil, who, a few days later, also attended a meeting where workers representing 22 trade unions declared in favor of the eight-hour day and the general strike.[86] According to the anarchist weekly *La Révolte*, "in the course of the discussions . . . the Chicago 1886 strikes were naturally mentioned," but, unfortunately, accounts of the meeting leave us in the dark as to the terms in which the American event was discussed. It is clear, however, that even though the American precedent was not the only source of inspiration for the French trade-unionists, it did have an influence on it as the first and most relevant example of massive and simultaneous work stoppage in several large cities of a single country.[87]

At the same time, the dearth of explicit references to the Chicago events by the Guesdists should hardly be a surprise considering the factional struggles that plagued the revolutionary movement. Indeed Guesde's followers were too eager to dissociate themselves from their anarchist rivals in France to pay even lip service to their American counterparts. Yet a few significant clues may be picked up here and there hinting at the existence of an unacknowledged link between the American events and the strategy defined by the *Parti ouvrier français*. For instance when, in February 1889 the *Fédération nationale des syndicats* (under Guesdist control) with the help of the POF initiated a movement aiming at the shortening of the workday, Raymond Lavigne (later to author the First of May resolution at the 1889 Marxist congress) issued a circular letter in which he urged the French workers to remember "the great movements in England and in America in the course of which hundreds of thousands of workers, on the same day, at a given time simultaneously resorted to a similar form of action."[88]

More generally, as noted by Marjorie Murphy, "the strike, the bomb, the trial, and the sentencing had forced [within the ranks of the various French socialist factions] a discussion over the role of trade unions in political action, especially the Knights."[89] There are also reasons to believe that the disastrous outcome of the Haymarket explosion was one of the factors that led the French anarchists to question the strategy of direct action in the fall of 1886.[90] And, as regards the socialists, even if few of them were prepared to admit it, the memory of the American events of 1886 must have loomed large in the early celebrations of May Day. Paul Lafargue himself, a prominent Guesdist, later admitted that it was "the U.S.A. which, through their immense strike for the eight-hour workday, [had] inaugurated the series of May 1 demonstrations."[91] Moreover, given the fact that French socialists were by the late 1880s determined to steer clear of all dangerous connections with violence and reckless revolutionism, Haymarket was certainly one factor – among many others, and difficult to assess separately – in the slow and uneven process through which their movement changed into a social-democratic party rooted in the political life of the nation.

In the case of Spain, the American influence was much clearer, since the existence of a link between 1886, the USA, and May Day was not only taken for granted but also considered as seminal by the anarchists who dominated the labor movement. Yet, it had been for the Marxist-inclined *El Socialista* to show the greater sense of premonition when publishing in its issue dated June 11, 1886, a "Letter from America" signed R. [Rosenberg?] which predicted: "May 1 will become a day of international celebration for the workers everywhere in the world, exactly as July 14 is for the bourgeoisie of all countries." The Spanish revolutionaries were all the more attentive to what was occurring on the American scene as the eight-hour day was their main goal too. As early as September 1886, an "Interim 8-hour committee" was set up by the anarchists, mustering 57 workers' societies in the Barcelona area, which was later to lead the great strikes of 1890 and 1891 in many cities.[92] Its aim was to organize a general strike to impose the eight-hour workday, and, beyond that, to pave the way for the Revolution. Considered in this respect, the execution of the Chicago anarchists could be seen as something other than a tragedy: "We think that to be hanged for the same cause as Parsons, Engel,

Fischer, and Spies, and to die like Lingg is more than glory, it is the apotheosis."[93] Simultaneously, the socialists associated with an initiative from the *Centro Obrero* of Barcelona, which had decided to "undertake an active campaign, so as to obtain from governmental authorities a law limiting the workday to 8 hours."[94] The response was favorable, and by the end of 1887, 136 trade societies had signed the initial demand.[95] Despite the disputes over strategy between socialists and anarchists, the eight-hour movement gradually gained momentum, and the Unions' Congress organized by the moribund FTRE (IWA) on May 18, 19, and 20, 1888, could feel confident enough to proclaim that

> The eight-hour day is the war-cry of all workers of the civilized world; it has already led great masses of workers in Belgium, France, and the United States, as well as the glorious Chicago martyrs, to stand up; all the workers' organizations of Europe and America are going to the conquest of the 8 hours; in view of this international movement, the Spanish workers cannot remain inactive.[96]

As soon as the decision had been made by the Paris congress to call for international action on behalf of the eight-hour day on May 1, 1890, the Spanish anarchists set to work to make sure that the day would be a success, and the headline of *El Productor* on April 18, 1890, was as explicit as it could be: "*Huelga general!* (general strike) . . . May 1 will be a great day. The Chicago victims originated it! They deserve full satisfaction for their sacrifice!" And indeed the May Day demonstrations were imposing, as not only the anarchists, but also the socialists, appeared in full force. In the course of the following years, libertarian newspapers never failed to remind their readers of the American precedent. Here is for instance what *El Productor* wrote on May 18, 1891, in its "Historical Sketch of the May Movement":

> Now that the world proletariat is interested in the 8-hour day, the anarchists who are part and parcel of this movement, cannot stay away from it; on the contrary, for our honor and for our glory some anarchists have been the organizers of the resistance, and died in Chicago on the republican gallows, and it is thanks to the anarchists that the workers' demands for May Day have obtained such a resounding echo.

Clearly, French and Spanish militants, anarchists, and socialists *did not* have the same perception of the origins of May Day, and *could not* assign the same importance to the American precedent in the complex chain of events that had led to its celebration. Similar differences existed everywhere in Europe, and this is something that has to be reckoned with when one tries to assess the legacy of the 1886-87 events.

Indeed, controversies hardly subsided with time. Soon after the First of May had been set up as an international labor day, French socialists and anarchists started trading insults and accusations, the latter claiming that the politically minded socialists were "stifling" the movement by their "dull" demonstrations.[97] Gradually, some anarchists developed an alternative strategy which pointed to the American 1886 events as a precedent to be studied and emulated: whereas the socialists in 1890 and 1891 had been content with demanding that a law should be voted to enact the eight-hour day – with no practical results – the Americans had chosen to rely on economic action and on mass strikes to impose *de facto* the shortening of their workday. The main spokesman for this revision was Emile Pouget, the famous *Père Peinard.*[98] Initiated as early as 1890-91, his reflections on the American precedent of 1886 progressively led him to regard it as nothing less than a model for the Europeans to emulate. Towards the end of the 1890s, a considerable fraction of the European labor movement, equally disgusted with blind anarchist terrorism and the lackluster parliamentary routine of the social-democratic parties, was precisely looking for an alternative strategy which would be feasible, efficient, and revolutionary at the same time. This led to the emergence of the syndicalist movement and to a reconsideration of the meaning and of the goal of May Day. Here is how Pouget saw things:

> . . . Let us imitate the Americans!
>
> The tactics which, in 1886, enabled them to obtain the eight-hour day quickly is still an excellent one – it is even the only efficient one. It consists in wanting and acting;
>
> . . . The workers of the United States showed us the way. Let us be capable of following in their footsteps.
>
> . . . Once the Americans no longer wanted to work over eight hours, they chose May 1, 1886, as being the date on which such reform should apply, and they firmly pledged to each other not to work more than eight hours from that day onward.
>
> Let us follow their example![99]

Elected vice general secretacy of the French *Confédération générale du Travaille* (CGT) in 1901, and in charge of its weekly *La Voix du Peuple*, Emile Pouget, thanks to his acute sense of propaganda and education, so to speak raised the American example to the status of a doctrine, the idea of direct and simultaneous mass action conceived as a preparation for the general strike, thus providing the CGT and a number of other European unions[100] with a new strategy for action. At the CGT congress held in Bourges in 1904, Pouget contributed to the decision to launch a vast movement aiming at imposing the eight-hour day as from May 1, 1906. However, after scoring some successes the syndicalist movement ebbed away throughout Europe. Of special interest, from the viewpoint of this paper, is the fact that the memory of the U.S. labor upheaval of the mid-eighties, explicitly described as an example to be followed, had been a crucial reference point in discussions about strategy within an important fraction of the European labor movement.

Much remains unknown about the origins of May Day, and, concerning even the limited field of study that has been explored in this essay, more work of investigation will be necessary to achieve fully satisfactory conclusions. The authors, however, will feel fully rewarded if it appears that they have been able to throw new light on some aspects of the links between the United States labor movement and European working-class organizations at the end of the nineteenth century – a largely uncharted field as of yet – bringing to the fore the need to study those links more closely.

Notes

From *Storie e Immagini del lo Maggio* (1990). Reprinted by permission of the publisher.

The authors would like to express their warmest thanks to Jeremy Gladstone, and Jeffrey Hopes for their valuable assistance in the preparation of the English-language version of this essay.

1. See M. Perrot. "The First of May 1890 in France: The Birth of a Working-class Ritual," in P. Thane *et al.* (eds.), *The Powers of the Past: Essays for Eric Hobsbawm* (Cambridge and Paris 1984), p. 143. This of

course does not mean that the international First of May can be reduced to the conscious objectives of its initiators, since on the one hand it had roots in the rich associations which the month of May in general and May Day in particular traditionally had for working people, and, on the other hand, it acquired a dynamic of its own, sparking off all kinds of forms of expression unanticipated by its promoters. See *ibid.*, pp. 143-144. But that does not detract from the legitimacy of making a specific research topic of the circumstances under which plans for an international demonstration of working people on May 1 were originally devised and subsequently, elaborated upon.

2. *Workmen's Advocate* (New Haven, Conn.), 10 August 1889.

3. Lavigne's resolution did not provide for the *annual* observation of May Day by the working-class of all countries. It was left for subsequent congresses of the Second International to fix the character of May Day as a yearly event. See M. Dommanget, *Histoire du Premier Mai* (Paris 1972), pp. 109 ff.

4. On the paternity of the resolution see the first-hand account by G. Deville, "Historique du Premier Mai," *Le Devenir Social* II (Avril 1896), pp. 289-309. Also Dommanget, Chapter v. On the contribution of American protagonists, see the pathbreaking article by S. Fine, "Is May Day American in Origin?" *The Historian 16:2* (Spring 1954), pp. 121-134. For additional information and comment see P. S. Foner, *May Day: A Short History of the International Workers' Holiday 1886-1986* (New York 1986), pp. 40-43; C. Collomp, "L'American Federation of Labor et la IIe Internationale: Vers l'isolement politique et idéologiques," *Les Cahiers d'Encrages 1:4* (mai 1988), pp. 29-40; H. Perrier, C. Collomp, M. Cordillot and M. Debouzy, "The 'Social Revolution' in America? European Reactions to the 'Great Upheaval' and to the Haymarket Affairs," *International Labor and Working-Class History 29* (Spring 1986), pp. 38-52; M. Cordillot, "Les Reactions aux événements de Haymarket en Europe: données et problèmes," paper presented at the International Colloquium *In the Shadow of the Statue of Liberty*, Paris 22-25 October 1986 (publication forth coming).

5. Dommanget, chap. iv.

6. Deville, p. 298. See also Dommanget, pp. 11-114.

7. H. David, *The History of the Haymarket Affair* (New York 1936); P. Avirch, *The Haymarket Tragedy* (Princeton 1984); D. Roediger and F. Rosemont (eds.), *Haymarket Scrapbook* (Chicago 1986).

8. Perrier *et al.*, "The 'Social Revolution' in America," *passim.*

9. Needless to say the movement of the 1880s was heir to an already long tradition. As early as the 1860s American working-class organizations had shown interest in bringing about some kind of international cooperation across the Atlantic, if only to regulate emigration to North America. Thus in 1869 the National Labor Union sent Andrew Cameron to the Congress of the International Workingmen's Association in Basel, Switzerland, mostly in order to arrive at an understanding with the IWA on the subject of immigration. J. Commons *et al.*, (eds.), *A Documentary History of American Industrial Society* (New York 1958), IX, pp. 341-350.

10. D. N. Lyon, "The World of P. J. McGuire: A Study of the American Labor Movement, 1870-1890" (University of Minnesota, Ph.D. 1972), p.

157; L. Valiani, "Dalla Prima all a Seconda Internazionale," *Movimento Operaio*, 1954, pp. 32-33.

11. *Workman's Advocate*, 10, 24 November, 1, 15, 22 December 1888, 15 June 1889. For background information, see Valiani, pp. 35-50.

12. *Workman's Advocate*, 30 June, 29 September, 24 November 1888. See H. Perrier, "The Socialists and the Working Class in New York, 1890-1896," *Labor History* 22:4 (Fall 1981), pp. 488-489.

13. *Workman's Advocate*, 4 May, 1, 15 June, 13, 20, 27 July, 3, 10, 24 August 1889.

14. The Order's membership, after increasing sevenfold in a single year (with an apex of 700,000 in July 1886), underwent a sharp decline from late 1886 through the summer of 1889. Then for almost three years the membership levelled off at just over 120,000. See R. Oestreicher, "A Note on Nights of Labor Membership Statistics," *Labor History* 25:1 (Winter 1984), pp. 102-108.

15. *Journal of United Labor* (Chicago), 21 May 1887, 25 February, 25 October, 8, 15, 29 November, 6 December 1888, 21 March 1889. Cf. Marianne Debouzy, "Les ouvriers américains à l'Exposition de 1889," *Revue de l'Economie Sociale*, xix (1989).

16. Knights of Labor General Assembly, 1888, *Proceedings*, p. 74; *Journal of United Labor*, 24 January, 21, 28 February, 9 May 1889.

17. *Ibid.*, 28 February 1889.

18. *Ibid.*, 14 March, 9 May 1889.

19. *Ibid.*, 14 November 1889. In his report Bowen explained that on reaching Paris he discovered there were going to be two distinct congresses, and that he chose the Possibilist one, "though having strong personal inclinations to unite with others," because it seemed more in keeping with his mandate.

20. "The vote of the General Assembly was that I attend the World's Fair only, and I could not see that any gain would accrue to the Order on either side of the Atlantic from such a step. To cross over and visit the Exposition would be very pleasant, but it would leave whoever went open to the charge of going on a junketing tour, and there are those who would be uncharitable enough to make such remarks. On the whole, I believe that I did the best thing possible for the Order and for myself in not attending the Paris Exposition." *Ibid.*

21. "The statement that I feared to go because of the gathering of socialists at that point has no foundation, for I was not elected to attend their congress, and would have had nothing in common with them had I gone to Europe." *Ibid.*

22. *Journal of United labor*, 15 November 1888. The fact that secessionist elements from the Order had sent a representative to Paris (see below, note 44) may have been one more factor in Powderly developing a hostile attitude toward the Paris international congresses.

23. The AFL had a membership of 138,000 in 1886 and 225,000 in 1890. L. Wolman, *The Growth of American Trade Unions, 1880- 1923* (New York 1924), pp. 32, 122.

24. FOTLU Convention, 1882, *Report*, p. 22.

25. FOTLU Convention, 1884, *Proceedings*, pp. 22-24.

26. AFL Convention, 1887, *Report of Proceedings*. p. 9.

27. FOTLU Convention, 1884, *Proceedings*, pp. 22-24.

28. AFL Convention, 1887, *Report of Proceedings*. pp. 9-10, 17, 25-26.

29. AFL Convention, 1887, *Report of Proceedings*. pp. 29.

30. AFL Convention, 1888, *Report of Proceedings*. p. 17. Cf. B. Mandel, *Samuel Gompers: A Biography* (Yellow Springs 1963), p. 113.

31. AFL Convention, 1888, *Report of Proceedings*, p. 21. At the meeting of the AFL's Executive Council on May 14, 1890, the organization's line of conduct was thus specified: no delegate would be sent "direct from the Federation to the Industrial Congress in Paris" (at that date, and apparently until the very eve of the Paris congresses, the Americans did not know that there were going to be two), in view of the fact that the congress would be "of a very discordant character," being "composed of diverse and conflicting schools of thought"; but, on the other hand, some "local bodies of the Federation" would "send delegates." The latter turned out to be Federal Labor Union No. 2714 and Tile Layers' Union No. 2690, both of which, upon learning in Paris that two separate congresses had been called, refused to present their credentials to either body. *Carpenter*, 15 June, 15 August, September 1889.

32. Mandel, p. 113.

33. This is apparently the reason he stressed in his letter to the Paris congresses (see below).

34. Mandel, pp. 112-113.

35. Collomp, "L'American Federation of Labor et la IIe Internationale," p. 33.

36. AFL Convention, 1888, *Report of Proceedings*, p. 11.

37. *Ibid.* pp. 28-29. See also S. Fine, "The Eight-Hour Day Movement in the United States, 1888-1891," *Mississippi Valley Historical Review* 40 (December 1953), p. 443.

38. AFL Convention, 1888, *Report of Proceedings*, p. 29.

39. AFL Convention, 1889, *Report of Proceedings*, pp. 15-16, 20, 29-31.

40. *Carpenter*, September 1889, 15 March 1890; Fine, "The Eight-Hour Day Movement," pp. 48-452,

41. AFL Convention, 1889, *Report of Proceedings*, p. 15.

42. Gompers, *Seventy Years of Life and Labor* (Reprint, New York 1967), 1, p. 297. An English-born jeweler who had emigrated to the United States in 1865, McGregor had been active in socialist circles in the early 1870s. By the middle of the decade he had deserted the socialist cause while remaining active in the labor movement. In the late 1880s he served as Gompers' secretary.

43. L. L. Lorwin, *Labor and the International* (New York 1929), pp. 71, 118-120. See also *Carpenter*. September 1889.

44. "Congrès international ouvrier socialiste, Paris, 14-21 juillet 1889," in *Histoire de la IIe Internationale* 6-7. (Geneva 1977), p. 24; "Protokoll des Internationalen Arbeiter-Congresses zu Paris," *Ibid.*, pp. 177-178. Kirchner is also listed as a delegate from Germany. Ahles is incorrectly listed as

a delegate of the "United Brotherhood of Iowa," but in fact he represented a splinter group of the Knights of Labor. According to Busche, he had come "all the way from Iowa to have the congress pass resolutions against Powderly," but "went home before the close of the congress without even presenting his condemnatory resolutions." *Workmen's Advocate*, 24 August 1889. See also Fine, "Is May Day American?," p. 122, note 6.

45. Fédération des Travailleurs socialistes de France, "Compte Rendu du Congrès international ouvrier socialiste," in *Histoire de la IIe Internationál, cit.*, pp. 214-215. *Journal of United Labor*, 15 August, 14 November 1889; *Typographical Journal*, 15 August 1889. As members of the Typographical Union, Waudby and Crowley were members of an affiliate of the AFL, but they by no means formally represented the Federation. Crowley was also a delegate to the International Typographical Congress which was then meeting in Paris. Waudby may also have been a member of the Knights of Labor. Fine, p. 129. Also *Ibid.*, p. 122, note 7, and p. 123, note 8.

46. "Protokoll des Internationalen Arbeiter-Congresses," in *Histoire de la IIe Internationale, op.cit.*, pp. 117-119, 162-163; *Workmen's Advocate*, 24 August 1889.

47. "Protokoll des Internationalen Arbeiter-Congresses," pp. 172-173. In the reports on the Paris congresses published in the SLP's press the call for an international eight-hour demonstration was mentioned only marginally, which is hardly surprising since the Rosenberg-Busche faction had from the start deprecated the AFL eight-hour campaign, arguing that "an eight-hour movement can only be successful when the masses organize themselves as an independent political party upon the platform of the Socialistic Labor Party." *Workmen's Advocate*, 25 February, 10, 17, 24 August 1889.

48. "Compte Rendu du Congrès international ouvrier socialiste," in *Histoire de la IIe Internationale, cit.*, pp. 244-245, 264-265; *Journal of United Labor*, 15 August, 14 November 1889.

49. *Journal of United Labor*, 14 November 1889. See also "Compte Rendu du Congres international ouvrier socialiste," cit pp. 264-271.

50. "Protokoll des Internationalen Arbeiter-Congresses," cit., p. 59; Deville, "Historiques," p. 301.

51. "Compte Rendu du Congrès International ouvrier socialiste," *op.cit.*, p. 230. According to this source, "A delegate from the AFL read an address from that federation. Following an observation by Citizen Dénéchaud [a French delegate], who remarked that this citizen was not a delegate to the congress, he left the platform," Dommanget (*Histoire du Premier Mai*, p. 117), does not think that the unnamed delegate may have been McGregor, being rather inclined to believe that he was one of the two typographers, Waudby or Crowley, but his thesis is unsubstantiated. It is worthy of note that in 1932 Waudby, although in 1889 he had been a delegate to the Possibilist congress, claimed to have been the originator of the May Day resolution at the Marxist one. Fine, "Is May Day American?," pp. 129-130. See also the letter from McGregor in *Carpenter*, 15 September 1889.

52. For Gompers' version of why this letter has not been saved, see *Seventy Years*, p. 297. Gompers' account of the whole story in his autobiography (*Ibid.*, pp. 296-298) is generally unreliable. There is also a brief reference to the letter in his President's report to the AFL 1889 convention (*Report of*

Proceedings, p. 15): "In my letter I took occasion to refer, among other matters, to our Eight-Hour movement." See also *Carpenter*, 15 June 1889; *Typographical Journal*, 15 August 1889; AFL Convention, 1891, *Report of Proceedings*, p. 14.

53. Our (M.C. & H.P.) translation from the French minutes, as quoted in Deville, "Historique," p. 301. See also "Protokoll des Internationalen Arbeiter-Congress," p. 59 (in this text – the German translation of Jules Guesde's original report on the Marxist congress, which has not been published in French – McGregor is erroneously designated as "George M. Hugh").

54. "Compte rendu du Congrès international ouvrier socialiste," p. 275. Our translation from the French.

55. Gompers, *Seventy Years*, pp. 297-298. *American Federationist* (May, 1894), p. 52; Foner, *May Day*, p. 41-42.

56. Dommanget, *Histoire du Premier Mai*, p. 117; Fine, "Is May Day American in Origin?," pp. 131-132.

57. This is corroborated by an unpublished letter of Jules Guesde (n.d., probably April 1897, quoted in Dommanget, *Histoire de Premier Mai*, pp. 111, 117), in which he reconsiders the origins of May Day allegedly on the basis of "all the evidence pertaining to the international congress" which he had thought "forever lost" and recovered during a removal. Guesde writes: "Moreover, the AFL English-language report – and not the delegates, as the Federation had sent none – definitely provided the dates."

58. AFL Convention, 1888, *Report of Proceedings*, pp. 28-29; Fine, "The Eight-Hour Day Movement," p. 443; Fine, "Is May Day American?," pp. 131-133.

59. *Carpenter*, January 20, 1891, quoted in Fine, "The Eight-Hour Movement," p. 444. This policy, away from the tradition of applying political pressure to achieve social legislation, became increasingly characteristic of the major unions' policy from the early 1880s onward. See, for instance, FOTLU leader Frank Foster's statement before the 1884 convention: "This much has been determined by the history of the national eight-hour law – it is useless to wait for legislation in this matter. In the world of economic reform the working classes must depend upon themselves for the enforcement of measures as well as for their conception. A united demand for a shorter working day, backed by thorough organization, will prove vastly more effective than the enactment of a thousand laws depending for enforcement upon the pleasure of aspiring politicians or sycophantic department officials." FOTLU Convention, 1884, *Report*, p. 20.

60. Perrot, "The First of May 1890 in France," pp. 144-146.

61. "Historique du Premier Mai," p. 299. See also J. Guesde, "Le Premier Mai et ses origines," *Le Socialiste*, 7 mai 1889.

62. Let us add four more elements which, as far as the delegates were concerned, caused the similarities, even superficial ones, between the American and the European approaches, to conceal the differences on which they had no time to dwell. Firstly, the great confusion prevailing during debates. Secondly, the fact that, far from occupying a central place in the Marxist congress, the vote on the May Day resolution was hastily dispatched without the participants having a clear conception of the historic character of their deci-

sion: to wit the scanty place awarded to the motion in official accounts and in retrospective comments made by eyewitnesses. Thirdly, there was a five-day delay between the reading of Gompers' letter and the debate on Lavigne's resolution (with nothing to indicate that McGregor was present at the session). Fourthly, Gompers, addressing socialists for whom he felt no tenderness but towards whom he had to be diplomatic for tactical reasons, was not inclined to stress the specificities and the limits of the American plan, but rather what it contained which could lead the Europeans to support it.

63. "The First of May 1890 in France," pp. 145 ff.

64. Deville, "Historique du Premier Mai." See also J. Guesde, "Le Premier Mai et ses origines," *Le Socialiste* (Paris), 7 May 1899.

65. Quoted in Ph. S. Foner, *History of the Labor Movement in the United States*, II (2nd ed., New York 1975), p. 183.

66. *Ibid.* pp., 183-184.

67. Gompers to August Keufer, 9 may 1890, quoted *Ibid.*, p. 182.

68. Gompers to Eleanor Marx Aveling and W. Thorne, 19 February 1891, quoted *Ibid.*, p. 183.

69. *The People* (New York), 26 April 1891; Foner, *May Day*, p. 56.

70. AFL Convention, 1890, *Report of Proceedings*. pp. 12-13, 20-24; Foner, *History of the Labor Movement*, pp. 281-287; Perrier, "The Socialists and the Working-class in New York," pp. 490-491.

71. *Report of Proceedings*, p. 13.

72. "Congrès international ouvrier socialiste tenu à Bruxelles du 16 au 23 août 1891," in *Histoire de la IIe Internationale*, vol. 8, pp. 126-127.

73. *Histoire de la IIe Internationale*, vol. 8, p. 245; vol. 9, p. 200; vols. 10-11, p. 248. See also AFL, 1891 Convention, *Report of Proceedings*, pp. 24-26; Gompers, *Seventy Years*, p. 390.

74. Mandel, *Samuel Gompers*, p. 117; Gompers, *Seventy Years* I, pp. 366-367.

75. Lorwin, *Labor and the International*, p. 120.

76. J. Grossman, "Who is the Father of labor Day?," *Labor History* 14 (December 1973), pp. 612-623.

77. Foner, *May Day*, p. 76.

78. *American Federationist* 3 (May 1897), p. 52.

79. M. Cahill, *Shorter Hours*. (New York 1932), p. 186.

80. Foner, *May Day*, p. 76.

81. This date was celebrated mostly by anarchists, but also by some socialists. See Perrier *et al.*, "The 'Social Revolution' in America?," pp. 45 ff.

82. "Compte Rendu du Congrès international ouvrier socialiste," pp. 228, 241, 272-273, The procession was led by Annie Besant. *Workmen's Advocate*. 27 July 1889.

83. *L'Intransigeant* (Paris), 27, 30 November 1886; *Le Socialiste* (Paris), 4 December 1886; *Der Sozial Demokrat* (Zurich), 18 November 1887. See also M. Murphy, "And they sang the Marseillaise," *International Labor and Working Class History*, 29 (Spring 1986), pp. 28-37; R. C. Sun, "Misguided

Martyrdom," *Ibid.*, pp. 53-67; A. R. Carson, *Anarchism in Germany* (Metuchen, N.J., 1972), p. 379.

84. "Report of the international Trades Union Congres, Heldn London, on November 6, 7, 8, 9, and 10, 1888," in *Histoire de la Ile Internationale*, 6-7, p. 301.

85. F. D. Nieuwenhuis, *Van Christen tot Anarchist* (Amsterdam 1920), p. 135.

86. For details about the European reactions to the Haymarket, see the special Haymarket issue of *International Labor and Working Class History*, Spring 1886 (especially articles by Perrier *et al.*, R. C. Sun, and J. H. M. Laslett).

87. *La Révolté* (Paris), 12 November 1887; R. Brécy, *La Grève générale en France* (Paris 1969).

88. *Le Cri du peuple* (Paris), 27 January 1889.

89. Murphy, "And They Sang the Marseillaise," p. 36.

90. *La Revolte* (Paris), 4 September 1886.

91. Quoted in Dommanget, *Histoire de Premier Mai*, p. 44.

92. G. Brey, *Seis Estudios sobre el Proletariado Andaluz, 1869-1939* (Cordoba, 1984), p. 98.

93. *El Productor* (Barcelone), 2 December 1887.

94. *El Socialista*, 17 December 1886.

95. *El Socialista*, 30 December 1887.

96. *Acracia* 30 (June 1888), pp. 622-623.

98. See C. De Goustine, *Emile Pouget, let matins noirs du syndicalisme* (Paris 1972).

99. Pouget, "Le Premier Mai," *La Voix du Peuple*, 1 May 1901. Our (M. C. and H. P.) translation.

100. See, for example, the leading article in *El Productor*, 23 November 1901: "The Chicago Martyrs and the General Strike."

IV

A Nation "Intended for a Race of Free Men"

Part IV deals with ideological changes at the end of the nineteenth century. These changes involve the system of political beliefs and values inherited from the early Republic, the conception of citizenship, the definition of civil liberties, and the relationship of workers to politics.

1. Republicanism interpreted and reinterpreted

In recent years republicanism has been the "missing link" which historians have attempted to recover in order to understand the political behavior of American workers in the nineteenth century. After recalling the methodological problems involved in the approach to this topic, Linda Schneider focuses on the evolution of republicanism and its reinterpretation in the 1880s. Nick Salvatore warns us against the confusions and ambiguities of this notion which has meant different things to different people and has been put to various uses by historians.

Linda Schneider sees republicanism as a "very flexible and enduring substratum of belief in American culture, readily interpreted by workers". Labor republicanism came out of artisan republicanism. Its political rhetoric was strongly equalitarian in tone, and its labor theory of value was based on a conception of workers as independent producers who had inalienable rights. Ironworkers, for instance, saw themselves in such terms. With social and economic changes in the 1870s the contradiction between capitalist relations and republican equality grew sharper. The crisis of artisan labor brought about a reinterpretation of republicanism. It lost some of its radicalism and became a "defense of the stable community life built upon well-paid skills". Among skilled ironworkers republicanism became an ideological expression of institutionalized union power. In this perspective workers' citizenship meant the right to organize and the right to own property. Ironworkers saw themselves as property-owning citizens imbued with a sense of community. Linda Schneider then asks: was this sense of community infused or not with class consciousness? This question touches off a debate over the relationship between class and citizenship which Nick Salvatore then deals with.

He investigates further contradictory aspects of republicanism. For some people it implied a critique of social relations in the capitalist system while for others it presupposed harmony between groups and classes. Historians exploring the relationship between class and citizenship have come to opposite conclusions. For some historians the republican tradition was a major obstacle to the growth of class-consciousness while for others, the republican tradition appealed to egalitarianism and became a typically working class outlook. Nick Salvatore does not believe in a "working class republicanism" that would set apart workers from other groups in society. In his view, republicanism is an amorphous concept, whose content is vague enough to be used by different classes at different times. There have been successive versions of republicanism. Salvatore insists on the growing complexity of the republican tradition after the Civil War, as the conflict had deeply altered the relationship between republicanism and the state. The latter played a much broader role and assumed a much more positive image as an institution. It was from then on identified by many groups with the republican heritage.

Salvatore also deals with the racism that came to permeate the many different cultures of the white working people during the post-war period. His analysis converges with that of Catherine Collomp: it was racism that provided white workers with a "common basis for developing a collective identity". Racial exclusion became a fundamental principle of most labor organizations.

Thus Salvatore cautions historians "against exaggerated claims for republicanism", for at least two reasons. First, racism and egalitarianism coexisted within the political culture. Second, the republican tradition was reinterpreted in American nineteenth century popular culture as a sign of America's exceptionalism. Thus his conclusion confirms Linda Schneider's and goes even further: the shift to conservatism was such that the republican tradition became a basis for the defense of the status quo.

2. The new ideology of citizenship

As was seen in the previous section citizenship was central to the ideology of republicanism. Like the ideology of which it was a part, it was interpreted differently by different groups and reinterpreted politically at the end of the century. Sections 2 and 3 of Part IV examine the content of this concept from different points of view. Catherine Collomp focuses on the redefinition of citizenship by labor leaders and Hartmut Keil looks at it from the vantage point of German socialist immigrants.

The issue of citizenship was part of the debate on immigration. It played an important role in the argumentation of labor leaders who opposed unrestricted immigration. They considered "new" immigrants neither capable nor worthy of becoming citizens. What did they mean? How did they define citizenship?

Catherine Collomp shows that to understand citizenship as it was conceived by labor leaders, one has to take into account the problem of the identity of the American working class in the 1880s and 90s as well as organized labor's search for legitimacy.

At a time when the working class was divided along ethnic lines and constantly expanding with the influx of immigrants, labor leaders were confronted with the difficulty of building up a collective working class identity. They were intent on "nationalizing" the working class. In their eyes the instrument of this nationalization would be trade unions. This national integration of the working class was made more complex by the fact that, because of deep changes society was going through, the nation was in the process of redefining its national identity. How then, in this context, could one make workers part of the nation in a country where a large fraction of the working class consisted of foreigners, of recently arrived immigrants, coming in increasing numbers from Southern and Eastern European countries? Who was a worker in the eyes of labor leaders? What kind of work made someone a potential citizen?

In Gompers's view citizenship was identified with skilled work (craftsmanship) and material achievement. Only unionized workers – i.e. white skilled workers – could hope to meet the standards required for citizenship. There was more than a touch of racism in that view and something peculiarly American: ultimately citizens were defined as consumers; only those who had enough money to spend on commodities and thus attain a certain standard of living proved their ability to be American citizens.

There was also something deeply ideological in this conception: citizenship meant adhering to the American creed and the American way of life. In this respect Powderly was outspoken, for he asserted that "America was intended for a race of free men" and since not all men were "capable of enjoying, appreciating and perpetuating the blessings of good government", the best was not to let them in.

Paradoxically labor leaders were pushing for a selective, exclusionary conception of citizenship that was going to be advocated systematically by elite political leaders at the turn of the century.

Whereas labor leaders thought that not everybody was worthy of enjoying "the blessings of good government", many radical immigrants, starting from different political assumptions harbored doubts about these blessings and did not have the same faith in or respect for the vote. Hartmut Keil's paper focuses on the ambivalence of German socialist immigrants towards citizenship. He brings into relief some of the contradictions they faced.

German socialists, including marxists, had been strongly influenced by the republican liberal tradition, to the point that Social Democrats incorporated some of its elements in their own political tradition. Yet German socialists were divided on the usefulness of the franchise. Whereas Social Democrats pinned their hopes on electoral activity, Marxists were of the opinion that political rights without economic independence were meaningless. On the whole German socialist immigrants seem to have chosen to become citizens and use their political rights, though they were highly critical of the evolution of American society and of the way political institutions were manipulated by capitalists.

The papers on German and Hungarian socialist immigrants show that these radicals were caught on the horns of the same dilemma: they were torn between the will to americanize their movement and the fear of diluting its radicalism. The answer to this problem varied not only with the political hopes and tactics of each group but also with the life strategies of its members.

3. Citizens' rights challenged

In radicals' eyes no doubt the trial of the Haymarket anarchists appeared more than any other event to explode the myth of America as a land of freedom and expose the United States as the "slaughterhouse of liberties" (cf. Vecoli).

Yet, as Risa Lieberwitz makes clear, workers had had ample opportunity to experience the limits (not to say the lack) of freedom both in the workplace and in their attempts at building organizations. The legal context in which unions operated made a sham of the right of association. "Unions had 'no legal status or authority' as collective rule-making entities", a recent study reminds us. "Their members were subject to indictment for criminal or civil conspiracy not only when the means they used or the ends they sought transgressed the law, but also whenever a court decided that their existence in a collective form was 'oppressive' to the rights of an employer."[1] Thus in the 1880s union members, already familiar with the notion of "criminal conspiracy" the courts had long been using against them,[2] were further criminalized by the American legal system.

As social unrest developed in industrial cities and the campaign for the eight-hour movement gathered strength, the *New York Times* proposed as the best way to settle the strike question "to indict for conspiracy every man who strikes and summarily lock him up. This method would strike wholesome terror into the hearts of the working classes. Another way suggested is to pick out the leaders and make such an example of them as to scare others into submission".[3] Viewed retrospectively, these proposals accurately reflect the climate of the time and the precariousness of workers' rights. The Haymarket trial was in fact the climax of a "wave of governmental action against labor activism throughout the U.S. during the spring of 1886"[4] including grand jury indictments, and violent suppression of strikes by police and militia.

At first the Haymarket trial may not have been perceived as an attack on freedom of speech, the aspect on which Risa Lieberwitz's paper focuses. A majority of workers and labor organizations had no sympathy for anarchism and were eager to dissociate themselves from "direct action" advocates. Had not the Haymarket defendants placed themselves outside the community of citizens, because of their appeal to violence? Yet with time the meaning of the event became clearer and so did its intimidating effects. Workers realized that though anarchism was being outlawed, it was the labor movement that was the target and, beyond that, such fundamental rights as were guaranteed by the Constitution.

Demonstrations took place, dissident voices were heard, labor leaders took up the protest. Most significant, perhaps, in the two years that followed the spring of 1886, "local labor reform parties, which enjoyed strong electoral support in manufacturing towns and cities all over the country"[5] were formed.

Yet citizens' political rights were threatened in the years that followed. As "new" immigrants reached America, republican ideals were being challenged and citizenship became more restrictive. These developments produced, according to Marie-France Toinet, a drastic change in working class political participation in the early years of the twentieth century.

The working class, she argues, had been very active politically up to that time. Challenging a commonly held assumption, she asserts that the political behavior of American workers in the late nineteenth century was not fundamentally different from that of European workers. Taking her cue from Leon Fink,[6] Marie-France Toinet insists, as do some of the other contributors to this volume, on the international dimension of American workers' political culture.

How then is one to account for the breakdown in working class political participation in early twentieth century? The politicization of the working class, its high level of participation in elections and its influence in political life scared the ruling class. Thus a number of preventive measures were adopted. The pretext was the curbing of corruption and the cleaning up of political life. The result was the curbing of elective democracy. A new series of measures was instituted that made for increasing worker abstentionism and limited working class influence in electoral politics. By the first decades of the twentieth century citizenship — in the sense of political participation — had become highly selective. As to the question raised by Marie-France Toinet concerning the absence of reaction on the part of the working class when its political rights were being restricted, there are many possible answers. Some historians may find that Marie-France Toinet's picture of the situation is exaggeratedly dark and that workers did fight by means of the vote for a number of reforms.[7] Others may account for the temporary quiescence of the working class in terms of the changing structure of American capitalism, the recruitment of a new labor force and the new strategies of the ruling class. Whatever the answer the vision of America as a country "where every working-man is a sovereign citizen: the equal before the law of every other citizen"[8] no longer retained the power to crystallize working class struggles.

Notes

1. Christopher Tomlins, *The State and the Unions*, Cambridge, 1985, p.46.

2. Cf. Philip Foner, *History of the Labor Movement in the United States*, New York, International Publishers, 1955, vol.2, pp. 25-27, 116-117. Cf. Henry David, *The History of the Haymarket Affair*, New York, Farrar and Rinehart, 1936, p.42.

3. *New York Times*, April 25, 1886, quoted in Henry David, *op. cit.*, p.40-41.

4. David Scobey, "Boycotting the Politics Factory: Labor Radicalism and the New York City Mayoral Election of 1886", *Radical History Review*, no. 28-30, 1984, p.282.

5. David Montgomery, "Labor and the Republic in Industrial America", *Le Mouvement social*, 111, April-June 1980, p.205.

6. Leon Fink, *Workingmen's Democracy*, Urbana, University of Illinois, 1983, p.21, 23.

7. Cf. Joseph Huthmacher, "Urban Liberalism and the Age of Reform"; *Mississippi Valley Historical Review*, XLIX, June 1962, pp. 231-241.

8. Eugene Debs quoted in Nick Salvatore, *Eugene Debs, Citizen and Socialist*, Urbana, Illinois University Press, 1982, p.81.

Republicanism Reinterpreted: American Ironworkers, 1860-1892

Linda Schneider

In American labor history a growing literature has called for a "synthesis" that would unify the myriad local studies of the new labor history, linking abundant data to advances in theoretical understanding. Old preoccupations have dominated these calls for synthesis. A great many attempts to formulate theory have been organized around the perpetual question of "American exceptionalism."[1] Too often in this discussion, rich and detailed historical evidence has been collapsed into rigid ahistorical dichotomies. Too often, the vivid body of data on working-class republicanism has been used simply as evidence for or against the existence of class consciousness among American workers, and given little further theoretical interpretation. In labor history, our exposition of historical evidence has been far ahead of our conceptual apparatus in subtlety and sophistication.

These problems have not gone unnoticed. In the last few years we have seen calls by some labor historians for the "historicization" of the notion of working-class republicanism, tracing changes in republican ideology as the nation moved away from the revolutionary era.[2] Others have suggested that labor historians utilize a more complex set of concepts instead of the usual dichotomies of class consciousness vs. hegemony, or class analysis vs. individualism, or class consciousness vs. community consciousness. They have suggested more sophisticated concepts for exploring the dynamics of class feeling and behavior, like Charles Tilly's linked triad of "the organization of production/class formation/class action."[3] Still others have urged that labor historians break out of the grip of dichotomous thinking about American exceptionalism by separating the question of party formation from that of class consciousness, through the use of the concept of political mobilization.[4]

Tilly's triad of the organization of production (which I will call class relations) /class formation /class action is a good starting point for thinking about concepts of class, because it moves away from the usual dichotomies. But Tilly's scheme suggests a linear progression from class relations to class formation to action, that has all too often been mechanically and teleologically assumed. We find ourselves so often locked into arguments that take for granted that capitalist class relations produce classes, and that these classes 'ought' to take action. In the absence of specific class actions – i.e. labor party formation – we infer a lack of class consciousness, and then search for the hegemonic condition, the competing individualist ideology, or the conflicting loyalties to community that aborted class consciousness. The Thompsonian alternative to this line of reasoning has been to search out characteristically American working-class action and consciousness and steadfastly refuse any attempt to assess the degree of class consciousness of American workers, in comparison to those of other nations.[5]

It is time for labor historians to unlock the linked concepts of class relations/class formation/action; to investigate, instead of assuming their connections. A dynamic picture of "class" and ideology would trace a constant interaction between the flexible cultural tradition upon which historical actors draw, the class relations which shape their relationships with others, and the events of conflict during which ideology is mobilized in the service of class action. Rather than assuming a one-way flow of causality (from relations to formation to action), we must see that people modify their consciousness in response to changing social relations, but they choose from among themes available in their culture. Class consciousness is expressed when workers enter into class conflict, but it also directs and may limit class actors' targets and goals. The connection between class formation and action is not automatic: class sentiment must be mobilized and a crisis in class relationships, or by political organization and leadership. We need to investigate those circumstances under which class ideologies find little expression in class action, and those under which workers whose class consciousness appears limited, nevertheless take militant class action. Further, we need to be aware that consciousness does not necessarily precede action; though shaped by cultural tradition and the experience of class relationships, consciousness is often sparked to life only in the midst of class action.

It is, of course, a great deal easier to sketch out theoretical considerations than it is to put them to use in analyzing real historical events. Nevertheless, with this caveat, I would like to try to apply some of these concepts to my own case study data on American western ironworkers, examining interconnections between the changing social relations of capitalism, the development of republican ideology and the relationships between workers and their industrial employers during several moments of conflict.

Republicanism was a very flexible and enduring substratum of belief in American culture, readily interpreted by workers, as changing class relations altered their situations and perceptions. Republican sentiments "were readily mobilized in crisis to support class conflict, but the assumption and limitations of republican ideology also shaped workers' actions. In the mid-nineteenth century, artisan ironworkers, stung by the indignities of wage labor, made of republicanism a radical critique of some aspects of capitalist relations. By the end of the century, iron and steel workers who had reached accommodation with market institutions, reinterpreted republicanism into a less radical defense of the stable community life built upon well-paid skills. In both instances, quite different forms of republican ideology supported militance in class action.

Throughout the first half of the nineteenth century, iron was manufactured in the United States under essentially preindustrial conditions and for agricultural uses. In every part of the country, small, temporary, rural foundries smelted iron with charcoal. The pig iron they produced, once forged into wrought iron "merchant bar", was bought by the local farmer or blacksmith to turn into agricultural goods: horseshoes, wagon parts, tools. Artisan conditions began to change in the 1850s and '60s, when iron manufacture was industrialized. Iron works were increasingly concentrated in urban centers, and larger plants were built that combined foundry work, forging and the final rolling or casting. They produced finished goods and machinery to satisfy a new industrial demand. Markets widened: raw materials were brought to central locations from which goods were widely shipped.[6] These changes together created a distinctive, contradictory set of class relationships for ironworkers.

New technology fundamentally shaped the relationship between ironworkers and their employers. The centerpiece of new industrial organization in ironmaking was the use of coal instead of charcoal. Coal, shipped in large quantities, made it possible to manufacture iron in huge amounts, in a central, permanent facility. But iron made with coal was of lower quality, containing more impurities, than iron made with charcoal. At the same time, greater quality control was needed for the production of industrial goods, than had been needed for all-purpose agricultural wrought iron. Because of these difficulties, coal-based technology, though cheaper and more efficient, was adopted slowly, resulting in an industry very unevenly developed, local rolling mills and forges co-existing with vast modern enterprises.[7]

The key to solving the new technical problems lay with labor. Only a very skillful workman could, with inferior materials, produce iron with rigorous quality control. No technical cadre of management existed who possessed the necessary knowledge and, increasingly, iron manufacturers themselves were no longer skilled ironmasters who worked alongside their men, but investors from other fields, totally ignorant of the production side of the iron business. Chemical analysis of iron did not yet exist. The iron manufacturer had to rely on the skill and experience of his men. Iron manufacturers now recruited a workforce composed of skilled craftsmen who were able to make the new processes work. These men were largely skilled British ironworkers, thousands of whom immigrated to the United States in this period. Starting in the 1850s, American manufacturers recruited skilled men in Wales, They were gradually joined in the iron mills by thousands of Irish immigrants.[8]

These craftsmen were a special group, proud of their skills, enjoying the recognition of employers and other workers, and founding upon their indispensability a considerable degree of independence on the job. Out of their labor struggles in the 1850s and '60s came a system under which ironworkers exerted critical control over the number of apprentices trained and helpers employed, and over the promotion of these younger men. Workers and employers arrived at a "contract" system for iron manufacture. Employers contracted with skilled puddlers and rollers for the job to be done. These men then organized and directed the work in their departments. The skilled men, not the employers, supervised, hired and fired the less-skilled members of work crews, and paid them out of their own wages, which they received on a tonnage (or piecework) basis. Ironworkers were accustomed too to setting their own standards of "a fair day's work for a fair day's wages." Puddlers and roll hands limited the amount of iron to be produced in a day and came and went at the hours they pleased (although by custom these were long.)[9]

Not only did skilled ironworkers control the work process, but in addition they bargained for a degree of control over pay. Many ironworkers secured a "sliding scale" in accordance with which their pay varied with the market price of iron. Once having negotiated a scale, employers had little control over wages. The tonnage rate was pegged to the market price of iron; then workers decided among themselves what part of that sum should be paid out to each. Thus, both the division of pay and the division of labor were out of employers' hands. Through the 1870s, with little further change in the technology of ironmaking, skill retained its importance, and workmen were successful, through unionization, in institutionalizing the artisan character of their work. This history stands in contrast with that of shoe or cotton workers in the same period, for whom mechanization profoundly changed the character of work experience, displacing skilled artisan labor.

But though ironworkers in this period had no complaints against mechanization, their protests nevertheless had much in common with those of other artisans forced into the "wages-system". Exposed to wide fluctuations in demand for iron and for labor, skilled ironworkers became very sensitive to their dependence as wage workers. It was this aspect of the new class relations of industrial capitalism which struck them as most objectionable.[10] By the 1870s, we find skilled ironworkers in a contradictory situation. On the one hand, the existing technology put a premium on skill, making possible increased autonomy on the job, and increased power as organized workers. But, at the same time, an integrated national economy was forming, and this created fundamental market insecurities which ironworkers struggled to control. With improved transportation, labor markets widened, enabling employers to import workers from great distances away during strikes. Manufacturers as well as workers lost the protection of geographic barriers, and competition increased, both for small firms confronted with new modern rivals, and between large new companies themselves. As money markets too became national in scope, and manufacturers' dependence on borrowed capital grew, the industrial economy became increasingly subject to serious financial panics. The iron industry was doubly vulnerable, since its prosperity was closely tied to the demand for rails, and railroad financing was a notoriously shaky affair. The Panic of 1873, and the ensuing six years of depression (precipitated by the crash of the Jay Cooke Company in its attempts to finance the Northern Pacific Railroad) hit iron producers hard. By 1874, more than one third of the nation's iron furnaces, and more than one half of the rail mills had shut down. Competition among iron manufacturers for remaining business intensified as they cut prices and costs.[11] Throughout the industry, workers were widely laid off, and employers sought to cut wages and impose a primitive industrial discipline. They attacked the unions which protected stable wages and limited hiring of lower-paid helpers.

Strikes developed troughout the iron and coal industries at this time, as workers resisted wage cuts, attacks on unions, blacklists, evictions from company housing, payment in company store credit and disciplinary codes. For example, at the huge, modern Cambria Iron Works in Johnstown, Pennsylvania, lowered wages were paid in store goods and credit. A lockout followed attempts by miners to organize (the roll hands were organized already) and the new contract required repudiation of unions. Workers could be fired, evicted and blacklisted for infractions like insubordination, quarreling and drunkenness. In the Ohio Valley, owners of the many small iron mills there joined together to reduce wages also and threaten a blacklist.[12]

In the crisis that followed the panic of 1873, ironworkers were driven to articulate their class sentiments in industrial conflict. They drew on old ideological themes of artisan republicanism and British radical republicanism. From these they chose some elements and reinterpreted others as they sought to understand and resolve the conflicts of their industrial era. The labor republicanism they voiced merged two strands of thought; one, a political rhetoric which condemned the new forces of capitalist market economy as inimical to the American republic of equals; and the other, a labor theory of value, which stressed the importance of the worker in production, and the independence, dignity and security which were his due. These two themes met in the accusation that employers threatened the American republic. As a class, employers were growing too powerful, becoming an aristocracy which undermined republican equality. And by reducing workers to dependency, employers destroyed the independent citizenry upon which the republic rested. In their republican rhetoric, ironworkers linked unionism to the preservation of American values. Mill owners, they argued, denied the rights of citizens, and by their opposition to unions, and their other arbitrary acts, they threatened liberty, equality and independence. Strikers in Johnstown condemned Cambria Works owner Daniel Morrell, for trying to rob them of "that which every American citizen has a right to Liberty and Union." The ironclad oath, said the president of the small union of iron and steel roll hands at Johnstown, "is an insult and an outrage upon the liberty and freedom of the men of Johnstown." Having identified unionism with American values, labor leaders and editors went on to express a dramatized amazement that such values could be denied in the United States. "What is republicanism worth," asked the popular *National Labor Tribune*, if while it gives men political rights and liberties it permits them to be robbed of their property inherent in their labor?" Employers were tyrants, said striking workers, bent on making slaves or serfs out of their employees. The tyranny of the Cambria Company managers, said the strikers' committee there, was worse than that of the "slave owners of the South or of the former Czar of Russia, as the serfs had at least the right to their own opinions."[13]

Animating their republican rhetoric was ironworkers' radical perception that the commoditization of labor created dependence. Ironworkers' comments on the threat of dependence were heavily laden with emotion, pervaded with a tone of injured dignity of indignation and defensive pride. "The tendencies of the times are to crowd down labor, dictate to the poor and compel them through fear of starvation to submit. Thus they will degrade us...," lamented the *National Labor Tribune*. "We would rather go hungry and be free than feast and be slaves, which would be the case should we submit to our *would-be masters*," declared a "Roller" from the Ohio Valley. The resolutions of the Ohio Valley manufacturers were terms "odious to the nostrils of the freeman" and the Cambria Company ironclad oath "an insult and an outrage". Ironworkers complained repeatedly of "oppression," of being "imposed upon" and treated without respect. In addition, the skilled men often asserted a further, psychological loss, namely that disrespectful treatment by employers threatened or "insulted" their manhood.[14] Resisting "degradation" at employers' hands, ironworkers described themselves as freemen, independent laborers; intelligent, self-educated, industrious and a bulwark of the nation. Workmen claimed respect for their skill and the vital role they played in production. "We trade unionists," declared the *Vulcan Record*, the journal of the puddlers' union, "understand perfectly well the important part we as laborers are performing. We demand to be respected by our employers and not degraded by their avarice and selfish greed."[15]

These two ideas: a belief that labor was the crucial foundation of production, and a conviction that workers, treated as a commodity in a system of market relations, were debased from their former status as equal citizens, are the radical core of working-class republicanism to which many labor historians have pointed in arguing that American workers did indeed forge a class-conscious ideology in the nineteenth century. And certainly that is true, as far as it goes. Ironworkers saw indignity, dependence and degradation in market production; their perceptions flowed from their experience of capitalist class relations and were sufficient to sustain them in a period of intense organizing effort and many strikes. Impelled by their radical perceptions, ironworkers raised basic questions concerning the organization of industry. First, they called the system of labor incentives into question. Was labor to be treated as a commodity, responsive to market incentives and constraints, or were independent craftsmen to regulate the conditions of their employment? Then, they asked how was production to be regulated? Ironworkers wanted to control their industry in the interests of stability, job preservation and the maintenance of customary wages and profits. In contrast, employers were becoming aware of the possibility of expansion as a goal, of maximizing profits, (or minimizing losses) relative to the current market situation.

But though they opposed the commoditization of labor, ironworkers were not anti-capitalist, nor did they question the institutions of private property. Their view of employers wavered: sometimes immoral, greedy enemies, ironmasters were at other times seen as victims, jointly with workers, of inimical market forces. They heard with interest "producerist" plans, discussed by labor leaders and editors, to control both employers' greed and market forces. Such strategies, known as the "harmonization" or "equalization" of labor and capital were carried out by ironworkers as they negotiated contracts and attempted to form cooperative enterprises. These plans reflected both poles of the labor republicanism of this era: a labor theory of value and also a "free labor" ideology which linked workmen and employers. Harmonization was based on the belief that labor played an important role in production, for which it deserved compensation. Labor and capital were "virtually partners in production," and each deserved its rightful share of the profits. The independence of labor could be secured by "the establishment of its right to determine and assert its own value..." Ironworkers took practical steps towards securing these "just dues" or "fair wages" in negotiating sliding scales. The scale arranged that as the price of iron went up, wages would also rise, giving workers a share in increased profits. Workers protested their willingness to share in ill-fortune too, taking wage cuts along the scale when prices fell.[16]

But more was sought than simply a fairer division of profits. Labor journalists explained that at the bottom of the conflicts between workers and employers lay the fact that labor and capital held different "theories of value." "Capital," said the *National Labor Tribune*, "determines the rate of wages by the ratio of the supply of labor to the demand for it. Labor on the other hand asks that the value of a day's labor be determined by the ratio between the supply of labor and the profits arising from labor."[17] The sliding scale exemplified labor's principle in the sense that it was a profit-sharing scheme rather than a method of wage-payment. In this respect, it was meant to free the worker of the dependence and lack of control over his fate which stemmed from the determination of wages by supply and demand. Ironworkers' desire to escape the market determination of wages was also reflected in the setting of bottom prices on scales. It was understood that if the price of iron declined below the minimum, the contract would be renegotiated. The scale minimum represented the principle that wages should be determined by a standard of living, not supply and demand.[18] In the 1870s, ironworkers saw capitalist market relations as incompatible with republican equality, and they saw unions as the agent which would preserve liberty and independence for workmen. But their vision was by no means anti-capitalist and their goal a profit-sharing "partnership" between labor and capital.

A great deal of the influential work elucidating republicanism has discussed labor ideology in the confrontation between artisan trades and industrializing capitalism, mostly before 1875.[19] Those concerned with historicizing the study of republicanism should be interested to ask, what happened to labor republicanism after the first crisis of artisan labor? In each industry, as artisans were replaced by a new generation of industrial workers, was labor republicanism altered? For western ironworkers, the answer is yes. In the twenty years after the Panic of 1873, skilled ironworkers expressed shifting values and new industrial priorities in a reinterpreted republicanism.

Ironworkers in the prospering western industry found the years after the 1870s depression to be good ones. During this decade, the Amalgamated Association of Iron and Steel Workers unionized almost all the iron mills of Allegheny County, Pennsylvania. Though there were several strikes and lockouts, employers and workers were able to reach a smooth accommodation. Unionized workers continued to control the apprenticeship system, passing on their skills and ideology to younger workers. Union pay scales were extended and Amalgamated Association contracts further institutionalized the power of skilled workers through innumerable work rules. Output restrictions and the control of the mill committee over work procedures remained unchallenged. Employers accepted union power in this period because it was advantageous to them. Union scales standardized labor costs and processes restraining competition. The sliding scale eased the impact on manufacturers of economic contraction and falling prices.[20]

Such cooperation between labor and management was not to last. During the same period in which union power was recognized and institutionalized, a process of industrial change began which was gravely threatening to the skilled men and their union. The threat was in the new steel industry where intense competition spurred cost-cutting through mechanization. Technical innovation was very successful in steel manufacture, but union workrules and procedures slowed the introduction of new technology.[21] Scholars now recognize the Homestead Strike of 1892 as the first signal of the end of an era, the first major defeat of craft unionism in steel against the forces of mechanization and non-union labor regimentation. But to iron and steelworkers at the time, the seriousness of employers' challenge to craft control was not apparent. While steelworkers in the '90s were aware of the progress of mechanization, an adjustment mutually advantageous to labor and capital seemed possible. Mechanization, though it sometimes did away with jobs, allowed the men to earn high wages under existing tonnage agreements. Insensitive to the dangers of mechanization, workers focussed their opposition on employers' attempts to lower tonnage rates. Steelworkers were not troubled either by the threats which an earlier generation had perceived in market institutions. The early shock of confrontation between artisan labor and industrial capitalism had worn off. The skilled workers who struck at Homestead in 1892 were dedicated union men who earned high wages and enjoyed a respect status. But these Amalgamated men expressed little identification with the indispensability of their skills.

Without a belief in the primacy of labor, without opposition to wage labor, what was left of their republicanism? In the Homestead crisis, skilled workers made republican claims and used republican symbols. Their ideological links to the past are clear. Strikers claimed they were "entitled to those rights which are the principles of organized labor and which are inseparable from their citizenship." As it had in earlier periods, the *National Labor Tribune* portrayed employers as a growing aristocracy, "a privileged class, with privileges hardly less than those held in monarchies." The old themes of serfdom and slavery, dependence and outraged manhood were still played upon at Homestead. Non-union men who supported the strike declared it "an injustice to the mechanical department and day laborers and an insult to their manhood to ask them to work under guard, as we believe that in this free land, all men should be free." The company wished to destroy the union, said labor spokesmen, and force "submission", "uncomplaining submission," "positive dependence upon the beck and nod of employers" upon their workmen.[22]

But while we find continuities in imagery and issues with the republicanism of the 1870s, by the 1890s there was a change in the tone of steelworkers' republicanism. The distinctive emotions of injured dignity and defensive pride so characteristic of the 1870s, were much weakened in the '90s. In many cases republican notions of citizenship and rights, slavery and dependence seemed to have become simply familiar formulas for expressing discontent.

Passion flowed instead into new themes, drawn from the other half of the republican tradition, the ideology of the republic of equals. At Homestead in 1892, the sense of possession in jobs, stemming from a craft identity, was being replaced by a sense of possession in the *place*, a commitment to the town where workers hoped to build the good life of which their jobs were a necessary part. New ideological themes reflected the changed conditions of steelworkers' lives. Other satisfactions were taking the place of the waning rewards of craftsmanship. As work routines passed out of steelworkers' daily control, the pleasures of good wages and home comfort, of respect and consequence in a worker-dominated town gained importance. In community life, as in the mills, respect and equality appeared linked to union power. In Homestead and other mill towns, social life revolved about the Amalgamated Association lodges. In these lodges, in volunteer fire departments, boat clubs, and singing societies, craft workers experienced in daily life the republican society, of "manly" productive equals that they idealized. Locally produced music, painting, poetry and theater gave craftsmen's own lives and local dramas artistic expression. Through the 1880s the union worker found all about him confirmation of his central role in the republic.[23]

During the Homestead strike a new ideological theme emerged: the worker as a property-owning citizen. Strikers spoke passionately about the Homestead conflict as a case of home-owner citizens defending their dwelling place. Homestead's workmen claimed a vested right to live and work in the town because they had laboriously made homes there. They objected to their employer's attempt to control hiring and wages as undermining domestic security. This "defense of home" was invoked to justify workers' part in the July 6th battle with Pinkerton guards. Strikers depicted that melee as the legitimate and lawful resort of citizens to arms, rather than a bloody mob action. The hated Pinkertons were described as "hireling offscourings" paid to shoot down upright, honorable and peaceful citizens who were standing for their rights and their homes." The widely known song about the Homestead strike claimed: "no one can come and take our homes for which we have toiled so long/ No one can come and take our places — no, here's where we belong..."[24]

Measured against an "essentialist" yardstick, Homestead's republicanism was less radical than that of ironworkers twenty years earlier. Accepting market institutions, it failed to challenge any of the basic economic institutions of capitalism. But it would be a great mistake simply to toss the republicanism of the Homestead era into the scrap heap of "false consciousness" as a result. Steelworkers at Homestead were prepared to fight about the inequities produced by a capitalist economy. They saw themselves engaged in a struggle with employers over the distribution of income, fighting for the high wages which supported a desirable family and community life. In a sense they were less individualistic in their values than earlier ironworkers, for they no longer sought to become 'independent freemen'; rather, they defended the union whose power brought high wages. As workmen's skills lost their primacy in steel production; as their belief in the illegitimacy of market forces faded, the republican tradition of class sentiment accommodated these altered realities. Republican values alerted steelworkers to threats to the "republic of equals" which they identified with their own community. "Community consciousness", so often portrayed as the opposite of "class consciousness", was infused at Homestead with class sentiment and inspired class action.[25] Furthermore, the events of the Homestead Strike admirably demonstrate that it will not do to make class consciousness and class action march too closely in lockstep: though the republicanism of Homestead's workers was less than radical by Marxist standards, it was invoked in a particularly militant, and violent confrontation in which an entire working-class community, including the local government and police force, mobilized against employers' strikebreaking forces.

Notes

1. Among recent influential calls for synthesis are David Montgomery, "To Study The People: The American Working Class," *Labor History*, 21 (Fall 1980); David Brody: "The Old Labor History and the New: In Search of an American Working Class," *Labor History*, 20 (Winter 1979); David Brody, "Labor History in the 1970s: Toward A History of the American Worker," in *The Past Before Us: Contemporary Historical Writing in the United States*, ed. Michael Kammen (Ithaca, 1980). Much recent work debates American exceptionalism; see Sean Wilentz, "Against Exceptionalism: Class Consciousness and the American Labor Movement," *International Labor and Working Class History*, 26 (Fall 1984) pp. 1-24 and Responses by Nick Salvatore, pp. 25-30 and Michael Hanagan, pp. 31-36, and by Steven Sapolsky, *Ibid.*, , 27 (Spring 1985) pp. 35-38; also Reply by Wilentz, *Ibid.*, , 28 (Fall 1985), pp. 46-55. Also, David Montgomery, "Why Is There No Socialism in the United States? Report on Conference in Paris," *Ibid.*, , 24 (Fall 1983) and John Patrick Diggins, "Comrades and Citizens: New Mythologies in American Historiography," *American Historical Review*, Vol. 90, No. 3 (June 1985).

2. See Sean Wilentz, "Artisan Republican Festivals and the Rise of Class Conflict in New York City, 1788-1837," in *Working Class America: Essays on Labor, Community and American Society*, eds. Michael Frish and Daniel Walkowitz (Urbana, 1983).

3. For example, see David John Hogan, Class and Reform: *School and Society in Chicago, 1880-1930* (Philadelphia, 1985) preface, pp. xiii-xix; and Charles Tilly, "Neat Analyses of Untidy Processes," *International Labor and Working Class History* 27 (Spring 1985).

4. See Tilly and Hanagan. Also, Richard Oestreicher formulates the importance of the concept of political mobilization in his unpublished

paper, "Working Class Political Behavior and Theories of American Electoral Politics, 1870-1940," presented at the Organization of American Historians Annual Meeting, April, 1986.

5. The two poles of this debate may be seen as Thompsonian vs. Marxist, with Herbert Gutman and Sean Wilentz representing the Thompsonian side. See David Hogan, *Class and Reform*, preface. Wilentz summarizes his rejection of Marxist "essentialism" in "Against Exceptionalism," pp. 2-3. Gutman's Thompsonian approach was very clearly expressed in Michael Merrill, "Interview With Herbert Gutman," *Radical History Review*, 27 (1983), pp. 202-222. Books which measure American working class republicanism against a Marxist standard of class consciousness include Alan Dawley, *Class and Community: The Industrial Revolution in Lynn* (Cambridge, Massachusetts, 1976); Daniel J. Walkowitz, *Worker City, Company Town: Iron and Cotton Workers Protest in Troy and Cohoes, New York 1855-84* (Urbana, 1978) and Brian Greenberg, *Worker and Community: Response to Industrialization in a Nineteenth-Century American City, Albany, New York, 1850-1884* (Albany, 1985).

6. The most informative sources on the history of the iron industry are several articles by Louis C. Hunter: "Factors in the Early Pittsburgh Iron Industry," in *Facts and Factors in Economic History* (Cambridge: Harvard University Press, 1932); "The Influence of the Market Upon Technique in the Iron Industry in Western Pennsylvania up to 1860," *Journal of Economic and Business History* 1 (February, 1929): 241-81; "Financial Problems of the Early Pittsburgh Iron Manufacturers," *Ibid.*, 2 (May, 1930): 520-44; "The Heavy Industries Before 1860," and "The Heavy Industries Since 1860," in Harold F. Williamson, ed., *The Growth of the American Economy* (New York: Prentice-Hall, 1946), pp. 210-88, 467-95. Other data may be found in Peter Temin, *Iron and Steel in Nineteenth Century America* (Cambridge: M.I.T. Press, 1964); William A. Sullivan, *The Industrial Worker in Pennsylvania 1800-1840* (Harrisburg, 1955) and Louis M. Hacker, *The World of Andrew Carnegie, 1865-1901* (Philadelphia, 1968).

7. Hunter, "Factors in the Early Iron Industry," p. 438-39; "The Influence of the Market," p. 279; Temin, p.3.

8. Rowland T. Berthoff, *British Immigrants in Industrial America* (Cambridge, Massachusetts, 1953), pp. 64,66.

9. Greenberg, pp. 36-39; Walkowitz, pp. 87-89, 95-98. Also, Jesse S. Robinson, *The Amalgamated Association of Iron, Steel and Tin Workers*, Johns Hopkins University Studies in Historical and Political Science, vol.38 (Baltimore, 1920).

10. Wilentz stresses opposition to wage labor as the kernel of American working-class consciousness in the nineteenth century: "Against Exceptionalism," especially pp. 6-15.

11. Williamson. pp. 533, 752-3; Cochran, p. 133; Edward Kirkland, *Industry Comes of Age* (New York, 1961), pp. 4-5; Hacker, p. 404; Herbert Gutman, "Industrial Workers Struggle for Power," in *The Underside of American History*, Vol. II, ed. Thomas R. Frazier (New York, 1974), p.17; Kirkland, p.7.

12. See the detailed articles by Herbert Gutman chronicling these strikes: "Two Lockouts in Pennsylvania 1873-1874," *Pennsylvania Magazine of History and Biography* 83 (July 1959), pp. 307-26; and "An Iron Workers' Strike in the Ohio Valley, 1873-74," *Ohio Historical Quarterly*, 68 (October 1959), pp. 353-70.

13. "Committee," Johnstown, to the editor, June 17, 1874, *National Labor Tribune* (hereafter noted as *NLT*), June 20, 1874, p. 1; David A. Plant, Columbus, to the editor, April 22, 1874, *NLT*, April 25, 1874, p.1;

"The Johnstown Imbroglio," *NLT*, May 23, 1874, p.2; "Committee," Johnstown, to the editor, June 24, 1874, *NLT*, June 27, 1874, p.1.

14. "Workingmen in Council," *NLT*, Mar. 21, 1874, p. 1; To the editor, *NLT*, Mar. 7, 1874, p. 2; To the editor, Mar. 1, 1874, *Cincinnati Commercial*, Mar. 4, 1874, p. 3; David A.Plant, Columbus, to the editor, Apr. 22, 1874, *NLT*, Apr. 25, 1874, p. 1.

15. "Where We Stand," *Vulcan Record*, Dec. 31, 1873, p. 45.

16. *Ibid.*, pp. 42-43.

17. "Trades' Unions and Capital," *NLT*, May 9, 1874, p. 2; *ibid.*, May 23, 1874, p. 2.

18. See, for example, Carroll D. Wright, "The Associated Iron and Steel Workers," *Quarterly Journal of Economics* (July, 1893), pp. 408. 420.

19. Alan Dawley, *Class and Community*; Paul Faler, *Mechanics and Manufacturers* Sean Wilentz, *Chants Democratic: New York City and the Rise of the American Class 1788-1850* (New York 1984); Bruce Laurie, *Working People of Philadelphia, 1780-1850* (Philadelphia, 1980); Daniel Walkowitz, *Worker City, Company Town* ; Brian Greenberg, *Worker and Community*. Many recent studies have looked further into the last quarter of the nineteenth century and even into the early twentieth century. See Nick Salvatore, *Eugene V. Debs, Citizen and Socialist* (Urbana, 1982); Richard Oestreicher, *Solidarity and Fragmentation: Working People and Class Consciousness in Detroit, 1875-1900* (Urbana, 1986); Francis G. Couvares, *The Remaking of Pittsburgh: Class and Culture in An Industrializing City, 1877-1919* (Albany, 1984).

20. David Brody, *Steelworkers in America: The Nonunion Era* (New York, 1960), pp. 50-52; John Fitch, *The Steel Workers*, The Pittsburgh Survey (New York: Charities Publications Committee for the Russell Sage Foundation, 1910), p. 87; Katherine Stone, "The Origins of Job Structures in the Steel Industry," *Radical America* 7 (November-December 1973), pp. 21-26.

21. Stone, p. 25; Brody, p. 3.

22. *NLT*, Sept. 3, 1892, p. 1; *NLT*, Aug. 27, 1892, p. 1; "Statement of Homestead Employes" to the *Pittsburgh Dispatch*, submitted by George Rylands, a strike leader, as part of his testimony before the House investigating committee, U.S. Congress, House of Representatives, Committee on the Judiciary, *Investigation of Homestead Troubles*, H. Rept. 2447, 52 Cong., 2nd sess., 1892-93, p. 185; *NLT*, Nov. 26, 1892, p.4.

23. Francis Couvares describes this local life vividly for Pittsburgh in *The Remaking of Pittsburgh.*

24. *NLT*, July 16, 1892, p. 4; George Swetnam, "Songs of a Strike," *Pittsburgh Press*, Feb. 5, 1967; Jacob A. Evansohn, "Folk Songs of an Industrial City," in *Pennsylvania Songs and Legends*, ed., George Korson, (Philadelphia, 1949) pp. 445-6.

25. See Brian Greenberg, *Worker and Community*, pp. 2-3. For historians as diverse as Paul Kleppner and John Bodnar, loyalty to community and ethnic/religious identity have been seen as running counter to working-class political identity and action. Paul Kleppner, *The Cross of Culture: A Social Analysis of Midwestern Politics, 1850- 1900* (New York, 1970); John Bodnar, *Immigration and Industrialization: Ethnicity in an American Mill Town 1870-1940* (Pittsburgh, 1977); and *Workers' World: Kinship, Community and Protest in an Industrial Society 1900-1940* (Baltimore, 1982).

Some Thoughts on Class and Citizenship in America in the Late Nineteenth Century

Nick Salvatore

From the perspective of traditional American political thought, the juxtaposition of the terms class and citizenship appears quite paradoxical. As commentators from Alexis de Tocqueville to Louis Hartz have noted with a combination of awe and even disbelief, Americans have had the good fortune to have been "born free" in an environment rich in resources. As a result, many have argued, the possibilities both perceived and achieved in America have been judged simply superior to the historical experiences of other societies. While the level of sophistication in this analysis has varied greatly (from Michael Rogin's trenchant interpretation to Daniel Boorstin's celebratory messages), the idea itself serves as the foundation for the assertion that America is the exception to both the European experience in general and to Marx's prophetic vision in specific. In this view class divisions have had little sustained effect on the consciouness of Americans for the fact of a common citizenship, rooted in the republican heritage of the American Revolution, has assured this "chosen people" at a minimum both of inclusion into the body politic and of opportunity for advancement.[1]

It is no secret that much of the social history of the past two decades has challenged the methodological assumptions and empirical research that girds this analysis. There are now untold numbers of studies that examine the rates of social mobility, standard of living, ethnic experience, family life and related topics concerning the lives of non-elite Americans. These studies suggest that the image of a homogeneous America projected, if at times glumly, in the earlier literature was misleading. But for many the new history bears additional intentions. One central theme would assert an historically powerful connection between the meaning of republicanism and the consciousness of class. Specifically, much attention has focused on the nature of the republican tradition that emerged from the eighteenth century and the concrete way in which Americans of different classes adopted different (if not mutually exclusive) understandings of this tradition in the nineteenth century. More than a methodological critique, some efforts in this vein seek to develop from these ideas a new interpretative analysis of all American historiography.

For working people this republican heritage, it has been argued, empowered them in their confrontations with employers and provided them with an important sense of public worth independent of elite approval. John Kasson caught this point with power and precision when he juxtaposed, in his discussion of technology and nineteenth century republican values, the moral order of the emerging factory system with the equally moral and prophetic power of that republican tradition. In a 1816 poem entitled, *The Manufacturer's Pocket-Piece: or the Cotton-Mill Moralized,* Kasson tells us, Walton Felch saw in the discipline of the factory the necessary check on a tendency to republican excess by the "lower orders". "Learn hence," Flech admonished his countrymen, "whatever line of life you trace,/ In pious awe your proper sphere to grace." In sharp contrast were the female textile workers of Lowell who, in defence of their 1834 "turn-out," appealed to a different understanding. Equating the textile manufacturers with the Tory sympathizers of the American Revolution, the poetess wrote: "Yet I value not the feeble threats/ Of Tories in disguise,/ While the flag of Independence/ O'er our noble nation files." As Kasson makes clear both uses of republican ideas can be traced back to the eighteenth century.[2]

While the impact of this new approach has been quite important, it has yet to supplant older interpretations. In a completion of an historiographical circle, challenges are now directed at the methodological assumptions and empirical research that informs this new work. Central to this discussion is the meaning of republicanism as a political tradition, social experience and prophetic vision. In the remainder of this essay I would like to discuss some of these issues in the hope that we might better understand the symbolic power of that enigmatic statue that occupies such a prominent place in New York Harbor.

It is important to remember that the terms class and republicanism are historically distinct conceptions. It is not just that one (republicanism) chronologically preceded the other but rather the two terms address quite different orderings of society. Briefly, a Marxist understanding of class pinpointing working people, defined largely by their relationship to the means of production, as the group or class that possessed the historic responsibility to transform society. That specific group with its prophetic task held interests quite separate from other classes in society, even if that "objective reality" might not always be subjectively clear. In contrast, republicanism was a broader and less precise term in nineteenth century American culture. From its inception republicanism in America was rooted in a political identity, was compatible with a social system that encouraged state intervention in the economy or one that applauded laissez-faire, and was a central pillar of the belief that America was exceptional. As Eric Foner has suggested, republicanism presupposed at first a decentralized, pre-industrial economy organized largely around commercial and artisanal activity. For artisans, moreover, their control of the work process both assured a sense of economic independence and allowed the time necessary to engage in political activity. But such activity was not encouraged in order to advance the interest of a specific group or class. Indeed, class divisions, sectional strife or party conflict were widely thought inimical to the republican experience. As Foner notes, it was Tom Paine who described the "public good" — the central end of republican thought — as the "good of every individual collected."[3] Most importantly, the conception of work within a republican vision was broad enough to include manufacturer and artisan; optimistic enough, in an expanded capitalist economy, to largely ignore the possibilities of alienation and instead to focus on a still recognizable Calvinist work ethic; and nationalistic enough to see in the promise of America, rather than in any specific class, the potential to transform historical experience. Those who would violate these precepts — middle men, speculators, bankers, lawyers and the like — by defining private interest as public good were widely perceived as the threat to American republicanism.[4]

Class and republicanism, then, are not interchangeable when applied to the nineteenth century. This truism is readily acknowledged by historians who understand the republican tradition as a major barrier to the formation of class consciousness. This is what I think Alan Dawley meant, in part, when he described the equal rights tradition (i.e., republicanism) as the "nail in the coffin of class consciousness." Appeals to a political identity that would ignore or transcend class distinctions can only be frustrating to one who posits class consciousness as the only sufficient response. Some nineteenth century Americans also encountered this problem. Although not a Marxist Jonathan Fincher, editor of the influential *Fincher's Trades Review*, also complained of a republican tradition that would give priority to a political rather than an economic consciousness. "Once absorbed in politics...," Fincher wrote in 1863, "the duties of block, ward or township committees absorb the time that would be devoted to the family and to the Trades' Union. The rights of labor are made subordinate to the claims of this or that candidate."[5] But such distinctions are perhaps not always recognized by those historians who would emphasize the transforming power of the republican tradition for nineteenth century working people. As Mary Ryan has noted in another context, it is possible "to stretch the term *republic* perilously thin."[6]

The reasons for this emphasis on republicanism as an analytical paradigm for understanding the experience of American working people are diverse. For some it reflects a recognition that Friedrich Sorge was correct when, in his 1871 report to Karl Marx and the International Workingmen's Association, he wrote that, despite industrial development, "the consciousness of the [American] workingman of his own class-condition does not keep step with it."[7] But how then to account for the evident class conflict that occurred, in cycles of dramatic tension, throughout the nineteenth century without recourse to liberal theory or analysis? To discover a working class republican tradition, especially as understood through the more supple Marxist framework of E.P. Thompson, has provided one answer.[8] As the spate of recent books and dissertations whose introductions acknowledged both republicanism as the path and E.P. Thompson as the guide attests, there is something that is simultaneously both old and new in these efforts. At its most repetitive, it does recall the more florid excesses of the Popular Front era in the United States when citizens replaced comrades as the Communist Party's preferred image. But this republican analysis is also something new. At its best, these attempts, based on extensive scholarship, seek to uncover, through social and cultural analysis, central aspects of the lives of non-elite Americans. While this approach has touched off serious debate,[9] it has also provided for some of the more innovative and exciting new histories. Intellectually, moreover, these efforts at republican synthesis seek to go the Progressive historians one better. Where much of the work of the Progressive historians focused on the self-interest falsely presented as public good by elites, the present emphasis insists that non-elites, and especially the working class, possess their own interests which are broadly synonymous with the public good. To argue that working people had an "agenda" quite distinct from other classes in society requires a reinterpretation of major themes in American historical writing. In terms of republicanism it is to take an idea that has long been recognized as a potent legitimizing factor for dissent — precisely that appeal to the egalitarian tradition of the American Revolution — and to make that idea stand for the perception of the majority, at least among the non-elite.[10] Conceptually, this is necessary for the older paradigm, one that held that dissent served to recall the majority to the path of democratic "righteousness," supports a liberal interpretation of capitalist democracy. A republican synthesis, then, offers a third way between a rejected liberal analysis and a traditional Marxism perceived by most as largely untenable.

But does it work (the classic American question!)? Can republicanism be so surgically separated into distinct social positions that even roughly correspond to class division? Is it possible or meaningful to refer, in the late nineteenth century, to a working class republicanism that in some way defined that group of Americans as separate and distinct from other groups in society? I think not. That republicanism remained a source of inspiration for some is incontestable, and the public career of Eugene V. Debs attest to that power. But Debs himself did not come to this understanding until his late 30s; and, more importantly, he and his comrades were able to convince more than a minority of America's workers to join their efforts. Yet republicanism was not an unknown idea to the majority of working people. Rather, as Debs himself had until almost 40 years of age, the majority of native-born American workers (and immigrants as well, as they became acculturated) interpreted that republican tradition differently. As Robert E. Shalhope has noted of an earlier period in American history, Americans "quickly formed a persuasive ideological attachment" to republicanism, but one which "rested on such vague premises. Only one thing was certain: Americans believed that republicanism meant an absence of an aristocracy and a monarchy. Beyond this agreement vanished..."[11] In what follows I would like to suggest (in a necessarily incomplete fashion) some of the difficulties with republicanism as a paradigm for the American experience.

Eric Foner has accurately described the social and economic context which structured one aspect of the republican impulse in the era of the revolution. One can, moreover, trace that tradition over the next generation or two with a certain clarity. The workers that John Kasson and Thomas Dublin noted, and whom Sean Wilentz has highlighted, obviously existed. But even in this ante bellum period there were already evident many ways to adapt that tradition to contemporary events. As Bruce Laurie, Alan Dawley and Paul Faler have all noted, even among a *relatively* homogeneous working class in the early nineteenth century there existed quite distinct uses of American traditions which were by no means all separate from the middle class norm.[12] This tradition became even more complex in the post-bellum years.

Although now somewhat out of favor with social historians, George Fredrickson's book, *The Inner Civil War*, remains a valuable aid in understanding these matters. The book is subject to the criticism, as one of my graduate students archly put it, that the historical argument rests upon evidence from "six guys in Boston." Even so, Fredrickson's intellectual framework is instructive. Essentially he argues that the Civil War marked a turning point in the manner in which Americans perceived the state and their relationship to it. In the ante-bellum era, an anti-institutional individualism informed the political culture and the state itself played a relatively small role in the daily lives of individual Americans. In this context, Fredrickson suggests, loyalty to a concept of republicanism did not necessarily require fealty to the specific governmental body that represented the republican ideal at that moment. It was, after all, Thomas Jefferson who argued that America could profit from revolutions every twenty years. But the experience of the Civil War changed that relationship between republicanism and the state in two ways. First, in denying the South its right to secede, political discourse in the North insisted that the republican ideal was indistinguishable from the republican experience the North was then defending. Abolitionist agitation; the religious search for a more ideal community; the alternative vision offered by the occasional labor reformer —these voices became quite muted as sources of protest during these years, as even Ralph Waldo Emerson accepted a trustee-like position at the United States Military Academy. Second, in this process, loyalty to the state, to a particular understanding of republicanism of the heritage of the American Revolution, grew in a specific way and affected many of all classes in the North. The states as defender of the Union now demanded the loyalty of patriotic Americans. Earlier understandings of citizenship did not totally disappear, of course — evidence of those prior conceptions abounds in the histories of the labor, socialist, and progressive movements, for example. But as Fredrickson explains in his important discussion of loyalty during this era, "the ultimate America to which allegiance was due" gradually changed. As the war experience involved more and more citizens in its web, the focus of their allegiance centered not on "some vague and improbable democratic utopia but [on] the organized and disciplined North that was going to war before their eyes."[13]

This is the context, I would suggest, that must be recalled when discussing the meaning of republicanism in the post-

Civil War years. In contrast with David Montgomery's analysis, I think it is more than possible that many working people and Radical Republicans alike could agree both that labor was an issue "of paramount national importance" and that, as N.P. Banks noted in 1866, "It is to the State... which represents the people, the laboring classes should appeal, and many appeal with absolute certainty of protection."[14] This "absolute certainty" did not necessarily require a conception of the state as a neutral and impartial body whose sole responsibility was to assure republican rights in the abstract. The protests of working people during the depressions of 1857-58 and 1873-79, for example, in New York, Philadelphia and other cities suggests a popular perception of an interventionist state with specific responsibilities to workers. But such a vision also did not necessarily require, in the minds of those demonstrating, a conscious political desire to transform the democratic capitalist state in order to achieve that vision. Both the traditional Marxist and the newer republican syntheses assume the need for such a transformation, although in different ways. But Fredrickson's analysis, developed further with specific reference to the complex and intimate relation between working people and the political apparatus of the mainstream political parties in the nation's cities and towns, indicates a different possibility for the late nineteenth century. The positive image of the state as an institution that emerged from the Civil War, and the broad equation of that state with the heritage of the American Revolution, might indeed have formed the actual scaffolding that encompassed the emerging protest and demonstrations of late nineteenth century workers.[15]

If this is even a partial truth, however, one must give evidence of its validity beyond the musings of those "six guys from Boston." These ideas concerning republicanism, the state and the protest tradition were not just "in the air," although the political culture of post-Civil War years did pulsate with them. But working people were also affected by these currents in their political activity, economic relations and associational life. Briefly I would like to suggest how one aspect of working class associational life very well might have reinforced these political ideas.

Although research on the social and cultural dimension of the Masonic lodge is still emerging, it is possible to discuss some aspects of the lodge experience in the decades following the Civil War. The anti-Masonic fervor of the 1830s was quite past and Masonry was an expanding and influencial national association. Masons saw themselves as representing the best of American traditions and thus could, as Lynn Dumenil has written, be critical on occasion of contemporary life. Nationally, Masonry was a multi-class organization and the evidence available at present suggests that many local lodges were similarly structured. Men joined the Masonic movement for a complex set of reasons that ultimately reflected upon their perception of themselves and their relationship to others within their community. Masonic membership affirmed a fraternity with other men in that community and signalled a special bond that could transcend social economic distinctions. The private lodge world of ritual and symbol marked these men as different, as distinct if not special; while the public celebration of that otherness, in the Masonic parades and festivals that permeated nineteenth century public life, proudly affirmed the Masonic role as exemplar for the community. Further, Masonry also demarcated the line between native and alien, if in a complex fashion. Immigrants were more than welcome to join Masonic lodges but acceptance as members was frequently dependent upon recognition of the immigrant's "desire," as one Masonic lodge stated in 1854, "to become *Americanized* as speedily as possible in language, habits and feelings."[16]

In terms of republicanism, moreover, an examination of the proceedings of the Grand Lodge of the Massachusetts Masonic movement between 1850 and 1870 indicates that these lodges were one institution which spread a specific understanding of the relationship between the state and the republican tradition. As sectional tension increased during the 1850s and armed conflict grew plausible, Massachusetts Masons (including amongst their ranks many active abolitionists) stressed a defense of the state as central to preserving the republican heritage. Although they reached out to Southern Masons as fraternal brothers, and as late as 1860 publicly promoted the mutual visitations between Massachusetts and Virginia lodges as a way to defuse sectional tensions, the local and state Masonic officers consistently reaffirmed the need to preserve "our own happy, prosperous and united country — united by the glorious recollections of the past and the hopes of the future."[17] Following the Civil War, that renewed sense of loyalty to the state as the defender of this republican tradition gained additional support from these Massachusetts Masons, many of whom were themselves Union Army veterans. As the members of Old Colony Lodge, of Hingham, Massachusetts, wrote in september 1865:

> And now that the strife is over, and the sword returned to its scabbard, may we not expect that the same institution [Masonry], co-extensive with the whole domain of our land, which has so mitigated the cruelties of war, shall also act no small part in the earnest and difficult work of a national "Reconstruction," of restoring to health and wholeness our dismembered country... a union of states under one constituted head.[18]

What occurred with the Masonic movement quite possibly found further expression within other organizations. Like Masonry, the organization known as the Grand Army of the Republic was a multi-class mass movement with an important private and public presence in post-Civil War America. Research in the records of GAR posts needs to be done but, based on newspapers' accounts of their parades and public ceremonies, the identification by these veterans of the institutional state with that republic heritage seems clear. The close association of the GAR with the political campaigns of the Republican Party, and the persistent complaints by Democratic opponents about the Republican waving of the "bloody shirt," suggests as well the partisan purposes to which this identification could be put. Similarly, an examination of the Knights of Columbus, an organization with broad influence among Irish Catholics of all classes in the late nineteenth century, indicates similar attitudes — although, again, more research is needed. What is sharply evident, however, is the need for caution in interpreting the republican tradition. However stirring, the statements of such labor spokesmen as Ira Stewart or Eugene Debs or the episodic activities of some groups of workers in a given city does not therefore transform either the historical experience of workers or the earlier interpretation of American historiography.[19]

Discussing the Masonic movement raises another difficulty with republicanism as an interpretative synthesis. Among nineteenth century Masons, as among most voluntary associations within the white working class community, a very clear and acknowledged racial divide existed. Historians may have had a tendency to reify racism, as Barbara

Fields has argued in her powerful essay, but there is no denying the fact that racist attitudes permeated the varied cultures of white working people following the Civil War.[20] As Alexander Saxton has painstakingly shown, whether working people were Democrats, Republicans or socialists, motivated by producerism, trade unionism or republicanism, all but a handful continued to reflect the dominant racial and racist views of American society. Moreover, as Saxton noted and Gwendolyn Mink has explored recently in detail, the racial objectification of Afro-Americans, Chinese and other non-White immigrants actually provided white workers with a common basis for developing a collective identity, for establishing some of the parameters of their political culture and for creating institutions of major importance in their lives. Indeed, the common bond between three of the four national working class institutions following the Civil War – the National Labor Union, the American Federation of Labor and the American Railway Union – was the clear racial exclusion each demanded.[21] As one delegate to the 1867 convention of the National Labor Union stated, the delegates had gathered "to legislate for the good of the entire laboring community." There was therefore "no necessity for the foisting of the subject of colored labor" on the convention. "Blacks would combine together of themselves and by themselves," Baltimore carpenter William Cather argued, with the support of the majority of the delegates, "without the assistance of whites. God speed them; but let not the whites try to carry them on their shoulders."[22] Less than twenty years later delegates to the American Railway Union's convention, flush with victory over James H. Hill and enthusiastically girding for battle with George Pullman, actually proclaimed as a sign of their organization's *innate democratic nature* the delegates' overwhelming rejection of Eugene V. Debs' motion that the Union eliminate the color line for membership.[23] Although some Americans in all classes did transcend the dominant attitudes on race, the voluminous evidence that does exist concerning the majority position should caution against arguments quickly made about the centrality of class in assessing the historical fortunes of black and white working people.[24]

It is important to recall these points, however briefly, because they might act as a corrective to exaggerated claims for republicanism. Racist attitudes and a commitment to egalitarian democracy were not antithetical whithin the political culture. These attitudes limited and circumscribed, for the overwhelming majority of nineteenth century white Americans, those appeals to a more universal identity, whether couched in the rhetoric of class, republicanism or producerism. Even the Knights of Labor, who struggled to include the black worker, drew the line at the Chinese. At a minimum, however, republicanism as an interpretative framework must directly confront, in its varied historical specificity, the meaning of race in American culture across all social classes.

Finally, and in even more abbreviated fashion, I would mention another difficulty with efforts to elevate republicanism as a variable alternative to either liberal or Marxist historical analysis. At the core of the republican tradition is, of course, the legacy of the American Revolution and its egalitarian tradition. Yet it was precisely this legacy, reinterpreted in nineteenth century popular culture and in much of that era's literature as well, that marked America as different, as exceptional, among the world's nations. This tone is evident in the attitude of the Lowell striker John Kasson referred to as it is in the studies of nineteenth century culture by John William Ward and Henry Nash Smith.[25] Moreover, this belief in American exceptionalism influenced even those committed to political change. Richard F. Hinton, an American citizen appointed in 1867 as the International Workingmen's Association's special representative in America, wrote in a 1871 article that the IWA appeal was most potent "in countries where feudalism has graven most deeply dividing lines." In contrast, in America "the freedom of the ballot naturally leads men to organize for success through that potent instrumentality." Although the IWA emphasis on "social and economic issues" modified this impulse at first, Hinton (like Sorge) reported that the movement in the United States "has now fairly assumed the distinctive American character. In Europe all such movements are perforce revolutionary; in the United States they are reformatory."[26] That Sorge lamented what Hinton applauded reflects their quite different cultural and ethnic backgrounds. This understanding of the republican tradition itself as the mark of America's exceptional conditions was widespread and not without its irony. It fueled Eugene Debs' growing opposition to corporate America, as expressed in his moving speech upon release from jail in 1895, even as it had motivated his earlier laudatory comment on opportunity in America: "Nothing like it," Debs wrote in 1883, "was ever known before."[27] A commitment to the republican experiment as the exceptional feature of American political culture motivated many Americans of all classes to resist the social changes consequent upon industrialization and immigration, as they felt the exceptional qualities could not withstand a pluralistic society. Simutaneously, many among those very immigrants saw in the hopes for their children's future, if not in their own reality, the key to what made America different from their European experience: "We [the children of the immigrants] were the only conceivable end to all their striving," Alfred Kazin wrote of his parents' generation. "We were their America."[28] It was this pervasive irony that confounds one-dimensional interpretations that Irving Howe referred to recently when he wrote, following an extended and sympathetic examination of the familiar "objective factors" traditionally brought out to "explain" American exceptionalism, that he nonetheless did not reject the concept of exceptionalism. Switching his focus "from material conditions to the character of American culture," Howe then stated:

> Exceptionalism among us took primarily an ideological or a mythic form, a devotion to the idea that this country could be exempt from the historical burdens that had overwhelmed Europe. It seems obvious that so distinctive a culture, defining itself through an opposition to, even a rejection of, Europe, cannot finally be understood apart from the shaping context of special historical circumstances: it did not arise merely as an idea in someone's head, or an Idea in a collective Head.[29]

In conclusion, let me restate my skepticism that republicanism understood as an interpretative synthesis will provide an effective framework for understanding nineteenth century America. At a minimum, before republicanism as a theory replaces earlier understandings it must, to borrow an analogy from a scientific discussion, "sink a huge anchor in details."[30] We need to know more about working people's associational life, religious commitments and ethnic activities in ways that do not simply assume the existence of a separate culture based on class. Further, we must explain how working people could largely remain committed to mainstream political activity even when they mounted militant challenges in the economic arena. In short, we need an analysis subtle enough not to attempt to force a varied social and cultural history into a preordained mold and supple enough to entertain contradictions without funnelling them toward an imposed teleological end.

Tom McCormick, a twenty-four year old Vietnam-veteran, suggested the need for this appreciation of historical irony when, in December 1971, he and sixteen fellow veterans of the war seized the Statue of Liberty and held it for almost two days. That enigmatic lady has been "since we were children... analogous in our minds with freedom and an America we love," he explained. Their experiences in Vietnam shook that faith, as they found freedom equated with racism and inequality. Therefore, McCormick stated for the group, they occupied the Statue: "Until this symbol again takes on the meaning it was intended to have, we must continue our demonstrations all over the nation of our love of freedom and of America."[31] From the Protestant jeremiad of Cotton Mather to the Fourth of July speech of many a nineteenth century politician or labor man, to recall America to its ideal condition was to be critical of contemporary reality even as one affirmed most profoundly one's connection to the culture and society criticized.

Notes

1. See Alexis de Tocqueville, *Democracy in America* (New york, 1960); Louis Hartz, *The Liberal Tradition in America* (New York, 1955); Michael P. Rogin, *The Intellectuals and McCarthy* (Cambridge, 1968); and Daniel Boorstin, *The Americans,* 3 vols. (1958-1973).

2. John Kasson, *Civilizing the Machine* (New York, 1976), pp. 80-93; Thomas Dublin also notes this republicanism in *Women At Work* (New York, 1979). For more detailed analysis see Eric Foner, *Tom Paine and Revolutionary America* (New York, 1976); Sean Wilentz, *Chants Democratic: New York City and the Rise of the American Working Class, 1788-1850* (New York, 1984); Leon Fink, *Workingmen's Democracy: The Knights of Labor and American Democracy* (Urbana, 1983); Linda Schneider, "The Citizen Striker: Workers' Ideology in the Homestead Strike of 1892," *Labor History,* 23 (Winter 1982), 47-66; Nick Salvatore, *Eugene V. Debs: Citizen and Socialist* (Urbana, 1982).

3. Foner, *Tom Paine,* pp. 37-39, 87-89, 98-106; David Montgomery, *Beyond Equality: Labor and the Radical Republicans. 1862-1872* (New York, 1867), chapter 5.

4. See Chester McArthur Destler, *American Radicalism, 1865-1901* (Chicago, 1966), pp. 1-31. The cordwainers' trial in Philadelphia in 1806 is an early example of this understanding. See John R. Commons, et al., *History of Labour in the United States* (2 vols., New York, 1918), I, 141-

142. See a related discussion of New York City bakers in Howard Rock, *Artisans of the New Republic: The Tradesmen of New York City in the Age of Jefferson* (New York, 1979), pp. 184-197; Wilentz, *Chants Democratic*, pp. 134-140.

5. Alan Dawley, *Class and Community: The Industrial Revolution in Lynn* (Cambridge, 1976); see also Bruce Laurie, *Working People of Philadelphia, 1800-1850* (Philadelphia, 1980); *Fincher's Trades Review*, October 10, 1863. Within a decade Fincher himself succumbed to the pull of politics and was elected to the Pennsylvania State Assembly.

6. Mary Ryan, "Thinking Class," *American Quarterly*, 37, 1 (Spring 1985), 144.

7. Friedrich Sorge to Conference of Delegates, International Workingmen's Association, August 20, 1871, in Records of the Central Committee, North American Federal Council, Letterbooks, International Workingmen's Association Papers (micro-film edition, Catherwood Library, NYSSILR, Cornell University)

8. See Sean Wilentz, "Against Exceptionalism: Class Consciousness and the American Labor Movement," *International Labor and Working Class History*, 26 (Fall 1984), 1-24.

9. See the early exchange between James H. Huston, "An Investigation of the Inarticulate: Philadelphia's White Oaks," *William and Mary Quarterly*, 3rd Series, XXVIII, 1 (January 1971), 3-25 and Jesse Lemisch and John K. Alexander, "The White Oaks, Jack Tar, and the Concept of the 'Inarticulate'," *William and Mary Quarterly*, 3rd Series, XXIX, 1 (January 1972), 109-142. For more recent criticisms see John P. Diggins, "Comrades and Citizens: New Mythologies in American Historiography," *American Historical Review*, 90 (June 1985), 614-638; Rowland Berthoff, "Writing a History of Things Left Out," *Reviews in American History* 14 (March 1986), 1-16.

10. This is precisely what Herbert G. Gutman argued concerning Protestantism and American workers: "Protestantism and the American Labor Movement: The Christian Spirit in the Gilded Age," in his *Work, Culture and Society in Industrializing America* (New York, 1976), 79-118. For a recent dissenting view, see R. Laurence Moore, *Religious Outsiders and the Making of Americans* (New York, 1986).

11. Salvatore, *Eugene V. Debs*, chs. 1-5 esp.; Robert E. Shalope, "Toward a Republican Synthesis: The Emergence of an Understanding of Republicanism in American Historiography", *William and Mary Quarterly*, 3rd Series, XXIX, 1 (January 1972), 72.

12. Laurie, *Working People of Philadelphia*; Alan Dawley and Paul Faler, "Working class and Politics in the Industrial Revolution: Sources of Loyalism and Rebellion," *Journal of Social History*, 9 (1976), 466-80.

13. George M. Fredrickson, *The Inner Civil War: Northern Intellectuals and the Crisis of the Union* (New York, 1965), 150, and *passim*. See also James H. Kettner, *The Development of American Citizenship* (Chapel Hill, 1978), especially 334-350.

14. Quoted in Montgomery, *Beyond Equality*, 233.

15. Montgomery, *Bevond Equality*, ch. 6; Leah Hannah Feder, *Unemployment Relief in Periods of Depression: A Study of Measures Adopted in Certain American Cities, 1857 through 1922* (New York, 1936), 31-35, 41-46. Samuel Gompers, *Seventy Years of Life and Labor* (2 vols., New York, 1925), I: 94-97; Leon Fink, "The Uses of Political Power: Toward a Theory of the Labor Movement in the Era of the Knights of Labor," in Michael H. Frisch and Daniel J. Walkowitz (eds.), *Working Class America: Essays on Labor, Community and American* Society (Urbana, 1983), 104-122.

16. Proceedings, *Grand Lodge of the Most Ancient and Honorable Fraternity of Free and Accepted Masons of the Commonwealth of Massachusetts, 1854* (Boston, 1855), 14-16. On nineteenth century Masonry, see Lynn Dumenil, *Freemasonry in American Culture, 1880-1930* (Princeton, 1854).

17. Proceedings, *Grand Lodge of the Most Ancient and Honorable Fraternity of Free and Accepted Masons of the Commonwealth of Massachusetts, 1850* (Boston, 1851), 19-20.

18. Proceedings, *Grand Lodge of the Most Ancient and Honorable Fraternity of Free and Accepted Masons of the Commonwealth of Massachusetts, 1865* (Boston, 1866), 21-24, 86-87.

19. See, for example, accounts of the three day encampment of the Massachusetts GAR in Worcester *Evening Gazette*, September 4, 5, 6, 1883. See also Paul Kleppner, *The Cross of Culture: A Social Analysis of Midwestern Politics, 1850-1900* (New York, 1970); Christopher J. Kauffman, *Faith and Fraternalism: The History of the Knights of Columbus, 1882-1982* (New York, 1982), chs. 4, 6.

20. Barbara J. Fields, "Ideology and Race in American History," in J. Morgan Kousser and James M. Mcpherson (eds.), *Region, Race, and Reconstruction: Essays in Honor of C. Vann Woodward* (New York, 1982), 143-177.

21. There is no space to examine the more complicated history of the Knights of Labor on this point. In general see William H. Harris, *The Harder We Run: Black Workers Since the Civil War* (New York, 1982); Sterling D. Spero and Abram L. Harris, *The Black Worker* (New York, 1968); Sidney H. Kessler, "The Organization of Negroes in the Knights of Labor," in John H. Bracey, Jr., August Meier and Elliott Rudwick (eds.), *Black Workers and Organized Labor* (Belmont, California, 1971), 6-25.

22. Alexander Saxton, *The Indispensable Enemy: Labor and the Anti-Chinese Movement in California* (Berleley, 1971), esp. ch. 2; Gwendolyn Mink, *Old Labor and New Immigrants in American Political Development: Union, Party, and State, 1875-1920* (Ithaca, 1986); Commons, et al. (ed.),

23. *RailwayTimes*, July 2, 15, 1894.

24. See, for example, Armstead L. Robinson, "The Difference Freedom Made: The Emancipation of Afro-Americans", in Darlene Clarke Hine (ed.), *The State of Afro-American History: Past, Present and Future*, (Baton Rouge, 1986), esp. pp.61, 69.

25. See John William Ward, *Andrew Jackson: Symbol for an Age* (New York, 1955); Henry Nash Smith, *The Virgin Land: The American West as Symbol and Myth*, (Cambridge, 1950).

26. See Minutes, General Council, International Workingmen's Association, 24, October 1, 1867, in the George Howell Collection; Richard F. Hinton, "Organization of Labor: Its Aggressive Phases", *Atlantic Monthly*, XXVII, (May 1871), pp.544, 556-557.

27. Salvatore, *Eugene V. Debs*, pp.50-55, 153-155.

28. See John Higham, *Strangers in the Land: Patterns of American Nativism. 1860-1925*, (New York, 1967); Kathryn Kish Sklar, *Catherine Beecher: A Study in American Domesticity*, (New Haven, 1973); Alfred Kazin, *A Walker in the City*, (New York, 1951), p.56.

29. Irving Howe, *Socialism and America*, (New York, 1985), p.133.

30. Stephen Jay Gould, "Cardboard Darwinism", *New York Review of Books*, September 25, 1986, p.47.

31. *New York Times Magazine*, May 18, 1986, p.43.

Unions, Civics, and National Identity: Organized Labor's Reaction to Immigration, 1881-1897

Catherine Collomp

Organized labor's reaction to immigration at the end of the nineteenth century has been described in several ways. Historians such as Arthur Mann and Herbert Hill, who wrote during the 1950s and 1960s, severely criticized the exclusive and restrictionist attitude of labor unions. Mann and Hill argued that organized labor's reliance on racist ideology was an anomaly incompatible with the unions' self-ascribed mission to build a broad working-class movement regardless of creed, color, and nationality.[1] These studies, however, failed to place the workers' reactions in the context of the whole nation's reaction to an immigration coming from new and culturally different countries. Thus labor unions were blamed for not overcoming the prevailing assumptions of white and Anglo-Saxon superiority.[2]

In a different perspective, A. T. Lane has analyzed the AFL's support of a literacy test (a measure aimed at reducing the number of non-Anglo-Saxon immigrants) as a response to an economic problem. He has argued that it was during times of economic recession, especially during the first decade of the twentieth century, that the AFL demanded a literacy test. Lane has interpreted this demand as the AFL's view that regulation of immigration was a solution to temporary unemployment and economic exploitation.[3] Other historians have studied particular aspects of the hostility toward foreign immigration. Alexander Saxton's work on the anti-Chinese movement in California and Charlotte Erickson's study of the abolition of the contract-labor system have greatly forwarded our knowledge of the reaction to two specific sources of immigration and have provided fundamental avenues of research. But by limiting the geographic scope of his study to California, Saxton has left the impact of the anti-Chinese movement on national labor organization to be studied by later historians and Erickson did not go beyond 1885.[4] Moreover, little work has been done so far on the history of the support by the Knights of Labor and the AFL of the literacy test (this form of immigration restriction had been advocated by mainline labor leaders as early as the beginning of the 1890s). Until recently, no comprehensive study had been undertaken to analyze the successive and various forms of hostility toward all new immigrants (Oriental or European) during the last two decades of the nineteenth century.

Gwendolyn Mink has to a considerable extent filled this gap. In a broad synthesis dealing with the consequences of the split between old (unionized) labor and new immigrants between 1875 and 1920, she has convincingly shown the centrality of the issue of immigration restriction for the labor movement and for American labor politics. She has emphasized the impact of immigration on organized labor and has demonstrated that this impact made its way into the realm of politics and led to the party realignment that occurred in 1896.[5]

My own research has not followed the path of political history. I have analyzed the evolution of organized labor's restrictionist attitudes and practices in order to establish a chronology of the unions' policies on immigration. Such an approach reveals the importance of immigration in the shaping of mainstream American labor organizations and of their ideological and political choices. By focusing on the last two decades of the nineteenth century, it can be seen that immigration restriction was a direct corollary of the organization of labor in its formative stage. This period was indeed the moment when, in the context of a more massive and culturally different immigration, the labor movement formed or reformed itself, adopting the stable structure of trade-unionism at the same time that the leaders spelled out the movement's policy concerning immigration. During these years the unions and their federations also affirmed their basic political assumptions: the Knights of Labor's belief in the soundness of American political institutions and the AFL's pseudo-political neutrality and defiance of socialism.

Thus the "free worker" ideology that stemmed from the demand for the exclusion of the Chinese or the restriction of the so-called new immigration must be placed in a larger context than merely a cultural or economic one. This ideology evinced labor's desire for integration into the body politic and the nation at large. But this incorporation process was rooted in the organic ties that the unions established among an ethnically divided working class. From this perspective, the national union's response to immigration can be seen as directly related to their attempts at defining their jurisdiction and constituency. And organized labor's restrictionist attitude can be regarded as both a cause and a consequence of the narrow scope of trade-unionism. Organized labor's policy was not an epiphenomenom but rather a directly constitutive element of its formation and ideology.

Between 1881 and 1897 not a single year passed that organized labor did not demand legislation to restrict immigration into the U.S. or demand that acts already existing be enforced more stringently.[6] These demands are coeval with the growth and decline of the Knights of Labor and with the birth of the AFL and the transformation of that body into the major workers' organization. When by the end of the 1890s the AFL had become a "mature" institution it had articulated and institutionalized three basic tenets in regard to immigration.[7]

In 1882, the people of California and the workers' organizations of the Pacific coast obtained the exclusion of the Chinese. From then on the two national labor organizations continued to lobby for the renewal of the temporary provisions of the original 1882 Act. As a result Chinese exclusion was renewed for ten more years, first in 1892 and again in 1902. The two labor organizations had also demanded that more stringent controls be incorporated into the laws and regulations concerning the immigration of Chinese workers.[8]

In 1885, the Foran Act abolished the contract-labor system. With the passage of this legislation, the Knights and the Federation of Organized Labor and Trade Unions (out of which the AFL grew) seemed to achieve another of their goals. But organized labor soon discovered that – even with the several amendments added to the Foran Act[9] – the alien contract-labor law did not have the desired effect of significantly reducing the increasing flow of "new" immigrants. And labor leaders started advocating more comprehensive legislation to restrict immigration.

T. V. Powderly, Grand Master Workman of the Knights of Labor, and AFL President Samuel Gompers urged the establishment of a literacy test, which Senator Henry Cabot Lodge proposed in 1891.[10] The Knights endorsed the Lodge bill at their 1896 General Assembly and the AFL did so at their 1897 convention. By the end of the 1890s, organized labor's policy on immigration had been articulated and had already achieved some of its goals. This policy remained unchanged until the literacy test was implemented in 1917.[11]

Anti-Chinese regulations, the Foran Act, and the proposed literacy test complemented each other and to a certain extent engendered each other. As Charlotte Erickson has shown, the rhetoric used to describe the "cheap contract laborers" was only a variation of the ways in which the Chinese had been excluded.[12] Similarly when it came to persuade labor audiences of the necessity to impose a literacy test, the new immigrants were described as "hordes of slavish, ignorant and unassimilable foreigners who like the contract laborers had not come of their own free will."[13] Moreover, went organized labor's argument, it was precisely because the Foran Act of 1885 had been misconceived, due to an overly narrow interpretation of contract labor, that there was a need for a broader legislative framework to restrict European immigration.[14] The leaders of organized labor aimed at maintaining or raising the status of American workers above the servility, the exploitation, and the dependency they attributed to the Chinese, to the contract laborers, and to the poor, unskilled "new" immigrants. For the principle of unregulated immigration they substituted the principle of the workers' freedom to command a decent standard of living. It was therefore the duty of "free workers" to oppose the "importation of the servile races" (as T. V. Powderly recalled in one of his autobiographical works).[15]

Exclusion, regulation, and restriction did not succeed each other in chronological order; their application and reinforcement were simultaneously demanded. In the 1880s organized labor, as we have seen, lobbied to obtain the renewal of the Chinese Exclusion Act, while simultaneously urging the passage of a law to prevent employers from contracting labor abroad. Similarly, in the 1890s the Chinese, contract labor, and literacy test issues overlapped in recurring and thematically similar paragraphs of Gomper's or Powderly's annual reports to their respective conventions.[16] Each of these issues was seen as an indispensable part of the necessary legislation to control immigration. Samuel Gompers was made to understand by visits to Ellis Island in 1894 that the Foran Act could not significantly reduce the number of immigrants from Southern or Eastern Europe.[17] But most AFL delegates, however, continued to believe that the abolition of the contract-labor system was the most important piece of legislation for the protection of the working class against the employers' unfair practices.[18] When the literacy test failed to obtain presidential approval, Powderly (now Commissioner General of Immigration) committed himself to a broader interpretation of the original Foran Act.[19]

The demand for immigration restriction had not only reached an automatic periodicity, as Alexander Saxton has suggested concerning Asian immigration,[20] but it was continuous and its scope became ever broader. It was also consistently negative. Never in labor literature were any positive qualities attributed to the Chinese, contract laborers or "new" immigrants: they were consistantly reviled for their apparent inability to command the "American standard of living."[21] And what organized labor advocated was not a quantitative device to reduce immigration but a qualitative one that, through an appropriate set of measures, could provide a means of selecting immigrants according to ethnic or social criteria. There are only a very few instances when organized labor tried to address the immigration problem by attempts to regulate the inflow according to the actual demand for labor (i.e., on strictly economic criteria).[22] By signing and supporting the manifesto of the Boston-based Immigration Restriction League, the Knights and the AFL were underwriting the declaration of League President Prescott Hall: "We do not complain of too many immigrants of a certain kind if they are first class."[23]

Organized labor's support of immigration restriction did not spring just from economic motives. The fact that underpaid Chinese workers provided competition on the job market that white workers could not sustain must not be underestimated. Also, in its original intention at least, the Foran Act had also been passed as a result of the replacement of striking American window-glass workers by English and Belgian workers recruited by contract; the members of the Knights of Labor L.A. 300 were determined to eliminate such activity, which they considered unfair competition.[24] Some labor leaders also suggested during the 1893-96 depression that immigration be suspended for a period of several years in order to assure employment for American workers.[25]

One can even argue that exclusion, regulation, and restriction were passed or advocated as a result of economic hard times. Anti-Chinese hostility culminated toward the end of the 1873-77 crisis, and the Foran Act was passed during the mid-1880s economic slump. And, finally, the campaign for the literacy test went into high gear at a time when many workers were suffering from hard tomes caused by the 1893-96 depression.

However these arguments offer only a partial explanation for the motives behind organized labor's commitment to limiting immigration. They do not explain why a literacy test was endorsed rather than a purely numerical limitation. Labor leaders never truly analyzed the economic competition of the Chinese, and after the passage of the 1882 Exclusion Act and its renewal in 1892 the Chinese population did not grow in the U.S. But the heinous comments on the Chinese presence were inversely proportional to the numbers that came to America. In the same way the Foran Act was passed without an accurate analysis of the contract-labor system; the impressionistic assumption was that "cheap laborers" were imported contract laborers and led the Knights to endorse the Window-Glass Workers' plea for a ban on the direct recruitment of labor abroad.[26] Furthermore, organized workers and their leaders were well aware that immigration dwindled in times of recession.[27]

Economic historians have argued that the last two decades of the nineteenth century should be regarded as a long depression in the U.S.[28] This interpretation, however, does not preclude the fact that immigration must be seen both as a sign of and a factor for economic development. The 1880s and the 1890s can be characterized as a transitional period in the evolution that led to increased monopolistic capitalism and to the development of factory production that entailed a continuous modification of the workers' role in the production process. The working class suffered from the social consequences of technological and capitalist transformations and not from a direct effect of immigration on wages and employment. A negative impact of immigration on wages has not been fully demonstrated. On the contrary it now seems certain that, owing to a general declining of commodity prices, workers' real purchasing power increased during the 1878-93 period. Both contemporary economists and recent historians have shown that labor's economic status did not decline while, by contrast, industrial capital yielded relatively "small profits" in this era when output often outgrew actual demand.[29]

In addition it has also been shown that, apart from the general economic conditions, unionization was the single most important factor that produced wage increases. Unionized skilled workers, who more often than not were immigrants themselves, enjoyed significantly higher wages than the unorganized unskilled.[30] And yet organized workers were the most vocal opponents of the principle of unregulated immigration. It was a legitimate fear of replacement that motivated skilled workers to demand that a limitation be placed on the influx of unskilled new immigrants. The skilled workers' relatively high level of remuneration made them, and their unions, direct obstacles to the employers' drive to lower labor costs. In the context of the slow rate of growth of benefits to be derived from capital ownership, employers were seeking ways to reorganize production by replacing the craftsman's skill with new technology and division of labor.[31]

This situation may explain why labor leaders did not address the question in real economic terms. Instead the arguments put forward to obtain legislation limiting immigration were of a moral or cultural nature, reinforced by the racial thinking so common to all segments of white society at the time. These cultural and racial arguments must be taken at face value for they are part of the general language and set values utilized by labor leaders in defining the ideology of the labor movement, its scope, and its identity. The restrictionist discourse must be analyzed not only in the context of the relationship between union leaders and their actual or potential members at a time when the labor movement was being formed, but also in the context of the interaction of the whole labor movement with the nation at large. This interaction has political repercussions. Throughout the last two decades of the nineteenth century, the limiting of immigration was the only issue about which the Knights of Labor and the AFL constantly lobbied the Federal government. Conversely reform of the immigration laws was just about the sole point on which Congress and the executive branch responded positively to labor's demands.

The AFL's distrust of the legislative process, and its insistence on direct action or collective bargaining to obtain progress in the matters of wages and working conditions considerably narrowed the platform of demands for which it sought nationwide reforms. Furthermore, many of the reforms advocated, whose purpose was to define the concept of a legitimate working class (e.g., a ban on convict labor, regulation of the workday of women and children), were discussed on the state level and not at the national one. Demands such as the eight-hour day for government employees involved lobbying by both the Knights and the AFL but only concerned a small fraction of the labor force – one that, indeed, did not belong to organized labor.[32]

But because immigration was a national issue it fell within the province of Federal government jurisdiction. Likewise, it was also a national problem for organized labor in as much as legislative reforms to restrict immigration not only contained the inherent promise of regulating the formation of the working class but also were intended to limit the ethnic fragmentation of the working population. Therefore limiting immigration had a double national and working-class dimension and that dimension explains the convergence of interests of the labor organizations and the Federal government. The major political leaders and parties all endeavored to capture the workingman's votes on an issue that went beyond working-class constituencies.[33]

As time went on organized labor was encouraged as its demands seem to have been answered favorably. The Chinese Exclusion Act was passed in response to Pacific Coast worker agitation,[34] and the Foran Act, for all its defects was passed using the very wording that the Knights' window-glass workers had drafted with the advice of a lawyer.[35] Further amendments to these two acts, although always insufficient from organized labor's point of view, also demonstrated congressional approval of the workers' demands.

In the 1890s, contrary to what happened in the previous decade, the proposed literacy test did not originate in the ranks of organized labor. The legislation was introduced by Republican Senator Henry Cabot Lodge in 1891. He had precipitated a debate in the *North American Review* on the evils of the new immigration and many writers had participated.[36] Samuel Gompers at the AFL's 1891 convention echoed Lodge's words by requiring the delegates to give their most "earnest and sincere consideration" to the problem. This speech urging the limitation of immigration was the first step in a campaign fought year after year. Gompers gradually moved the AFL to support a literacy test, and in 1897 the Federation endorsed the project at its annual convention by a vote of 43 to 18.[37] AFL members on this occasion were the last to support a measure that had been favorably received in the middle and ruling classes of the country.[38] Simultaneously, T. V. Powderly had also led the Knights to adopt the principle of a qualitative limitation of immigration. At the organization's 1892 convention he denounced the evils of free immigration, calling the delegates to resort to their "natural instinct of conservation." And in 1896 the Order strongly supported the Lodge-Corliss Bill that was pending in Congress.[39]

Therefore the Knights of Labor and the AFL, which had originally been the only institutions to demand the restriction of immigration, could now rank among other national institutions that were determined to regulate the process through which the American population was being formed. Labor now sided with middle-class reformers, liberal intellectuals, the Sons and Daughters of the Revolution, the Immigration Restriction League, spokesmen of the Democratic and Republican parties, and to a certain extent business leaders themselves to support an issue which obviously had cross-class implications.[40] Although the arguments of Gompers and Powderly that helped convince delegates of the soundness of the literacy test were not materially different from those that had led to Chinese exclusion or the abolition of the contract-labor system; the political and social sanction that the project now received could convince the two labor leaders of the soundness of their lobbying activity. And indeed the bill, which carried a majority in Congress, would have passed had President Cleveland not vetoed it at a time when steamship companies were renewing their campaign to prevent the Senate from overriding the veto.[41]

If immigration was the sole issue on which labor embarked for legislative action at the federal level, this endeavor was more characteristic of the leadership than of its constituents. This course of action provided labor leaders with knowledge of the technicalities of lobbying activity, and may also partly explain Powderly's selection as Commissioner General of Immigration when President McKinley rewarded him with an administrative function for services rendered during the Republican Party campaign of 1896.

But this course of action also indicates that the legislative process more directly concerned the leaders of organized labor than the local unions or the rank and file. Although little is known about the debates that may actually have taken place in local assemblies or unions, the available evidence suggests that the membership rarely was interested in such distant and broad issues as Federal legislation to restrict immigration. The membership was either only slightly concerned with the issue, or devised its own solutions to the problem by restricting admission to the assemblies or unions according to ethnic or qualification criteria. Some unions – especially those that combined a significant German membership and a socialist leadership – were clearly opposed to the literacy test for ideological reasons. The main exception to this generalization, however, is that of Chinese exclusion which was unanimously sought by all segments of organized labor and was implemented through exclusionary practices and constant harassment of the Chinese communities.[42]

This relative lack of interest in Federal legislation is further revealed by the fact that only a very small minority of the unions affiliated with the AFL actually supported the referendum on immigration restriction that the Federation leadership recommended at the 1896 Convention.[43] And even within those unions that actually referred the matter to their members, only a small number of locals replied,[44] and most of their members while favoring restriction did so without clearly indicating support of the Lodge-Corliss Bill. Furthermore, when at the 1897 AFL convention a vote was finally carried in favor of the bill, some supporters voted for it even though they had not been mandated to do so by their members or they even voted contrary to what had been expressed in the locals.[45]

A report issued by the New York Bureau of Labor Statistics clearly reveals that organized labor's leaders rather than the workers on the shopfloor supported the issue. In New York, a state where the pressure resulting from the constant flow of immigrants should have been more directly felt than anywhere else, 75% of the local unions, representing 60% of the 98,000 unionized workers in the state maintained that they were not adversely affected by immigration. And yet the Executive Bureau of the New York State Federation of Labor voted in favor of a five-year suspension of immigration.[46]

Thus the immigration question appears to have had a significant rhetorical function. As Joseph Buchanan noted in his autobiography, a speech to labor audiences in the Western states was not complete without mentioning the Chinese curse.[47] But such a ritual was also applied at the national level: indeed Gompers and Powderly never failed to devote a part of their annual reports to the Conventions or General Assemblies to the immigration question. Similarly their autobiographies each also contain a large chapter on the subject.[48] The fact that they addressed the problem to the Federal authorities and beyond their working-class audiences to the public opinion of the day, the fact that Gompers and Powderly were taking part in what was becoming a national debate on a sensitive political issue, explains the generally global and Manichean tone with which they addressed the situation.

In many respects the working class of the 1880s and 1890s with which Gompers and Powderly dealt can be regarded as a subnation. Many of its members were foreigners by birth; its institutions were not legally recognized; the workers' claims and struggles for a better standard of living were crushed by the full array of police and judicial powers. In the midst of constant ideological and economic repression as well as a struggle whose class dimension was not always clearly analyzed, the main problems labor leaders had to solve were those of unity and legitimacy. Organized labor's attitude toward the Chinese and toward the new immigrants reflects this quest for integration into the American nation.

The exclusion of the Chinese, abolition of the contract-labor system, and labor's support of the literacy test (devised to reduce the number of Slavic and Mediterranean immigrants) indeed provided a double process of assimilation. They enabled a working class divided along ethnic lines to define its common identity in racial, cultural, and national terms. And in so doing, its leaders also paved the way toward organized labor's integration into the American nation by adopting the dominant political culture and racial values of the United States.

Not only did first-generation immigrants represent a larger share of the working class (31%) than of the total population (14.4%) in 1890,[49] but they also constituted an even more disproportionate majority of organized labor. The labor movement drew its strength from ethnic communities. Over 50% of the members of the local trade unions and Knights of Labor assemblies in the states of Illinois and New Jersey were foreign-born immigrants and one may easily surmise that a large proportion of the American-born members were in fact second-generation immigrants.[50] This situation, a source of fear for many middle- and upper-class citizens,[51] was ultimately used as a justification for the political repression of the labor movement, a process that culminated in the trial of the Chicago anarchists.

Furthermore the labor movement of the 1880s was a fragile coalition of different ethnic groups whose organization was often established on the basis of language and ethnic identity in separate locals. If cultural and religious differences were carefully avoided in labor ranks, by contrast the difference between American or Americanized workers and immigrants not yet assimilated was emphatically denounced. It is therefore not surprising that the issue of immigration restriction was based on the recurring themes of cultural and racial similitudes or differences.

The Chinese were thought to be unassimilable because of an altogether impassable gulf between them and the American working class – hence the resort to the broad and reviling terms in which they were described. The "white" workers found their identity and sense of belonging by stressing their "caucasian" racial and Christian cultural heritage in opposition to the "pagan," "dirty," "rice (or rat) eaters" of the "yellow cloud of ruin."[52] Similarly when the first Italian and Hungarian workers came to work in the Pennsylvania mines they were commonly rejected for their eating and living habits, indeed for the very poverty that had brought them to America.[53] And finally when it was understood that the so-called contract laborers were only the forerunners of a long-lasting trend in immigration, the "new" immigrants were again rejected for their apparent lack of "civilization."[54] The use of racial terminology to describe the various nationalities by census takers and social commentators made it appear as if the social and cultural characteristics of these groups were permanently inbred and would not evolve in the American environment.

It was not only cultural but also political assimilation that was sought: labor's advocacy of immigration restriction paved the way toward its integration in the political mainstream. The common identity of the American working class was repeatedly stressed and enhanced by the frequent references of organized labor's leaders to the historical and political tradition of the American Republic. For instance, Powderly claimed that white workers were justified in using the boycott against Chinese-made products because this economic weapon had had glorious precedents in the making of the American nation. He called on white labor to engage in a new war for independence until "the hated Mongol shall be driven from our shores and until the banner of requited labor shall ride the breeze of Emancipated America."[55]

Such reminders were not only intended to create a collective memory, they also had a deeper meaning dealing with the question of national identity. Speaking against the recruitment of Hungarian miners, whom he barely afforded the status of human beings, Powderly insisted that America "was intended for a race of free men, and believing that, I will oppose the introduction of such men as are not capable of enjoying, appreciating and perpetuating the blessings of good government."[56]

In such language the themes of economic and political freedom were closely intertwined to convey the idea that American citizenship could only be based on a high standard of living and that by nature some people were unworthy of participating in the American body politic.

In their continuous campaign for the literacy test both the Grand Master Workman and Gompers (and other leaders of their organizations) laid emphasis on the incompatibility of the new immigrants with the very nature of American citizenship. At the 1896 AFL convention a special committee appointed to study the problem of immigration moved, among other propositions, that immigrants be screened by "stricter civil and educational qualifications for naturalization . . . , and that every immigrant landing on [American] shores declare his intention to become a citizen of the United States within one year after arrival."[57] Through spurious political analysis – which not only echoed Henry Cabot Lodge's words, but also urged for the recognition of the legitimate nature of organized labor – Gompers encouraged the delegates to the 1891 AFL convention to take a stand against unrestricted immigration. He said because the American forefathers had rejected the yoke of monarchical tyranny, American workers were justified in becoming intolerant of the practices of the "tyrannical autocrats of Europe who bolster up their miserable dynasties by forcing immigration and . . . literally dumping on our shores" immigrants who threaten the institutions of the American Republic.[58]

Thus the commitment of the AFL and the Knights to immigration restriction was presented as a new revolutionary war for Independence. This language did not fool the socialist members of the AFL but was in keeping with the successive steps that the Federation's leaders were taking toward political integration. For it must be kept in mind that these statements were made at the same time as the AFL leadership was waging an internecine war against socialism. An article published in the December 1894 issue of the *American Federationist* linked the two issues of immigration and socialism. Its author condemned free immigration because the poverty of the new immigrants was a "hotbed" for the development of anarchism and socialism.[59] And while Gompers was arguing that the Socialist Party platform was "un-American" and prevented the AFL from supporting it in 1890 and 1894, he also banned the use of the German language at annual conventions, thus making a twofold (political and cultural) move toward Americanization.[60] The desire to limit immigration to citizens of Anglo-Saxon nations was therefore part and parcel of a broader political platform that forwarded the political and cultural integration of the Federation into legitimate American institutions and the two-party system.

That this proposed integration implied class collaboration and was only a "blind thrown in the eyes of labor" is revealed by the fact that socialist-led unions were the most consistently vocal opponents of the Federation's support of the Lodge-Corliss Bill.[61] The arguments used by the socialist-led unions to denounce the AFL's attitude emphasized that the Federation's commitment to a restrictionist policy created a breach in the universal mission of the labor movement, that nationality of origin had not and should not impair working-class solidarity, and that the Lodge-Corliss Bill was only a "scheme of the Capitalists."[62]

Behind the qualitative restriction of immigration was a question of class and citizenship, which the Knights and AFL leaders gradually answered by stressing their common allegiance to American identity rather than a broad working-class identity. The United States in the 1890s was undergoing a process of redefinition of the national identity because of the combined effect of industrialization and heavy immigration. The organized labor movement played an active role in this process by emphasizing its American character and becoming an agent in the regulation of the components of immigration. In this respect citizenship, as an incorporating value, was a more potent factor than – and directly in opposition to – working-class identity, an ideology that reinforced the political and national consensus.

At another level of interpretation this incorporating process had roots in the unions' definition of their trade and constituency. We have stressed that the general discourse on immigration had a political and educational function more often conveyed by the leaders than by the rank and file. However, such rhetoric was part of a broader language and set of values that together can be read as corporative ideology. In the 1880s-1890s the trade-union movement adopted stable and durable structures. As industrialization proceeded, craftsmen and mechanics formed unions to protect their trades against unfair competition, the inroads of mechanization, and the division of labor. In the Gilded-Age-industrial-jungle of economic and social laissez-faire they formed organic corporate bodies of workers to create national unity in the trades, to establish codes of work, and to achieve the recognition of the dignity of labor. Actions to reduce the workday and regularly increase wages were part of this attempt to establish a deontology constantly threatened by new work process, regional competition, and the recruitment of a new labor force often inexperienced in industrial work. To obtain these goals the unions also regulated the labor force in their respective trades. The closed shop, rules of apprenticeship, and admission criteria thus contributed to form powerful islands of solidarity in each particular trade. These practices did not differ in meaning and consequence from what national labor leaders said or wrote for larger audiences. Together these symbolic or actual gestures formed what William Sewell has called the "corporative terminology."[63] In the context of rapid technological change and massive immigration workers formed organizations to protect themselves from the employer's greed just as much as they also protected themselves from the "cheap laborers" who embodied a permanent danger of degradation and exploitation. As Powderly formulated it: "The basic principle on which the Order was founded was protection, not protection from the manufacturers or employers alone, but from our own avarice and from cheap workmen also."[64]

In this respect the restriction of immigration was an organizing platform in itself and a direct corollary of the trade-unionist form of organization. As one cigar-maker put it when the AFL's support of the Lodge-Corliss Bill was being discussed: "If trade-unions have a moral right to restrict the numbers of apprentices to the natural wants and growth of the trade, then they have a right to ask for legislation to restrict immigration to a number consistent with the natural growth and development of the country."[65]

Although this statement did not allude to the ethnic bias through which immigration was to be restricted by the literacy test and that had been the most controversial element in the discussion on immigration at AFL conventions, it indeed corresponded to the practices of a majority of the unions affiliated to the Federation. Over one half (at least 22 out of 39) of the national unions represented at the 1897 Convention, when the literacy test was finally endorsed, still limited or tried to limit the admission of new members to those who had been trained by apprenticeship.[66] This form of industrial education, which also allowed regulation of the labor force, was the "pillar of trade-union organization" as some cigar-makers had said in other circumstances.[67]

Of course the skilled workers' insistence on apprenticeship as a necessary condition for admission to the unions was never intended as a restriction on the immigrants' membership. As previously stated, in the 1880s and early 1890s most union members were themselves foreign-born. And if – as in Europe – instead of coming from abroad, the majority of the new labor force had been of native stock, the unions that wanted to maintain traditional levels of workmanship would have been just as exclusive of unskilled workers. For instance the Cigar Makers' International union did not try to organize the unskilled American-born women who worked in the cigar factories of New York and Pennsylvania manufacturing cheaper brands of cigar. A three-year period of training at manufacturing cigars by hand remained a required qualification for admission to the union.[68]

But if apprenticeship was not in itself an exclusionary practice, it was often coupled to other admission criteria that were, criteria sometimes aimed at preventing recent immigrants from joining the union. The highly skilled trades, which had real control over the hiring of the labor force, resorted to criteria other than skill to protect their status. For instance in addition to apprenticeship, the glass workers limited the admission of new members by imposing an exorbitant initiation fee. They also required that applicants be naturalized citizens of the U.S. and generally reserved apprenticeship to the sons of actual members. As a result, by the end of the 1890s, the Window Glass Workers had not initiated any new foreigners for a period of years.[69] Or as one Flint Glass Workers' organizer maintained: "We reduce immigration by charging an initiation fee of 50 dollars to all foreigners while Americans have to pay only 3 dollars."[70]

Only a minority of the trade unions affiliated with the AFL or the Knights had such control over the industry they organized and thus were able to actually restrict membership without running the risk of engendering the formation of a dual union or the competition of unorganized labor. This situation characterized some unions in the metal trades (Iron Molders and Pattern Makers), some unions in the building industry (Masons and Granite Cutters), the typographical trades (International Typographical Union, Printing Pressmen), and all the unions of glass workers (Window Glass Workers, the American Glass Workers' Union, and the Glass Bottle Blowers). No wonder, then, that given these exclusionary practices the unions of skilled workers could boast of not having been adversely affected by immigrant competition.[71] Federal legislation was a measure that they logically supported but had anticipated by voluntarily creating their own protectionist barriers.

The situation was somewhat different in the trades that underwent a rapid dequalification process. In the garment and cigar industries, for instance, divided as they were between small shop, factory, and tenement production, the unions (United Garment Workers and Cigar Makers' International Union) adopted criteria of admission that recognized only the most traditional aspects of the craft and often relied on national or cultural differences to establish a boundry between what they saw as a legitimate form of work and unfair competition.[72] The line that separated small shop (or outside shop) unionized workers from factory or tenement, unorganized workers actually followed the line between the "old" and the "new" immigration. In this context national prejudice reinforced the perception of skill differences. Gompers formulated it clearly when, recalling his own experience as a New York cigar maker in the 1870s, he pondered the characteristics of American citizenship:

> When I went to work in David Hirsch's shop I found myself surrounded by fellow workers who spoke little but German. However I never thought of them as foreigners because they had iden-

> tified themselves with the effort to work out problems of our industry and participated in the common life of the city. But when Bohemians began to come to New York in large numbers and allowed themselves to be used by the employers to build up the tenement-house factory system which threatened to submerge the standards of life and work that we had established, *I felt that those tenement workers were foreigners*. The first step in Americanizing them was to bring them to conform to American standards of work, which was a stepping stone to American standards of life.[73]

The Cigar Makers Union did not organize the mostly Bohemian and Jewish tenement workers. Instead it resorted to legislative action at the state level to ban the tenement system of production (but ultimately to no avail) and excluded the tenement workers from membership in the union just as specifically as it excluded the Chinese cigar-makers.[74]

Gompers' conception of American citizenship, linked as it was to material achievement and a given (traditional) process of work, had far-reaching implications. It meant that work and citizenship were correlated dimensions but only in the most traditional forms of work that easily led to the trade-union form of organization. Thus craftsmanship alone – as opposed to factory or tenement work – was noble enough to be equated with American citizenship. This static and nostalgic conception of industrial work implied that the concept of American citizenship could not evolve with the new ethnic composition of immigration and the evolution of industrial work. And indeed Gompers and Powderly complained constantly of the incompatibility of the Chinese or "new" immigrants with the standards of American civilization.

Furthermore, in Gompers' philosophy, trade-union membership was a surrogate form of American citizenship. If this idea led to the positive recognition of the civic role of the labor movement as a respectable American institution, it also contained the inherent limits of the movement. For Gompers' statement meant that by virtue of their union membership organized workers were worthy of American citizenship and conversely because they were unorganized, the "new" immigrants were not fit for such national standards. This was a static syllogism that the AFL did not try to modify in the course of time. By the turn of the century over half of the unions affiliated with the Federation restricted membership by some criteria pertaining to skill and/or nationality of origin. With the important exception of the United Mine Workers, unions did not try to organize workers along industrial lines. Thus the interlocked concepts of trade-union membership and American citizenship did not evolve although the working class was still being formed and renewed by more massive immigration.

The negative reaction of the Knights of Labor and the AFL to immigration results from the fact that the labor movement crystallized around the narrow structure of trade-unionism at the same time as the working class was being augmented and transformed by the massive immigration of ethnically diverse people often new to industrial work and urban economic standards. If one believes – as can be verified in the history of all industrialized countries at the end of the nineteenth Century – that organization by trade is the first stage of labor organization, then it was inevitable that the labor unions would become the vectors of restrictionist policy, for organized labor's commitment to restricting immigration had roots in the organic unity that the trade-unions were creating among job- and wage-conscious workers in the various trades and crafts. In this respect hostility against socially and culturally different newcomers was at the same time the cement for, and the sign of, corporative ideology.

The fact that the Knights of Labor was mostly an aggregation of local and national trade organizations whose strength relied on the large number of skilled workers in their ranks[75] explains the fact that the Order's policy concerning immigration was not materially different from what the AFL unions advocated. And yet restrictionist actions did not only spring from the skilled workers' proclivity to protectionism. The presence of many unskilled workers in the Order did not prevent its leaders from demanding qualitative restriction of immigration. Similarly, notwithstanding the industrial nature and the predominantly foreign membership of their union, the United Mine Workers welcomed legislative measures intended to restrict immigration and the ethnic fragmentation of the working class.[76]

These developments allow us to maintain that, at the national level, immigration restriction based on an ethnically selective bias had further implications. It revealed the social and political role organized labor assumed in the nation. If America was a powerful nation-state – different in this respect from other countries where ethnic minorities asserted their separate nationalism – in the context of massive immigration it nevertheless had to adapt or redefine its national identity. And the problem of national consciousness was particularly acute for the working class, which more than any other segments of society suffered from ethnic division and class marginalization. The question of immigration provided an issue on which national consensus could be reached. In this context, the assertion of national identity was not only a strong factor of unity for the fledgling labor movement but also created the organic ties between a marginalized working class and the nation at large.

Labor organization assumed this nationalizing civic role because it also justified their existence as legitimate institutions. It was because they represented workers who aspired to the "American standard of civilization" that they could fight for their members' economic welfare. In Gompers' mind the nationalist assertion of American identity was not detrimental to the construction of working-class identity. However, the narrow scope of what he envisioned as a legitimate working class reinforced the most exclusive unions' sense of superiority, thus creating a wider gap between skilled and unskilled workers than in other countries.

The 1897 AFL commitment to a restrictionist policy concerning immigration was only one of several other moves that also revealed the social and political attitudes of the Federation, and that together shaped the twentieth-century trade-union movement. In 1895, Samuel Gompers gave up the pressure he had exerted on the southern branches of the International Association of Machinists to ban the color bar. Yielding on this issue meant that the AFL was now reflecting the nation's prevailing attitude on racial segregation.[77] In 1898, the AFL's eventual support of U.S. military intervention in Cuba gave some sections of organized labor the opportunity to transform what so far had been the expression of national identity into patriotic and nationalist assertion.[78] In the early 1900s, participation in the National Civic Federation was further proof of the AFL's integration into the political system. And when, at the 1901 AFL convention held at Scranton,[79] the delegates reaffirmed that (granted the exception of the United Mine Workers) the Federation would not encourage the formation of industrial unions, the AFL's neglect of the new immigrants was only a matter of consequence.

Notes

From *Labor History*, *29*, (Fall 1988), pp. 450-475. Reprinted by permission of the journal.

A first version of this paper was presented at the conference "In the Shadow of the Statue of Liberty" held in Paris (October 1986). I am indebted to Professors Ira Berlin, David Brody, Marianne Debouzy, and David Montgomery who read the paper and suggested some improvements.

1. Arthur Mann, "Gompers and the Irony of Racism." *Antioch Review*, 13 (1953), 203-214; Herbert Hill, "In the Age of Gompers and After, Racial Practices of Organized Labor," *New Politics*, 4 (1965), 26-46.

2. In an early paper, John Higham studied the concurrent changes in American society that led to the restrictionist policy: "Origins of Immigration Restriction, 1882-1897: A Social Analysis," *Mississippi Valley Historical Review* (1952), 7-88. See also *Strangers in the Land, Patterns of American Nativism, 1860-1925* (New Brunswick, NJ, 1955).

3. A. T. Lane, "American Trade-Unions, Mass Immigration and the Literacy Test, 1900-1917," *Labor History*, (1984), 5-26. See also his first study of the unions' support of the literacy test, "American Labour and European Immigrants in the Late Nineteenth Century," *American Studies*, (1977), 241-260. Since this paper was written Lane has integrated these two articles into a book which spans a longer time period; *Solidarity or Survival: American Labor and European Immigrants, 1830-1924* (New York, 1987).

4. Alexander Saxton, *The Indispensable Enemy, Labor and the Anti-Chinese Movement in California* (Berkeley, 1971); Charlotte Erickson, *American Industry and the European Immigrant, 1860-1885* (New York, 1957).

5. Gwendolyn Mink, *Old Labor and New Immigrants in American Political Development, Union, Party and State, 1875- 1920* (Ithaca, NY, 1986).

6. Knights of Labor General Assemblies, 1878-1897, FOTLU/AFL, proceedings of Conventions, 1881-1897, see especially Powderly's or Gompers' reports. The only year when Gompers did not mention the problem of immigration in his annual report was in 1893 when he stressed the problem of unemployment. When John McBride was a one-year president of the AFL, in 1895, he urged a more stringent application of the 1885 Foran Act (AFL, 1895 Convention, 14).

7. Leo Wolman considers that by 1897 the AFL had become a "mature" institution and that this year marks the beginning of "modern" trade-unionism in the United States, *The Growth of American Trade-Unionism, 1820-1923* (New York, 1924), 180.

8. FOTLU, 1882 Convention, 9, 17; 1885, 17; AFL, 1886 Convention, 10; 1887, 30; 1888, 10; 1889, 15; 1892, 39, 113; 1894, 12; 1900, 27, 142; 1901, 21; 1902, 20, 145, 228. See also "Chinese Exclusion" in AFL, *History, Encyclopedia, Reference Book* (Washington, DC, 1919), 174; Knights of Labor, *Journal of United Labor*, Aug. 1880, 1; 1883 General Assembly, 40; 1885, 11, 160; 1886, 190-191, 304-305; T. V. Powderly, *Thirty Years of Labor* (Columbus, OH, 1890), 424-429; George McNeill, *The Labor Movement, The Problem of Today* (Boston, 1887, A. M. Kelley reprint, NY 1971), 429-454.

9. Erickson, 148-166; FOTLU 1881 Convention, 4; 1884, 20; 1885, 16, 17; AFL Conventions, 1888, 122; 1889, 24, 27; 1890, 15, 30.

10. AFL, 1891 Convention, 15; Knights of Labor; 1892 General Assembly, 4-5.

11. AFL 1897 Convention, 51-53; Knights of Labor 1896 G.A. 15, 19. On the history of the enactment of the literacy test see H. P. Fairchild, "The Literacy Test and its making," *Quarterly Journal of Economics*, 31 (1917), 447-460.

12. Erickson, 157. See also U.S. Senate Commission on Education and Labor, *Labor and Capital*, 28th Congress 1885, I, 331-337, 791, 1139.

13. AFL 1890 Convention, 24, 27; 1891, 15; 1894, 12; Knights of Labor, 1892 G.A. 4-6; 1893, 25.

14. See Assistant Commissioner of Immigration Ed. McSweeney's article in the *American Federationist* (Dec. 1895), 173 and his testimony before the Industrial Commission, *Reports of the Industrial Commission*, 1901, xv; *Immigration*, 77; Powderly Papers, Powderly's correspondence, reels 72-75, 1895-1902.

15. Powderly, *Thirty Years of Labor*, 429.

16. See notes 8, 9, 10 supra.

17. AFL, 1894 Convention, 12.

18. AFL, John McBride's report, 1895 Convention, 14; 1896 Convention, discussion of the literacy test, 99.

19. Powderly Papers, Powderly's correspondence as Commissioner General of Immigration 1898-1902 (reels 74-75).

20. Saxton, 264.

21. See for instance Powderly's indictment of the Hungarian miners in the Connellsville region (PA) in a paper that was published in the *Scranton Truth* (June 1884), read to the 1884 General Assembly (575-578), and reproduced in G. McNeill, *The Labor Movement, The Problem of Today*. 419-420.

22. The most successful of these attempts was the creation of the Universal Federation of Window Glass workers with branches in Europe: see Erickson, 146-147; Knights of Labor, 1885 G.A. 31, 55.

23. Prescott Hall's testimony to the Industrial Commission (1901), xv. 62, 70.

24. Erickson, 139-148; *Journal of United Labor* (Jan. 1883).

25. For example, Grand Worthy Foreman Bishop suggested that immigration be suspended for 5 years, 1896 G.A., 19. See also New York State

Branch of the AFL recommendation that immigration be suspended for 5 years, in *Sixteenth Annual Report of the Bureau of Statistics of New York*, 1898, 1030.

26. Erickson, 145; Knights of Labor 1883 G.A., 459; Powderly, *Thirty Years of Labor*, 445.

27. Ed. McSweeney in the *American Federationist*, Dec. 1895, 174.

28. Jeffery G. Williamson, *Late Nineteenth Century American Development, A General Equilibrium History* (Cambridge, 1974), 94; B. Rosier, P. Dockes, *Rythmes Economiques* (Paris, 1893), 127-146; James Livingston, "The Social Analysis of Economic History and Theory: Conjectures on Late Nineteenth Century American Development," *American Historical Review*, 92 (Feb. 1987), 69-95.

29. J.G. Williamson and James Livingston, *Ibid.* See also: Clarence D. Long, *Wages and Earnings in the United States, 1860-1890* (Princeton, 1960), 118; Albert Rees, *Real Wages in Manufacturing, 1890-1914* (New York, 1961) 120-127.

30. J.R. Commons showed that unionization was the decisive factor that produced wage rises for the mine workers, Industrial Commission, 1901, xv, 405. Joseph Schachter has shown the same thing about the building workers: *Capital Value and Relative Wage Effects of Immigration into the United States, 1890-1930* (New York, 1977). 6. Peter Shergold, "Wage Differentials Based on Skill in the United States, 1889-1914, A Case Study," *Labor History*, 18 (1977) 485-508; Peter Shergold, *Working Live "the American Standard" in Comparative Perspective, 1899-1913* (Pittsburgh, 1982).

31, James Livingston, cf. note 28 above.

32. See Mollie R. Carroll, *Labor and Politics, the Attitude of the American Federation of Labor Toward Legislation and Politics*, (Boston, 1923); Louis S. Reed, *The Labor Philosophy of Samuel Gompers* (New York, 1930), 113-130.

33. Gwendolyn Mink has illustrated this point very clearly (71-161).

34. Saxton, *The Indispensable Enemy*; Elmer Clarence Sandmeyer, *The Anti-Chinese Movement in California* (Champaign-Urbana, 1973), 78-109.

35. Letter by James Campbell, president of L.A. 300 of Window-Glass Workers, in Powderly Papers, Powderly's Correspondence, Series B part 2, reel 80.

36. Henry Cabot Lodge, "The Restriction of Immigration," *North American Review* (Jan. 1891), 27-36; Lodge, "Lynch Law and Unrestricted Immigration," *Ibid.* May 1891, 602-612. For a detailed bibliography on the ensuing debate on immigration with reference to articles in *Forum, The North American Review and Century Magazine*, see Prescott Hall, *Immigration and its Effect upon the United States* (New York, 1906), 369-374.

37. AFL, 1891 Convention, 15; 1897, 51-53.

38. Higham, *Strangers in the Land* (New York, Athenum Edition, 1970) 97-105; "Origins of Immigration Restriction" *op. cit.*

39. Knights of Labor, 1892 General Assembly, 4, 1896, 15, 19. The Corliss amendment aimed at regulating the coming of Canadian workers who crossed the border to work in the U.S.

40. Higham, cf. supra note 38; Morell Heald, "Business Attitudes toward European Immigration, 1880-1900," *Journal of Economic History*, 13 (1953), 291-304.

41. Fairchild, "The Literacy Test and its Making."

42. Saxton, *The Indispensable Enemy*.

43. Only the Cigar Makers' International Union and the United Brotherhood of Carpenters and Joiners really carried the referendum and published its results in their journal, *Cigar Makers' Official Journal*, Nov. 1897. 10-11; *The Carpenter*, Oct. 1897, 4-5. See also A. T. Lane, "American Labour and European Immigrants."

44. For instance only 166 of the 783 local unions affiliated with the UBCJ answered the referendum (*The Carpenter*, Oct. 1897, 10.). Only about 5000 members of the CMIU (one fifth of its membership) answered the referendum (*CMOJ*, Nov. 1897, 10).

45. AFL 1897 Convention, 98.

46. *Sixteenth Annual Report of the Bureau of Labor Statistics of New York*, 1898, 1029-1040.

47. Joseph Buchanan, *The Story of a Labor Agitator* (New York, 1903), 276.

48. AFL Conventions, 1881-1897, reports of the President; Knights of Labor General Assemblies 1880-1897, reports of the Grand Master Workman; Gompers, *Seventy Years of Life and labor* (New York, 1925), II, 151-173; Powderly, *Thirty Years of Labor*. See also John Mitchell, *Organized Labor, Its Problems* (Philadelphia, 1903), 176-185.

49. Industrial Commission, 1901, xv, xxii, xxiii.

50. *Forth Biennial Report of the Bureau of Labor of Illinois*, 1886, 226-227; *Tenth Annual Report of the Bureau of Labor Statistics of New Jersey*, 1887, 25, 42-46.

51. See for instance the report of the Commissioner of the New Jersey Bureau of Labor Statistics on the composition of the labor movement (*Seventh Annual Report of the BLS of New Jersey*, 1884, "Immigration and the Labor Problem," 285-287).

52. Knights of Labor, 1886 G.A. 191.

53. See for instance P.J. McGuire's testimony in *Labor and Capital*, I, 337; or Powderly's paper in the *Scranton Truth* cf. supra note 21.

54. AFL, 1891 Convention, 15; Knights of Labor, 1892 G.A., 4-5.

55. Knights of Labor 1886 G.A., 190-191.

56. Knights of Labor 1884 G.A., 575-577.

57. AFL, 1896 Convention, 99.

58. AFL, 1891 Convention, 15.

59. *American Federationist*, Dec. 1894, 216.

60. AFL, 1890 Convention, 25, 27; Gompers, *Seventh Years*, II, 387; AFL, 1894 Convention, 42-43.

61. AFL, 1896 Convention, 99-100; 1897. 52-53; the former International Furniture Workers' Union (now affiliated to the UBCJ), the Journeymen

Bakers and the Brewers consistently opposed the literacy test (*The Carpenter*, Nov. 1897, 11, 14; *The Bakers Journal*, Aug. 15, 1897, 36, Dec. 1, 1897, 148); on the Brewers see John Laslett, *Labor and the Left* (New York, 1970), 17.

62. AFL, 1896 Convention, 99-100; 1897, 52-53. See also the Socialist Labor Party's organ, *The People*, Jan. 29, 1893, 2; Oct. 8, 1893, 1; April 29, 1894, 4; Dec. 10, 1896, 3; Dec. 17, 1897, 1.

63. See William Sewell's most seminal work, *Work and revolution in France, The Language of Labour from the Old Regime to 1848* (Cambridge, 1980).

64. Powderly, *Thirty years of Labor*, 429.

65. *Cigar Makers' Official Journal*, Dec. 1897, 8.

66. This figure was reached by comparing the national unions represented by the AFL 1897 convention and rules of apprenticeship in trade-unions as described by James Motley, "Apprenticeship in American Trade Unions," *Johns Hopkins University Studies in Historical and Political Science*, series XXV, no. 11-12, 1907, 53-55.

67. *Cigar Makers' Official Journal*, Nov. 1885, 9.

68. *Reports of the Industrial Commission*, 1901, xv "*Immigration*," 388.

69. F. E. Wolfe, "Admission to American Trade-Unions," *Johns Hopkins University Studies in Historical and Political Science*, series XXX, no. 3 (1912), 10-150.

70. *Sixteenth Annual Report of the Bureau of Labor of New York* 1898, 1036, 1068.

71. *Ibid.*, 1030.

72. On the limits of the CMIU's jurisdiction see Industrial Commission, 1901, xv, 385-388; G. W. Perkins, in "Regulation and Restriction of Output," *Eleventh Special Report of the U.S. Commissioner of Labor*, 1904, 572. On the United Garment Workers see Industrial Commission, 1901, xv, 316-317; Henry White, "The Sweating System," *U.S. Bureau of Labor Bulletin*, I (1895), 361-374.

73. Gompers, *Seventy Years*, II, 151, emphasis mine.

74. The CMIU 1891 constitution specifically excluded the tenement and the Chinese workers from the union's jurisdiction.

75. All recent studies on the Knights of Labor emphasize the role of the skilled workers in the Order's foundation and development and also stress the importance of local trade assemblies or local trade unions as basic units of organization within the Order. See for instance Jonathan Garlock, "A Structural Analysis of the Knights of Labor, A prolegomenon to the History of the Producing Classes," (unpublished Ph.D. diss., Univ. of Rochester, 1974); Richard Oestreicher, *Solidarity and Fragmentation, Working People and Class Consciousness in Detroit, 1877-1895* (Urbana, 1986); G.S. Kealey and Bryan D. Palmer, *Dreaming of What Might Be, The Knights of Labor in Ontario, 1810-1900* (Cambridge, MA, 1982); Leon Fink, *Workingman's Democracy: The Knights of Labor and American Politics*, (Urbana, 1983), 51-52, 75-76, 185.

76. John Mitchell, *Organized Labor, Its Problems*, 176-185. See also John Mitchell's testimony in *Reports of the Immigration Commission*, 1911, vol. 23, 369-375; vol. 41, 376- 431.

77. International Association of Machinists, 1895 convention, 33-34; Perlman, *The Machinists, A New Study in Trade Unionism* (Cambridge, MA, 1961), 8-18.

78. AFL 1898 Convention, 19, 20.

79. AFL 1901 Convention, 240.

An Ambivalent Identity: The Attitude of German Socialist Immigrants toward American Political Institutions and American Citizenship

Harmut Keil

The festivities surrounding the dedication of Bartholdi's Statue of Liberty on Thursday, October 28th, 1886 were duly noted by the *New Yorker Volks-Zeitung*, New York city's German-language labor paper. It reported on the event with the following headlines: "Freedom's Symbol. Unveiled by the Rich and by the Aristocrats. The Wage Slaves are Allowed to Stand By." Claiming that it was "the representatives from the idlers' and exploiters' ranks," the "hypocritic bourgeoisie" who dedicated the Statue with "great pomp, a lot of banners, salutes, two parades... and with an effusion of nice words," the paper took the celebration as "a characteristic symbol of our present condition — on the one hand the few living in luxury, their bellies filled, screaming Hurrah from their understanding of freedom — on the other hand the great mass of exploited and hungry, silent or resentful onlookers to this Belshazzar's feast."[1] While tacitly accepting the Statue of Liberty as a powerful symbol of the American people's aspirations, the *New Yorker Volks-Zeitung* openly attacked its appropriation and perversion by the Gilded Age plutocracy.

The dedication provided an ironic counterpoint to the agitation and strikes for the eight-hour day in spring and early summer of 1886, culminating in the fatal Haymarket events after May 1st and in the conviction of the anarchists in August. Haymarket had been the hoped for incident by businessmen and employers to launch a counterattack against the rising tide of trade and industrial unionism so successful and sweeping before the early May days. By fall, organized labor was on the defensive once more, with some of its leaders persecuted and many of its members threatened by blackmail and unemployment, so that its ranks were rapidly thinning out. Now the only alternative left to workers appeared concerted political action. Thus, the festivities around the unveiling of the Statue of Liberty took place at the height of the New York City mayoralty campaign, in which Henry George headed the United Labor Party ticket and where victory, as in other big industrial cities, seemed within reach.

German-American socialists were keenly aware of these contradictions, which they tirelessly exposed in their various publications. However, in certain ways they themselves revealed ambivalent perceptions of, and attitudes about the ideals of the American republic, on the one hand, and the realities of American life, on the other. This ambivalence needs to be explained.

This essay is based on four hypotheses:

1) German socialists shared a long liberal-republican tradition that was gradually incorporated into the emerging Social-Democratic movement in Germany. Republicanism thus became the historical antecedent of the socialist movement. Thus, they could readily identify with the ideals of the American Revolution.

2) Socialist immigrants impatiently observed the increasing discrepancy between revered political ideals and Gilded Age social and political realities. Their criticism resembled that voiced by American workers steeped in the tradition of American republicanism, socialist immigrants went beyond such criticism by their insistence on a class analysis of American society.

3) The liberal-republican tradition was not completely replaced by a Marxist analysis, however, since German so-

cialists did not easily discard their basic loyalties to the American political system as originally defined by the Declaration of Independence and the Constitution.

4) Socialists also referred to Marxist theory in justifying their acceptance of American social and political institutions. Having come as immigrants, they were to help build an American labor movement shaped by "indigenous" conditions. Therefore, they used the rights offered them as citizens of the Republic and attempted to rid their socialism of its "alien character". The "Americanization" of the movement, was thus of paramount concern.

The essay will be divided into two parts. First it will look at the image of the United States in Germany as a model of republicanism that took form in Germany and in the United States and at the emergence of a critical evaluation among German-American socialists of the realities of American society in relation to this model. In the second part, it will address German-American socialists' own conception of their role in American society and of their uses of American institutions and political rights.

1. American Society as Seen by German and German-American Socialists

1.1 The Liberal-Democratic Tradition

The perception that German socialists had of the United States was based on an abundant body of literature — travel and personal accounts, journalistic articles and pamphlets, political and historical writings, emigrants' guides, as well as fiction — that had been published since the War of Independence.[2] German socialists identified with the liberal and revolutionary tradition of the republican experiment.

American Independence was a tremendous boost for suppressed longings in Germany to be freed from the despotism and tyranny of feudal domination and absolutist monarchism. Such aspirations were projected on to the new republic by the literary tradition of the *Sturm und Drang* (Storm and Stress) period as well as by the Enlightenment, which hailed the American Revolution as a new stage in the progress of humanity.[3] The historical event of American Independence was rationalized into an ideological symbol of the Universal aspirations of mankind, while its practical result as codified in the American Constitution was soon accorded the rank of an inviolable political canon. Such a view of America did not mirror the reality of American institutions and life, but rather universal ideals to be aspired to in the European context of the Napoleonic era and the Wars of Liberation.

The emerging political liberalism in the repressive restoration period continued to center its attention on the American Constitution. In the opinion of liberals it had transformed their own as yet unattained ideals of personal and political rights and freedoms into a practical reality. "During the restoration period," observed a contemporary, "liberalism, in concentrating in its agitation and publications on America, was allowed one of its rare legal means of expression. It celebrated the republic with the star-spangled banner as the practical embodiment of its outlawed ideals."[4] Thus the United States became the symbol of political freedom; during the Hambacher Fest in 1832, which united diverse radical groups in a common demonstration for national unity and political rights, cheers were voiced on "the united free states of Germany" in obvious reference to the United States of America.[5] The radical democrats of the "Young Germany" movement helped popularize republican ideals in rousing poems and songs which often were but thinly veiled calls for action. Poems of the *Vormärz* period were later incorporated by the Social Democrats as an integral part of their revolutionary tradition and aspirations. Thus a general and basically uncritical enthusiasm for America's "great democracy"[6] prevailed among radical democrats as well as liberals during the revolution of 1848/49. At democrats' and workers' mass meetings the star-spangled banner was always displayed alongside the tricolore and the revolutionary red flag. Delegates to the meeting of the constitutional assembly in Paul's Church at Frankfort on the Main were exceptionally well informed on American constitutional as well as political and social issues.[7] It was especially the democratic left that pointed to the American federal system as an example to be followed and that asked for a new German federal state with a "constitution along the lines of North American with accompanying republican institutions."[8] Although the revolution of 1848/49 failed miserably to accomplish this goal, the liberal-democratic ideal of America which had guided its leaders and followers to a significant degree persisted right into the 1870s.

1.2 Popular Expectations

Parallel to the liberal-republican debate ran an underlying popular current of enthusiasm for the American Republic, grounded less in constitutional and political ideals than in hopes of material awards. Surpassing the former in importance in its long-term consequences, it led to mass emigration from Germany at the very moment when liberal aspirations had been shattered in the middle of the century. Fiction set the stage by popularizing the expectation that in America everything would turn out well; one only needed to live there for a while in order to return as a well-to-do, respected person. Novels, short stories as well as popular plays written and widely performed in the course of the nineteenth century presented the stereotypical "rich uncle from America" admired by relatives and friends upon his visit in the old country. Emigrants' guides often were no less biased, raising false hopes of easy settlement and quick material success in the new world. But it was above all the "reports of republican happiness spread by emigrated Germans in hundreds of thousands of letters among their fellow countrymen back home,"[9] often giving idealized accounts of public life and living and work conditions in the United States, that decisively shaped the masses' perceptions and expectations.[10]

Such expectations often ran contrary to the reality immigrants faced upon their arrival. But illusions were held tenaciously, to the exasperation of German-American socialists, who time and again pointed to the changed conditions in post-Civil War America. Apparently the liberal-democratic tradition died but a slow death, a fact that should not have come as a surprise, since it was continually being reinforced by the country's political ideology as well as its institutional mechanisms.

1.3 The Social-Democratic Incorporation of the Liberal-Republican Tradition

German Social Democracy incorporated some elements of the liberal-republican tradition while trying to come to terms with the strong undercurrent of favorable mass opinion toward the United States and its practical result, i.e.

mass emigration. It was the refusal of the German states (and after 1871 the German Reich) to grant fundamental civil rights, like the right to assemble, to associate, and to vote, that helps explain at least in part the unprecedented success of the Socialist Party in Germany. The new Erfurt program of 1891 in its second part still contained those very democratic demands that had partially been realized in the United States.[11] When evaluating the relative accomplishments of different nations with respect to civil and democratic liberties, German socialists continued to look favorably upon the American Republic.[12]

With respect to mass emigration from Germany to the United States, however, socialists took an ambivalent position. On the one hand, they blamed domestic economic, social and political conditions for the mass exodus, pointing out, however, that for lack of financial resources proletarians were not among the emigrants. While they were resolutely opposed to any legal restriction on emigration, they did not encourage the move abroad.[13] On the other hand, the attraction of the free republic for persons who were politically persecuted in Germany continued to be great. Since the 1820s, radicals of various persuasions who had been involved in revolutionary activities had chosen America for their temporary or permanent home. The Socialists were no exception; in the late 1870s and early 1880s, when the Socialist party was increasingly harassed by state authorities and when Bismarck's anti-socialist legislation of 1878 outlawed the organization and led to the expulsion of hundreds of socialists from their home towns, many of the persons affected chose to settle in the United States.[14] For lack of financial means of support for many members and their families, the party momentarily had to acquiesce, but it soon reiterated the position that it had held for several years: It was opposed to emigration, because "social grievances cannot be eliminated by mass emigration".[15] The resolution by the International Workingmen's Association on emigration, passed in 1873 by the General Council and stating that "emigration of workers does not contribute to the emancipation of the working class, but only transfers the battleground" was quoted with obvious approval by the party's paper *Volksstaat*.[16] The *New Yorker Volks-Zeitung* also opposed mass emigration, since this served as a "safety valve against the revolution" in Germany.[17] When some party leaders emigrated during the period of socialist persecution despite such warnings, these moves were openly branded as "desertion" and "cowardly acts." Instead, the "soldiers of the revolution" were admonished to "stay home;" it was their "duty to hold out on the battleground." Paraphrasing a sentence written by the poet Goethe, Wilhelm Liebknecht coined the famous rallying slogan: "Our America is in Germany!"[18]

It seems appropriate to refer to Wilhelm Liebknecht, rather than to Karl Marx, Friedrich Engels or Karl Kautsky, when writing about the impact of the liberal-republican tradition on the socialists' views of the United States. Liebknecht never entirely discarded the republican ideals dating from his revolutionary days in southwest Germany.[19] His positive attitude toward "the great Atlantic republic"[20] can be documented in his personal as well as his political life. Although his plans to emigrate to the United States did not materialize,[21] Liebknecht continued to show considerable interest in American political affairs.[22] Commenting on the Civil War, he expressed his admiration for the way the American people and its political institutions coped with this emergency. He pointed out enthusiastically that "nowhere else but in the United States is the citizen a free, self-determined, member of the commonwealth.... The state is not a hostile entity confronting the citizen, nay, it is completely bound up, it is identical with him." He showed complete trust in the mechanism of change of political power after Lincoln's death, since "the American Republic is based on a broad democratic foundation" and "the American Constitution is not a mere piece of paper." In his opinion "the example of the North American Union is pointed out to us by fate like the mirror image of our own defaults." Although conceding some years later that American institutions were not perfect, he still wished for similar institutions in Germany and Europe.[23]

In 1886, Liebknecht had an opportunity to visit the United States, when he was invited on a speaking tour by the Socialist Labor Party along with Edward Aveling and Eleanor Marx-Aveling. His beliefs were confirmed, and he was filled with a republican spirit of optimism, which he summed up in his travel account *Ein Blick in die Neue Welt* [A glance at the new world] in these words: "I find a public spirit, of which we have no understanding, an enthusiasm for justice, freedom, progress, the common good that I have not discovered to any approximate degree in the countries of the Old World."[24]

1.4 German-American Socialists' Criticism of American Society

By the time of Wilhelm Liebknecht's visit to the United States, German-American socialists could point to an almost twenty-year reevaluation of American society. They had observed closely the reality of political corruption and the negative consequences of rapid industrialization after the Civil War. The situation was made worse by economic depression, unsatisfied labor demands and ruthless use of force against workers on the part of the state and employers. Increasingly these analyses were guided by a Marxist approach. In their private and official correspondence as well as in newspaper articles.[25] Socialists who were active in the International Workers Association conveyed to their European comrades and to their local audiences a sense of the pervasive and inescapable logic and thrust of American capitalist development.

Fellow socialists in Germany were confronted with a new assessment of American society which diverged from Liebknecht's political idealism. In 1868, readers of Liebknecht's *Demokratisches Wochenblatt* (published in Leipzig) were informed by an American correspondent that

> the contrast between capital and labor in this country [i.e. the United States] is blatant... A revolution... is taking place in industrial progress; and this is happening so rapidly that a European observer must gaze in astonishment; and as a consequence the revolution must also spread over into the political realm and probably with a sudden force and vehemence that is so peculiar to the American national character.[26]

As if to confirm this opinion, the paper quoted from a speech by William H. Sylvis, the president of the National Labor Union, who had declared that "our people are ever more being separated into two classes, into the rich and the poor —into producers and nonproducers."[27] While criticism before the Civil War had been directed against the institution of chattel slavery, it now turned against "the other kind of slavery, worse than the one existing under the former slave system."[28] The correspondent of the *Volksstaat* (successor to the *Demokratisches Wochenblatt)* complained that the American Republic had been praised excessively in Europe, and that it was therefore difficult for immigrant workers to discard their high expectations.[29] The editor of the *Chicagoer Arbeiter-Zeitung*, who had himself looked into the depressed living conditions of Chicago's immigrant workers, described how immigrants came to the United States with unrealistic hopes, but became quickly aware of the fact "that, like in their home country, those without means were without rights, being oppressed by the rich here as well as there."[30]

Immigrant socialists sketched a bleak picture of American society in the German-language labor press. While acknowledging the "natural abundance of the continent" and the "auspiciousness of colonial, economic and social conditions" conducive to a political system "which rightly has served all peoples as an example," they also pointed out that opportunities for social advance had considerably worsened in the "model country of capitalism" and that an unbridled capitalist rule had been established, whose representatives were "more brutal by a good measure than their criminal likes living under monarchical rule." Thus America was no longer different from Europe.[31]

The mechanisms of the political system were harshly criticized. Although the right to vote was constitutionally guaranteed, it served as a "factor promoting the extension of the system of political exploitation, thereby advancing the moral contamination of the people's character." Underlying this development was the tendency to abuse the franchise for material gain and to seek public office for personal benefit. Large-scale corruption and election frauds were caused by such intentions. In addition, commentaries observed a "different method" of controlling the country's workers, an "inner reaction, which is the more dangerous, since its tricks often are not carried out openly in the name of the law, but under the mask of unlimited freedom.... The hydra-like opponent, whose superiority one feels, remains invisible and unassailable." Workers became "discouraged" and "disoriented" by this fact. Similarly, the increasing encroachments of the police against workers' meetings and "conspiracy laws" against workers' organizations were condemned. After the Haymarket tragedy in May 1886, comparisons between the United States and Bismarck's German Reich became frequent. The labor press saw this as a reactionary period, as a campaign against freedom of speech and of the press and against the rights of assembly and association. It denounced new laws and observed that these were in no way better than German authoritarian measures.[32]

As a result of such negative experiences, German-American socialists argued that the American political system should be modified in ways which, in addition to upholding the democratic rights written into the Constitution, would establish protections against the evils of the capitalist system. In a significant symbolic move, socialists used the centennial of the Declaration of Independence as well as of the Constitution to rewrite both documents for this purpose. Referring to old radical-republican traditions, they suggested that their development would lead to a true "social republic."[33]

2. German-American Socialists' Use of Political Rights: Franchise, Citizenship, and Immigration

Because of the absence of a continuing debate among German-American socialists on the practical implications of their general evaluation of American society, it is necessary to analyse the rare occasions when such questions were directly at issue in the broader context described above. The use of the franchise was an overriding concern. More than any other right, it symbolized the equal participation of all adult male citizens in the republic's political processes. German socialist immigrants were divided on the actual usefulness of the franchise. Marxists untiringly reiterated the fundamental principle that political rights without economic emancipation were meaningless. Such a view was not merely based on Marxist theory. During the 1870s, socialists, especially in Chicago and New York, learned by experience that the principle was corroborated by the reality of dirty electioneering, blatant disregard of voting rules, open buying of votes and outright fraud.[34] Thus the split in the Workingmen's Party in 1877 causing the withdrawal of many Marxist Internationalists from its ranks occurred over the question of the proper use of the franchise. Significantly, however, this was not discussed in terms of principle, but rather in terms of the tactics to be used in the American republican context.

German socialist immigrants obviously faced a dilemma. Not only did their party back in the German Reich insist on the right to vote in its program, but it also actively and impressively fought for it in local, provincial and national elections. In the United States, socialists admired the German party for the astonishing successes it scored at the polls; they contributed to its election funds, and considered its victories as inspiration for the Socialist Labor Party. Why should the party not follow the same pattern in the United States?[35] To justify these political activities, party members argued that Americans themselves held the election process in hight esteem as the proper means of political participation and that, therefore, they would not take seriously a party that rejected this central mechanism of the American political process.[36] Consequently, the SLP continued to present its candidates in the local elections at least, even if such concerted and repeated efforts rarely met with success. Participation was still justified on the grounds that elections could be used for purposes of agitation: people were more amenable to political issues at election time so that socialists could then hope for more attention in the market place of political ideas.[37] However they remained skeptical about the immediate benefits to be derived from elections for the SLP, especially since the majority system, which they attacked, would not be replaced by the system of proportional representation favoring small parties, which they demanded.

This basic acceptance of the institution of the suffrage was closely related to the views on citizenship held by the German socialist immigrants. The SLP was, of course, interested in registering as many votes as possible. The vote would certainly be increased by fellow immigrant socialists and workers who had favored the Social Democratic Party in the German Reich. Thus readers of the labor press were reminded before elections to request their citizenship papers in order to be allowed to vote.[38] When socialist immigration increased in the late 1870s and early 1880s as a result of the anti-socialist laws in Germany, an internal discussion occurred within the party in New York about the rights and duties of its members. Exiled socialists arriving in groups from Berlin and Hamburg and seeking material support from the SLP were asked to both join the party and apply for citizenship. In January 1880 the German branch reported to the New York Central Committee that it "has made it obligatory (by resolution) for new members to be citizens or at least to take out their papers before their temporary American card is exchanged for a regular membership card." When the American consul in Hamburg described socialists departing for the United States as dangerous and undesirable immigrants, sixty-five exiled socialists vehemently protested, pointing out that almost all of them had already declared their intention to become American citizens. Several years later, Johann Most confirmed such claims during a congressional hearing, extending them explicitly to anarchists as well. Even he had applied for citizenship but had been denied the privilege.[39]

Was the positive attitude toward citizenship prevalent among socialist immigrants and party members? While lack of adequate sources makes it impossible to come to definite conclusion, analysis of membership records of the SLP in New York for the three-year period from 1879 to 1882 supports the view that those socialists overwhelmingly sought citizenship.[40] Of the 781 members registered in the records, more than 86 percent had German names, documenting the well-known fact that the great majority had immigrated from Germany. Three-fifths (59.2%) of all members were citizens, and another fourteen percent had applied for it. Apparently many of those persons who did not belong to either category had immigrated only recently, as a look at the membership records of the largest branch (Branch 1, "German") indicates. Almost all of those registered early in the list were already citizens, whereas more of the later enrollments lacked designation. One may assume that these new members later also applied for citizenship.

The New York SLP in 1880 tried to curtail the rights of its new members, refusing to elect as delegates to the party convention those who were not yet citizens. This decision ran directly counter to the party's international orientation, and it was refuted after a heated debate. The New York delegates maintained that as a political party they had to adapt to national requirements, which made citizenship the precondition of the right to vote. The majority of delegates, however, wished to accord full membership rights to recent immigrants as well. Thus the resolution by Brophy that "all members shall be eligible to any office or position in the party" was accepted as article 6 of the General Rules.[41]

This incident may just have been an attempt by the established party members in New York to preserve their status against the multitude of newcomers from Germany. By using the criterion of citizenship for exclusionary purposes, they came dangerously close to a conservative policy restricting the rights of immigrants as well as immigration itself. Socialists averted such a course, however, in contrast to the Knights of Labor's and the American Federation of Labor's leadership[42] and to those German-Americans who had immigrated in the 1850s and who still considered themselves the true heirs to the liberal-democratic tradition. Having actively fought oppression in their fatherland in their youth, the majority of the latter had shifted their loyalties completely at the foundation of the German Reich in 1871, putting national unity above their republican ideals. After the Haymarket tragedy they participated in discussions of whether and how to restrict the country's liberal immigration policy. Milwaukee's and Chicago's German Societies were among those taking the initiative for raising the barriers of immigration, citizenship and suffrage, arguing that new immigrants were ignorant of American ways and institutions, did not know the language, and were merely bought by scheming politicians as voting cattle.[43] Being reminded of the fact that they themselves had been granted political rights soon after settling in Wisconsin in the 1850s, they claimed that conditions had changed and that it was no longer feasible to be so liberal. This view was supported by Hermann Raster, editor of the renowned *Illinois Staats-Zeitung* , who amidst the public outcry over the proposed restrictive measures within and without the German-American community, wrote in an editorial:

> The main question is and remains: Who shall rule this land? The native born and assimilated citizens of the country whose home is America, or fellows who, still standing in Europe with both legs, have not the slightest idea of the duties and rights connected with American citizenship —fellows who are yet by any means Americans, but are Polacks, Bohemians, or even German loafers and revolutionaries?[44]

Efforts at restricting immigration were widely condemned by the German-American socialist press, which repeatedly expressed its disdain for the German-American parvenus who had forgotten their own past, "tarnished the German name in this country beyond repair," and helped stir up "know-nothingism". These older political immigrants had thus outlived their political purpose.[45] On the issues of immigration and civil rights, socialist immigrants themselves now laid claim to being the true heirs to the German liberal-republican tradition in the United States, ironically taking on the role of its defenders against its former representatives.

Notes

1. *New Yorker Volks-Zeitung (= NYVZ)*, 29 oct. 1886.

2. For a general introduction to this literature cf. Hildegard Meyer, *Nord-Amerika im Urteil des deutschen Schrifttums bis zur Mitte des 19. Jahrhunderts. Eine Untersuchung über Kürnbergers "Amerika-Muden". Mit einer Bibliographie* (Hamburg, 1929); and Paul C. Weber, *America in Imaginative German Literature in the First Half of the Nineteenth Century* (New-York, 1926. Cf. also Rolf Engelsing, "Deutschland und die Vereinigten Staaten im 19. Jahrhundert. Eine Periodisierung", *Die Welt als Geschichte 18* (Stuttgart, 1958), 139; and Günter Moltmann, *Atlantische Blockpolitik im 19. Jahrhundert. Die Vereinigten Staaten und der deutsche Liberalismus während der Revolution von 1848/49* (Düsseldorf, 1973), P.39.

3. Ernst Fraenkel, ed., *Amerika im Spiegel des deutschen politischen Denkens. Äusserungen deutscher Staatsmänner und Staatsdenker über Köln und Gesellschaft in den Vereinigten Staaten von Amerika* (Köln/Opladen, 1959), p. 20. Meyer, *op.cit.*, p.8 and 10, and Engelsing, op.cit., p. 141.

4. Quoted in Engelsing, *op.cit.*, p. 146.

5. Meyer, *op.cit.*, p. 33f.

6. The term was used by the historianV. Raumer; it is quoted by Meyer, *op.cit.*, p. 44.

7. Cf. Eckhart G. Franz, *Das Amerikabild der deutschen Revolution von 1848/49. Zum Problem der Übertragung gewachsener Verfassungsformen* (Heidelberg, 1958), p. 105 and 139.

8. "Erster Bericht der demokratischen Partei der deutschen constituirenden National-Versammlung vom 1. August 1848," quoted in Franz, *op.cit.*, p. 105.

9. *Allgemeine Zeitung* , 16 Apr. 1848, quote in Franz, *op.cit.*, p. 108.

10. Thus, Gottfried Duden's *Bericht über eine Reise nach den westlichen Staaten Nordamerikas und einen mehr jährigen Aufenthalt am Missouri (1824-1827)*, published in 1829, triggered a real emigration fever; and

Gustav Koerner in his refutation *Beleuchtung des Duden- schen Berichtes über die westlichen Staaten,* published five years later, observed: "In many families it was read day by day on the eve of embarking for the New World, and became an authoritative source for their information;" cf. Weber, *op.cit.,* p. 115-119. Fraenkel, *op.cit.,* p. 35 emphasizes the "utopian expectations that wide masses of the German people had of America as a land of unlimited opportunities. In more than one sense for the lower classes of Continental Europe, the USA was the myth of the 19th century" the poet Johann Wolfgang Goethe wrote that "America was then (1775), perhaps still more than now (1818), the Eldorado of all who found themselves restricted in their present circumstances" *Dichtung und Wahrheit,* quoted in Weber, *op.cit.,* p.87.

11. Cf. "Programm der Sozialdemokratischen Partei Deutschlands," reprinted in. Institut für Marxismus-Leninismus beim Zentralkomitee der SED, ed., *Dokumente und Materialien zur Geschichte der deutschen Arbeiterbewegung,* vol.III: March 1871-April 1898 (Berlin, 1974), p. 383f. also Alfred Vagts, *Deutschland und die Vereinigten Staaten in de Welt-politik,* vol.I (New York, 1935), p. 512.

12. Vagts, *op.cit.,* p. 612f; and Fraenkel, *op.cit.,* p, 35f.

13. E.g. *Volksstaat,* No. 65, 14 Aug. 1872; No. 17, 26 Feb. 1873.

14. cf. Dirk Hoerder and Hartmut Keil, "The American Case and German Social democracy at the Turn of the Twentieth Century, 1878-1907," in *Why is there No Socialism in the United States? / Pourquoi n'y a-t-il pas de Socialisme aux Etats-Unis?* édité par Jean Heffer et Jeanine Rovet, Paris, EHESS, 1988, pp. 141-165.

15. *Volksstaat,* 4 Jan. 1873.

16. *Volksstaat,* 17 May 1873; cf also 22 Aug. 1873.

17. *NYVZ,* 1 July 1881; cf. also 10 Aug. 1880; 25 Apr. 1881, 10 July 1881; *The Sozialdemokrat,* published in Zurich, joined in this evaluation of the "emigration fever", which "we must deplore and fight"; 13 Feb. 1881.

18. *Volksstaat,* 25 Feb., 17 may 1873; *Sozialdemokrat,* 16 Jan. 1880; 20 Feb., 19 and 25 June 1881; *Verhandlungen des Parteitags der deutschen Sozialdemokratie in St. Gallen. Abgehalten vom 2. bis 16. Oktober 1887* (Hottingen-Zürich, 1888), p. 9; "Gegen die Ausreisserei," *Sozialdemokrat,* 13 Oct. 1888 *NYVZ, 3 Nov. 1878 and 13 Nov. 1880*
The slogan "our America is in Germany" appeared in the *Volksstaat* as early as 4 Dec. 1873. It derives from a remark by Lothario, one of the characters in Goethe's *Wilhelm Meisters Wanderjahre.* Having served in the American War of Independence, Lothario returns home to his old estate and exclaims: "Here or nowhere is America!" Cf. Weber, *op.cit.,* p.89.

19. For a general analysis of the views of European socialists on the United States, see R. Laurence Moore, *European Socialists and the American Promised Land* (New York, 1970). Liebknecht was attacked and ridiculed by Marx and Engels for his attitude; cf. Georg Eckert, ed., *Wilhelm Liebknecht. Briefwechsel mit Karl Marx und Friedrich Engels* (The Hague 1963), p. 21ff.; and Moore, p, 27.

20. "Die Botschaft des amerikanischen Präsidenten", *Osnabrücker Zeitung,* No. 189, 24 Dec. 1864; in: Georg Eckert, ed., *Wilhelm Liebknecht.*

Leitartikel und Beitrage in der Osnabrücker Zeitung 1864-1866 (Hildesheim, 1975), p. 257.

21. Liebknecht almost emigrated to Wisconsin in 1847. In later years he repeatedly toyed with the idea of emigrating to America. Wilhelm Liebknecht, *Erinnerungen eines Soldaten der Revolution* (Berlin, 1976), p. 16 and 82; Wilhelm Liebknecht, *Ein Blick in die Neue Welt* (Stuttgart, 1887, p. vi; Robert Schweichel, "Zum Gedachtniss Wilhelm Liebknechts", *Neue Zeit* 19/2 (1900/1901), pp. 539-44, 571-76, 602-608. George Eckert, ed., *Wilhelm Liebknecht. Briefwechsel mit deutschen Sozialdemokraten*, vol.I: 1862-1878 (Assen, 1973), p. 14f. F.A. Sorge, letter to Johann Philip Becker, 3 July 1867; To Karl Marx, 10 July 1867; to Becker, 11 July 1870, 25 Sept. 1870, in: F.A. Sorge papers, International Institute of Social History, Amsterdam; Sorge, letters to Liebknecht, 5 and 17 Apr. 1972, in Eckert, *Wilhelm Liebknecht. Briefwechsel mit deutschen Sozialdemokraten*, p. 414 and 417.

22. In the introduction to his travel account *Ein Blick in die Neue Welt*, p. vi Liebknecht himself states: "Since my early youth... I have not lost sight of the great republic in the west, and I have been following the development of American affairs with the greatest sympathy."

23. *Osnabrücker Zeitung*, No. 18, 7 June 1864; No. 299, 8 May 1865; No. 305, 15 May 1865; No. 574, 5 Apr. 1866; No. 601, 7 May 1866, in Eckert, *Leitartikel*, p.54, 381f., 387, 678, 705.

24. p. 271; quoted as translated by Moore, *op.cit.*, p.29.

25. Cf. Hoerder and Keil. *op.cit.*

26. *Demokratisches wochenblatt*, No.36. 5 Sept. 1868, p. 288.

27. *Ibid.*, No. 1, 2 Jan. 1869, p. 6.

28. *Ibid.*, No. 1, 2 Jan. 1869, p. 6.

29. *Volksstaat*, No. 38, 11 May 1870.

30. Quoted in *NYVZ*, 15 Feb. 1886.

31. "Die amerikanischen Arbeiter sind zum Vorkampf berufen", *Sozialist*, 26 Dec. 1885; cf. also *Chicagoer Arbeiter-Zeitung*, 17 July 1879; 9 Nov. 1886; *NYVZ*, 12 Sept. 1881; 4 Aug. 1882; 27 Feb. 1885; 27 Apr., 21 Aug. 1886; *Arbeiter-stimme*, 1 Jan. 1878; *Milwaukee'r Socialist*, 30 Nov. 1876.

32. *NYVZ*, 31 July 1878; 6 Jan. 1880; 17 and 18 May 1885, 5 March, 13 and 27 May 1887, 10 June 1890; *Volksstaat*, No. 10, 2 Feb. 1870; No. 29, 9 Apr. 1870; 18 May 1870; 13 Aug. 1973; No. 99, 17 Oct. 1873; *Sozialdemokrat*, 18 May 1882; *Chicagoer Bäcker-Zeitung*, 13 Apr. 1889. Robert Reitzel characterized the period as one of "modern inquisition", *Der arme Teufel*, 24 July 1886. For a more thorough analysis of the German-American socialists' perspective on the United States in the 1880s cf. Dirk Hoerder, "German Immigrant Workers' Views of 'America' in the 1880s", in this volume; for the repercussions of Haymarket cf. Hartmut Keil, "The Impact of Haymarket on German-American Radicalism", *International Labor and Working Class History*, No. 29(Spring 1986), 16-27; and Raymond C. Sun, "Misguided Martyrdom: German Social Democratic Response to the Haymarket Incident, 1886-87", *ibid.*, 53-67.

33. "Unabhängigkeits-Erklärung", F.A. Sorge Collection, New York Public Library, reprinted in Hartmut Keil, ed., *Deutsche Arbeiterkultur in Chicago von 1850 bis zum Ersten* Weltkrieg. Eine Anthologie (Ostfildern, 1984), p. 374ff.; "Die Sozialisten und das Centennial", *Chicagoer Arbeiter-Zeitung*, 1 and 2 May 1889; cf. also Carol Poore, "Whose Celebration? The Centennial of 1876 and German-American Socialist Culture", in: *Immigration, Language, Ethnicity*, vol. I. of *America and the Germans. An Assessment of a Three-Hundred-Year History*, Frank Trommler and Joseph McVeigh, eds. (Philadelphia, 1985), pp. 176-188.

34. Cf. Hartmut Keil, "The German Immigrant Working Class in Chicago, 1875-1890: Workers, Labor Leaders, and the Labor Movement", in Dirk Hoerder, ed., *American Labor and Immigration History, 1877-1920s: Recent European Research* (Urbana, 1983), p. 161f.

35. Cf. Hoerder and Keil, *op.cit.*

36. *Arbeiter-Stimme*, 3 Sept. 1876; *Chicagoer Arbeiter-Zeitung*, 6 Nov. 1886; Joseph Brucker, *Die Social-Demokratie und ihr Wisconsiner Wahl-Programm* (Milwaukee, 1877).

37. *Sozialist*, 14 Sept. 1889; *NYUZ*, 21 June 1880; 16 July 1886; *Chicagoer Arbeiter-Zeitung*, 24 Sept. 1888; Emil Kreis, letter to John Alexander, 29 Aug. 1883; to Ernst Lowa, 30 Sept. 1883; W.L. Rosenberg, letter to H. Autrich, 19 June 1884, Letter Press Copy Book, box 1, Socialist Labor Party papers, State Historical Society of Wisconsin.

38. Thus in *NYVZ*, 13 Oct. 1881.

39. *NYVZ*, 18 and 20 Sept., 10 Oct. and 21 Nov. 1881. Minutes, Central Commitee, SLP New York, Socialist Party Collection, Tamiment Institute, New York University. "Testimony of Johann Most". *Testimony taken by the Select Commitee of the House of Representatives to Inquire into the Alleged Violation of the Laws Prohibiting the Importation of Contract Laborers, Paupers, Convicts, and other Classes*, U.S. Congress, House of Representatives, 50th Cong. 1st Sess., Misc. Doc. No. 572 (Washington, D.C. 1888), pp. 246-253.

40. Minutes, Central Committee, SLP New York, Socialist Party Collection, Tamiment Institute.

41. Sozialistische Arbeiter Partei, *Platform, Statuten, und Beschlüsse, nebst einem kurzgfassten Bericht der Verhandlungen der National-Convention abgehalten in Allegheny, Pa., am 26., 27., 28., 29., 30., und 31. Dezember 1879 und 1. Januar 1880* (Detroit, 1880), p. 11 and 53f.

42. Cf. Samuel Gompers' and Terence V. Powderly's testimonies before the same committee that also heard Johann Most's testimony, *op.cit.*, pp. 390-402 and 496-506.

43. *Amerikanische Turnzeitung*, 19 June 1887, *Chicagoer Arbeiter-Zeitung*, 22 Dec. 1886; cf. also Keil, "Impact".

44. *Illinois Staats-Zeitung*, 20 Dec. 1886, quoted in Frederick Cotzhausen, *Historic Reminiscences and Reflections* (Milwaukee, 1906), p. 6f.

45. *Chicagoer Arbeiter-Zeitung*, 15 Dec. 1886; 18 Jan. 1887; *Amerikanische Turnzeitung*, 27 Nob. 1887; 13 Oct. 1889. For a general criticism of the '48ers cf. also "Die 'alten braven' Acht und Vierziger", *Vorbote*, 7 July 1878.

The Use of Criminal Conspiracy Prosecutions to Restrict Freedom of Speech

Risa Lieberwitz

Introduction

In a famous dissenting opinion, Justice Holmes expressed the potential power of speech to move people to action, stating, "Every idea is an incitement."[1] Indeed, the United States Supreme Court has reaffirmed the value of persuasive speech, stating that "free speech...may...serve its high purpose when it induces a condition of unrest, creates dissatisfaction with conditions as they are, or even stirs people to anger."[2]

While the need to protect the free expression of controversial ideas underlies the judicial protection of freedom of speech, government has also viewed the potential power of speech as dangerous. In particular, governmental suppression has been aimed at speech which challenges the legitimacy of the fundamental structure of capitalism. Criminal conspiracy prosecutions historically have provided a powerful weapon against groups advocating political or social change. In all political conspiracy prosecutions, the government's theory has focused on the defendants' speech, often charging a conspiracy to advocate or incite violence against the government.

The labor movement was the target of many criminal conspiracy prosecutions during the nineteenth century, beginning with the Philadelphia Cordwainers' Case of 1806, which was both the first criminal conspiracy trial in the United States, and the first recorded labor case.[3] Though toward the end of the nineteenth century, the government developed other weapons against organized labor, such as the labor injunction, criminal prosecutions have continually been employed against other political movements calling for fundamental social change.

In the Haymarket trial of 1886, the state government extended the conspiracy doctrine to its most extreme reaches. While the eight defendants were charged with murder, the government relied solely on a conspiracy theory, supported wholly by the defendants' expression of political ideas.

This article focuses on the Haymarket trial and the use of the doctrine of criminal conspiracy to convict the defendants because of their ideas. The Haymarket trial raises the crucial issue of the relationship between speech and action and the scope of freedom of speech for expression which may persuade others to take action. The article will also analyze legal developments addressing these issues since Haymarket to examine the level of progress in the scope of freedom of speech after one hundred years.

Criminal conspiracy

A conspiracy is defined as an agreement by two or more individuals to accomplish an illegal object, or to carry out a lawful object by illegal means. At common law, proof of an overt act in furtherance of the conspiracy was not required. While some criminal conspiracy statutes require an overt act, proof of a simple lawful act will suffice, such as making a telephone call.[4]

Specificity in describing criminal conspiracy is difficult, due to the primary focus on the agreement among the co-conspirators. As Supreme Court Justice Jackson stated, the modern crime of conspiracy is so vague that it almost defies definition... It is always 'predominantly mental in composition' because it consists primarily of a meeting of minds and an intent.[5] The abstract nature of the agreement as the major element of the crime is made even more ephemeral, as the government's burden of proof may be satisfied by evidence merely of an implicit agreement, shown by an implied mutual understanding, by tacit agreement, or by tacit consent.[6]

The vague and elastic character of criminal conspiracy is compounded by relaxed evidentiary rules unique to conspiracy trials, such as the co-conspirator exception to the hearsay rule. Under the hearsay rule of evidence, statements made out of court are not admissible at trial when offered to prove the truth of the content of the statements.[7] Under the co-conspirator exception, any out of court statements or acts by a co-conspirator committed in furtherance of the conspiracy are admissible in trial against all co-conspirators.[8] The co-conspirator exception has been justified by the difficulty of proving the state of minds of the defendants, which is essential to the element of the conspiratorial agreement.[9] However, as a result of this exception to the hearsay rule, each defendant found to be a conspirator is held liable for the acts and declarations of all other co-conspirators, whether or not the defendant was present or had knowledge of the acts or statements. Thus, on the basis of the statements and acts of others, a defendant may be convicted for conspiracy and for the substantive offense, though he did not participate in its commission.[10]

The ease of proof of conspiracy through the relaxed evidentiary rules has made conspiracy prosecutions the "darling of the modern prosecutor's nursery"[11] and a powerful weapon against political movements. The prosecution may use a "dragnet" approach to indict both leaders and members of a political organization for participation in a conspiracy against the government, which may be alleged to have existed over an extended period of time. Using association with a political group to prove a tacit agreement, the prosecution may then hold any group member liable for the acts or statements of all other members.

This method of proof in conspiracy prosecutions against political groups brings great repressive power against the defendants' freedom of speech and association.[12] While the government often relies on the defendants' declarations in any conspiracy prosecution, in a political conspiracy case, the defendants' statements are crucial to establish the revolutionary purpose of the "agreement." However, these statements in political trials are often in the form of political speeches, pamphlets, and editorials, for which the defendants may claim protection under the first amendment to the United States Constitution as expression on issues of public concern. Further, political conspiracy prosecutions, aimed at group activity, punish the defendants for exercising their first amendment right of association through participation in political organizations.

The first amendment problems in political conspiracy prosecutions are also related to the general principle that the government may constitutionally punish conduct, but not speech.[13] Any conspiracy conviction is for the "act" of agreement which, being "heavily mental in composition," is one step removed from conduct.[14] Punishment for an agreement to carry out a specific object may be justifiable in such cases as conspiracy to commit burglary, to fulfill the goal of preventing crime in its incipient stages. In political conspiracy cases, however, punishment for an agreement is even further removed from conduct and directly infringes on free speech protections. Since most political conspiracy trials involve an alleged agreement to advocate a position, such as an agreement to incite violence or to advocate revolution, the offense is then two steps removed from conduct.[15] In such cases, therefore, the conspiracy conviction punishes an agreement to engage in speech concerning political issues. Further, even in a political conspiracy case alleging an agreement to carry out an act such as the overthrow of the government, the "planning" stages of the substantive crime may consist primarily of constitutionally protected advocacy of political positions.

The Haymarket Trial

The Haymarket defendants, August Spies, Albert Parsons, Samuel Fielden, Michael Schwab, George Engel, Adolph Fischer, Oscar Neebe and Louis Lingg, were charged with the murder of an officer killed at the Haymarket, and with being accessories to the murder.[16] Under Illinois law, accessories to a crime could be charged and punished as principals.[17] Though charged with the murder, there was no evidence that any one of the defendants had thrown the bomb at the May 4 Haymarket meeting, nor that any of the defendants had participated in a plan to engage in violence at the Haymarket. Without such crucial evidence to support an allegation of murder, the State relied instead on a political conspiracy theory. Under this theory, the State intertwined conspiracy doctrine with the law of aiding and abetting by accessories to hold the defendants liable for the substantive crime of murder. The State's case consisted primarily of the defendants' political speeches and editorials, offered to prove a general conspiracy to overthrow the government through which the defendants had persuaded others to engage in violent acts, resulting in the bombing at the Haymarket on May 4, 1886.

The State's murder theory stretched conspiracy doctrine to its most extreme reaches. The State described the anarchist organization, the International Working People's Association (IWPA), as a conspiracy in itself, including the defendants as well as the IWPA's members worldwide. The government also alleged that the conspiracy had existed for years,[18] focusing chiefly on the three years prior to the Haymarket meeting.[19] This focus on the years between 1883 and 1886 corresponded to the IWPA's period of growth in the United States. The IWPA in the United States had its origins in the London Social Revolutionary Congress of 1881, which revived the anarchist wing of the International Workingmen's Association (First International).[20] The London Congress endorsed the doctrine of "propaganda by the deed", calling for actions of armed insurrection. Following the London Congress, the Chicago Social Revolutionary Congress was held in October 1881, attended by only twenty-one delegates, including Schwab, Parsons and Spies. The Chicago Congress took a militant stance, endorsing propaganda by the deed, but failed to achieve a unified organization of revolutionary groups. The arrival in 1882 of anarchist Johann Most in the United States and the Pittsburgh Congress of 1883 mark the starting points of the expansion of an anarchist movement in the United States. The Pittsburgh Congress adopted the name of the IWPA and produced the Pittsburgh Manifesto, described as "[a]n amalgam of socialist, anarchist, and other radical ideas... [which] embodied all the basic principles of the revolutionary socialist movement".[21] The Pittsburgh Manifesto was drafted by a committee of five delegates, including Most, Spies and Parsons.[22]

From 1883-1886, the IWPA made its greatest organizational progress in the United States, with Chicago as its largest and strongest center. To some extent, this expansion was fueled by the depression of 1883-1886, which created fertile ground for revolutionary ideas. The dissemination of anarchist theory was aided by the publication of pamphlets, leaflets and over a dozen anarchist newspapers and journals, including *The Alarm* and the *Arbeiter-Zeitung*, both published in Chicago. Chicago was also a center for the spread of ideas as the location of the IWPA's Bureau of Information. Further, the strength of the IWPA in Chicago was increased by its ties to the labor movement, reflecting the Chicago ideas of anarchist theory combined with revolutionary unionism. The revolutionary Central Labor Union, formed in Chicago in 1884 was closely tied to the IWPA, with membership of twenty-four unions by the spring of 1886.[23]

Haymarket defendants Spies, Parsons, Fielden, and Schwab were leaders of the Chicago IWPA. These defendants were also distinguished by their popularity and excellence as speakers at meetings and demonstrations, as well as their involvement with the labor movement, including the struggle for the eight-hour day. Neebe, Fischer and Engel were also well known in the anarchist movement. Neebe was an active organizer for the IWPA and the Central Labor Union. Engel and Fischer were founders and leaders of an ultra-militant minority group of the IWPA. Lingg, though having lived in the United States for a short time, was notable for his militance and as the only defendant definitely known to have manufactured bombs. Five of the defendants also edited and wrote for anarchist journals; Spies and Schwab for the *Arbeiter-Zeitung*, Parsons for *The Alarm*, and Engel and Fischer for the more radical *Der Anarchist*.[24]

This description of the period between 1883 and 1886 and the defendants' roles in the IWPA sets the stage for the State's case. Under the State's theory, the defendants' leadership and activities in the IWPA during its period of expansion in the United States proved a general conspiracy to overthrow "the existing order of society" and "the law by force," bring about "social revolution by force," and "excite the people... of this city to sedition, tumult and riot."[25]

The State further developed the theory that the general conspiracy was an umbrella for a specific conspiracy with the object of starting the revolution on May 1, 1886, during the strikes for the eight-hour day. Proof of the specific conspiracy was based mainly on the May 3 meeting of the armed groups of the IWPA, dubbed the "Monday night conspiracy." The State alleged that this meeting planned the opening blow of the revolution, by adopting defendant Engel's plan for armed defense of workers attacked by the police, and by scheduling the May 4 Haymarket meeting to protest the police killing of workers at the McCormick plant that afternoon. The specific Monday night conspiracy was essential to the State's case, under the legal doctrine of co-conspirator liability for acts and declarations by all other conspirators in pursuance of the objectives of the conspiracy. As all the defendants were alleged members of the general conspiracy, each would then be liable for the specific "plans" made at the Monday night meeting and the events at the Haymarket meeting, though only two defendants attended the Monday night meeting, six defendants were not present when the bomb exploded, and three defendants were not at the Haymarket at all. Thus, the State included each defendant in this web of conspiracy, despite the fact that some of the defendants did not know each other and some were political adversaries.[26]

Even with this entangled conspiracy theory, however, there was no proof of a plan to throw a bomb at the Haymarket, a connection between the members of the conspiracy and the person who threw the bomb, nor the identity of the bombthrower. The defendants' speeches at the Haymarket did not tie them to the bombthrowing, as the speeches by Spies, Parsons, and Fielden were, by all accounts, not inflammatory. Contrary to urging the crowd to take action, the speakers' comments showed restraint, such as Spies' statement that "[t]his meeting was not called to incite a riot," and Parsons' statement that he was not there "for the purpose of inciting anybody, but to speak out... to tell the facts as they exist..." Though Parsons told the audience to arm themselves, when someone called out, "We are ready now," Parsons answered, "No, you are not." Given the nonincendiary content of the speeches, the State attempted to overstate Fielden's obviously figurative statement before the police dispersed the meeting, as inciting the crowd to violence. Fielden told the audience to "throttle [the law], kill it, stab it, do everything you can to wound it — impede its progress."[27]

Without evidence of incitement from the Haymarket speeches, the State used the legal doctrine of accessories to bridge the gap between the conspiracy and the bombthrowing. The statutory definition of an accessory included an individual who, "not being present, advised, encouraged, aided or abetted the perpetration of the crime."[28] The State based its theory on the cumulative effect of the defendants' advocacy of revolutionary doctrine since 1883, alleging that the bombthrower had been persuaded by the revolutionary teachings to throw the bomb at the Haymarket, thereby making the defendants who had given the speeches and written the editorials guilty of aiding and abetting in the perpetration of the bombthrowing. The other defendants were also alleged as accessories, through the doctrine of coconspirator liability.[29]

To support its theory, the State brought in masses of evidence of the defendants' speeches, newspaper editorials and conversations during the three years prior to the Haymarket meeting, highlighting statements advocating revolutionary change, urging workers to arm themselves, and recommending dynamite as a revolutionary weapon, with instructions on its manufacture. The anarchist newspapers, the *Arbeiter-Zeitung* and *The Alarm* were special targets, as well as the IWPA's *Pittsburgh Manifesto*, Johann Most's *Revolutionary War Science*, and Spies' and Parsons' speeches at rallies and meetings. The State also focused on the so-called "Revenge Circular" written by Spies after the May 3 attack by police on workers at McCormick's factory and Fischer's circular announcing the Haymarket meeting. The "Revenge Circular," distributed on the evening of May 3, described the killing of the workers at McCormick's, opening with the call, "REVENGE! Workingmen to Arms!!" Though "violently phrased"[30] and "inflammatory,"[31] the "Revenge Circular" did not advise specific action. Fischer's circular had originally included the line, "Workingmen Arm Yourselves and Appear in Full Force." This line was removed from the circular at Spies' insistence; the line appeared in only 200-300 of the 20,000 circulars distributed.[32]

The key to the success of the prosecution's theory was the lack of required proof of an actual link between the defendants' speech and the action taken. As the State's own witnesses dispelled any contention that the speeches at the Haymarket could have incited such action, the State relied on the theory that advocacy of abstract revolutionary doctrine, expressed generally to the public, was sufficient at any time thereafter to incite action arguably consistent with that doctrine. The trial court assisted the State in reconciling the lack of evidence of actual incitement to action by one of the defendants to the unidentified bombthrower, by instructing the jury that neither piece of evidence was necessary. The court stated that the defendants would be guilty of murder if an unidentified person had been encouraged to commit murder by the defendants' public statements which "advised or encouraged the commission of murder, without designating time, place or occasion at which it should be done."[33]

On appeal, the Illinois Supreme Court affirmed the convictions, upholding the State's position on every point, including the theory that the defendants had incited the bombthrowing by advocating revolutionary doctrine over a period of years.[34] Why did the courts support convictions based solely on the defendants' speech on public issues? Certainly the political mood of the time and the fear of radicalism, overtly expressed by the capitalist press,[35] demonstrate that the Haymarket defendants could have been convicted on almost any evidence. However, the legal theory underlying the convictions reveals a vital issue of the relationship between speech and action and the scope of first amendment protection afforded to speech which may motivate the audience to unlawful action. This debate focuses on whether the first amendment protects such speech and the proximity between speech and action which may result in the loss of constitutional protection.

Though first amendment obligations were not explicitly extended to the states until 1925,[36] the right to freedom of speech has been an historically important tradition.[37] In Illinois, a free speech provision had been incorporated into the state constitution since 1818.[38] Yet, when faced with the issue of the relation between speech and action, the courts in the Haymarket case extended no protection to the defendants' political speech, despite the absence of any connection between their advocacy of revolutionary theory and the bombthrowing. Instead, it appears that the courts feared the potential of speech to incite the workers to action. The potential power of the IWPA's revolutionary doctrine was especially threatening, through the open endorsement of the doctrine of propaganda by the deed. Further, the idea of violent revolution was made more concrete by the recommendations of the benefits of dynamite and instructions on its manufacture found in the anarchist journals and literature. Indeed, the IWPA placed great faith in the persuasive power of ideas, seeking to educate and influence the workers through speeches, pamphlets and labor organizing. In a letter to *The Alarm*, one IWPA member clearly expressed the important link between ideas and revolutionary action, concluding, "From thought to action is not far, and when the worker has seen the chains, he need but look a little closer to find near at hand the sledge with which to shatter every link. The sledge is dynamite."[39]

By 1886, the ruling class in Chicago had also witnessed the influence of revolutionary ideas in the increased membership and visibility of the IWPA in disseminating information through its press, street parades and mass outdoor demonstrations. The IWPA's ability to reach the working class was also evidenced by the IWPA's close ties with the Chicago labor movement in the formation and growth of the Central Labor Union and the IWPA's active support of labor struggles, including the eight-hour movement. The ruling class could tolerate advocacy of revolutionary doctrine which did not persuade the audience.[40] However, rights of free speech were removed when radical ideas were translated into actions seeking societal change. Thus, despite the absence of evidence that the defendants had committed any violent acts or had advised any person to use violence at the Haymarket, the judiciary found the defendants guilty of murder because their ideas made them too dangerous.

Freedom of Speech after Haymarket

Other political conspiracy trials have raised similar issues concerning constitutional protection of speech which may motivate action. This issue was central to a series of Supreme Court cases reviewing conspiracy convictions for seditious speech offenses which, like the Haymarket trial, were the product of politically tense times; nine conspiracy convictions under the Espionage Act of 1917, during a period of national fear of criminal anarchy, and two conspiracy cases after WWII, during the McCarthy era paranoia about communism.[41] The Court's decisions show a progression from upholding convictions for conspiracy to advocate political doctrine unrelated to conduct, to extending first amendment protection to such advocacy unless the government proves a causal connection between speech and imminent danger of unlawful action.

Only speech which may constitutionally be prohibited may be the subject of a conspiracy charge.[42] In cases charging seditious speech, the Supreme Court has decided the first amendment issues under Justice Holmes' test of "whether the words used... are of such a nature as to create a clear and present danger that they will bring about the substantive evils that Congress has a right to prevent."[43] In applying the "clear and present danger" test in the WWI conspiracy speech cases, however, the Court majority sustained the convictions by merely presuming that the defendants' speech, alleged as overt acts in furtherance of a conspiracy to violate the Espionage Act, would create a danger of harmful conduct.[44] With regard to the evolution of first amendment doctrine, several of these cases are notable for the dissents of Justices Holmes and Brandeis, emphasizing the need to examine the surrounding circumstances in each case for objective evidence of an immediate danger of unlawful action resulting from the defendants' speech.[45]

In *Dennis v. United States*, decided during the McCarthy era in the 1950s, the Court sustained the constitutionality of the Smith Act, upholding convictions of Communist party leaders for conspiracy to teach and advocate the violent overthrow of the government and conspiracy to organize the Communist party for the same purposes.[46] The Court, in a plurality opinion, applied the same general assertions of the WWI cases, finding that "the requisite danger existed" to sustain the convictions, based on the need to prevent revolution, the highly organized and rigidly disciplined nature of the Communist party, "the inflammable nature of world conditions, similar uprisings in other countries, and the touch-

and-go nature of [U.S.] relations" with Communist countries.[47]

The Court narrowed the application of *Dennis* and the clear and present danger test in *Yates v. United States*, after "the paranoia and hysteria of the McCarthy era had abated"[48] and the membership of the Court had changed.[49] The *Yates* Court reversed convictions for conspiracy charges identical to those in *Dennis*, based in part on the failure to adequately instruct the jury that the defendants could not be punished for "advocacy of abstract doctrine," but only for "advocacy directed at promoting unlawful action" to overthrow the government.[50] Applying this distinction, the Court rejected the government's theory that the Communist party was itself a conspiratorial group, as the evidence showed that the Party merely advocated "the abstract doctrine of forcible overthrow," as opposed to "advocacy or teaching in the sense of a call to forcible action at some future time."[51]

The *Yates* holding that advocacy of unlawful action could constitutionally be prohibited left ambiguous the proximity between speech and action. The Court addressed this issue in *Brandenburg v. Ohio*, reviewing a conviction outside the normal pattern of political speech cases. The Court held unconstitutional a state criminal syndicalism statute, under which a leader of the Ku Klux Klan had been convicted for advocating the need for violence or unlawful methods to achieve political change.[52] The Court refined the clear and present danger test by narrowing the gap between speech and action, holding that the first amendment protects the "advocacy of the use of force or of law violation except where such advocacy is directed to inciting or producing *imminent* lawless action and is *likely to incite or produce* such action."[53]

Though *Brandenburg* provided broader protection for speech, the Court's decisions consistently assume the government's power to punish certain types of political speech. The government's ability to suppress speech directed to and likely to incite imminent lawless action leaves open an area subject to judicial manipulation. The vagueness of the "imminent" harm standard is exacerbated by the need to predict the likelihood of producing such harm even when the speech is not actually followed by action. Current Supreme Court doctrine would probably not permit the Haymarket murder convictions to stand, nor would a charge of conspiracy to commit murder be sustained. However, the possibility exists for a judicial finding that the Haymarket evidence would be sufficient to prove charges of conspiracy to incite violence and the substantive crime of incitement of violence. This possibility is created by the amount of judicial discretion provided under *Brandenburg*, and the opening left in *Yates* for punishment of "advocacy or teaching in the sense of a call to forcible action at some future time."[54] The potential for continued conspiracy prosecutions based on political speech during periods of political upheaval is revealed by the 1969 "Chicago Seven" trial.[55] With the development of the Black militance movement and the mass protests against the Vietnam War, the "Chicago Seven" were prosecuted for conspiring to violate the federal "Anti-Riot Act," passed in 1968 as a reaction against the civil rights movement.[56] The jury acquitted all defendants of the conspiracy charge, but found five defendants guilty of inciting others to riot.[57] On appeal from the convictions, the court found sufficient evidence of incitement to riot, though the government's case consisted primarily of the defendants' political speech and plans for protest demonstrations.[58] The court engaged in broad speculation regarding the intent and effects of defendants' speech, revealing the breadth of judicial discretion under the *Brandenburg* standard.[59]

Conclusion

The most striking similarity among political conspiracy prosecutions is the targeting of political movements which challenge the legitimacy of the social and economic structures, with the government's conspiracy theory focused almost exclusively on the defendants' speech on political issues. These trials usually take place during times of national tension, when the government fears the public's receptiveness to calls for change.

The power behind conspiracy prosecutions can be demonstrated from many aspects. A conspiracy charge in a case not involving a political prosecution does not punish illegal conduct, but merely an agreement to take unlawful action. In a political conspiracy case, the prosecution seeks to punish an agreement to speak, as in a charge of conspiracy to incite a riot, which is even further removed from any unlawful action. Additionally, regardless of whether the defendants are convicted, the prosecution itself has a "chilling effect" on the exercise of first amendment rights of speech and association. The government thereby achieves two goals; not only are those fearful of prosecution for expressing their political beliefs silenced, but the public also learns that it is dangerous to seek power through concerted action. Further, the government discourages individuals both from assuming leadership roles and from taking a minor part in political activity, for under the relaxed rules of evidence in conspiracy cases, less active participants in political organizations can be held liable for acts and declarations of their "co-conspirators."

Judicial treatment of the first amendment issues raised by political conspiracy cases reveals the courts' role in preserving the status quo. In the Haymarket trial, there was not even a pretense of establishing a causal relationship between the defendants' speech and the act of bombthrowing. The courts simply endorsed a general presumption that an unidentified person had been influenced by the defendants' political advocacy at some time. However, even the Supreme Court's broader protection of political advocacy restricts the boundaries of the first amendment to speech which is not likely to produce "imminent lawless action."

Judicial decisions on freedom of speech present the question of why speech is protected. Is speech protected *unless* it is "harmful" or *in spite of* the fact that effective advocacy can persuade the audience to act.[60] A meaningful theory of free speech must recognize and respect the potential power of speech by eliminating political conspiracy prosecutions, thereby extending constitutional protection to speech which results in unlawful action. Prosecution should be limited to criminal actions. Justices Black and Douglas expressed this view, stating in a minority opinion, [T]he First Amendment forbids Congress to punish people for talking about public affairs, whether or not such discussion incites to action, legal or illegal.[61] However, it is the very power of speech to influence fundamental societal change which motivates governmental suppression of effective advocacy of revolutionary ideas.

Notes

The author would like to thank David S. Bahn for his helpful comments and suggestions in the preparation of this paper

1. Gitlow v. New York, 268 U.S. 652, 673 (1925).

2. Terminiello v. Chicago, 33 U.S. 1, 4-5 (1949).

3. Castagnera, "The Doctrines of Civil and Criminal Conspiracy as 'Union Busting' Techniques in Labor Law Past and Present," 8 *Thurgood Marshall L. Rev.* 1, 7 (1982); Sayre. "Criminal Conspiracy," 35 *Harv. L. Rev.* 393, 413-16 (1922).

4. Filvaroff, "Conspiracy and the First Amendment," 121 *U of Pa. L. Rev.* 189-97, (1972); Note, "Conspiracy: Legitimate Instrument or Unconstitutional Weapon?" 3 *Colum. Surv. Hum. Rts. L.* 94, 96 (1970-71).

5. Krulewitch v. United States, 336 U.S. 440, 446-48 (1949) (concurring opinion); *see*, Filvaroff, *supra* note 4, at 191, n. 9.

6. Note, *supra* note 4, at 99.

7. *See*, McCormick's *Handbook of the Law of Evidence*, 729 (E.W. Cleary, ed.), 3d ed. 1984).

8. Church, "Conspiracy Doctrine and Speech Offenses: A Reexamination of Yates v. United States from the Perspective of United States v. Spock, *Cornell L. Rev..*, 569, 574 (1975); Filvaroff, *supra* note 4, at 192; Note, "Conspiracy and the First Amendment," 79 *Yale L. J.* 872, 877 (1970).

9. Church, *supra* note 8, at 574.

10. Filvaroff, *supra* note 4, at 192, 197-98; Note, *supra* note 8, at 877-78.

11. Harrison v. United States, 7 F.2d 259, 263 (2d Cir. 1925) *quoted in*, Filvaroff, *supra* note 4, at 193; Note, *supra* note 8, at 877.

12. Filvaroff, *supra* note 4, at 193; Note, *supra* note 4, at 113-17.

13. T. Emerson, *The System of Freedom of Expression* 16-18 (1970); Brandenburg v. Ohio, 395 U.S. 444, 456 (1969) (Douglas, J., concurring).

14. Church, *supra* note 8, at 575; Note, *supra* note 4, at 107-108; Note, *supra* note 8, at 888-89.

15. Church, *supra* note 8, at 575; Note, *supra* note 4, at 107-108; Note, *supra* note 8, at 888-89.

16. Brief on the Facts for Defendants in Error at 355, Spies v. People, 122 Ill. 1 (1887) [hereafter State's Brief on the Facts]; Spies v. people, 122 Ill. 1, 101-02 (1887); P. Avrich, *The Haymarket Tragedy* 234-35 (1984).

17. Spies v. People, 122 Ill. 1, 101 (1887). *appeal dismissed*, 123 U.S. 131 (1887).

18. Brief on the Law for Defendants in Error at 1-2, 9, Spies v. People, 122 Ill. 1 (1887) [hereafter State's Brief on the Law].

19. H.David, *The History of the Haymarket Affair* 289 (1936).

20. P. Avrich. *supra* note 16, at 58; H. David, *supra* note 19, at 55, 62-63.

21. P. Avrich. *supra* note 16, at 74; Avrich states that "[f]or a time the titles 'International Workingmen's Association' and 'International

Working People's Association' were used interchangeably, until the latter came to be the prevalent form." *Id.* at 76.

22. *Id.* at chs. 5,6; H. David, *supra* note 19. at chs. III, IV.

23. P. Avrich. *supra* note 16, at chs. 6, 7; H. David, *supra* note 19, at ch. V.

24. P. Avrich. *supra* note 16, at chs. 5-8; H. David, *supra* note 19, at chs. V, VII-VIII.

25. Brief for Plaintiffs in Error at 292 (*quoting* jury instructions) Spies v. People, 122 Ill. 1 (1887); H. David *supra* note 19, at 289-90.

26. P. Avrich *supra* note 16, at chs. 11, 13, 17; H. David *supra* note 19, at chs. VIII, XIV; D. Lum, *A Concise History of the Great Trial of the Chicago Anarchists in 1886*, at 67 (Arno Press ed 1969); State's Brief on the Facts, *supra* note 16, at 131, 137-45; Spies v. People, 122 Ill. 1, 225-30 (1887).

27. P. Avrich. *supra* note 16, at chs. 14, 17; H. David, *supra* note 19, at chs. XIII-XIV; D. Lum, *supra* note 26, at chs. II, III, VI, VII, Appendix I.

28. 38 *Ill. Rev. Stat.* div. 2, § 2, 3 (1874).

29. P. Avrich *supra* note 16, at ch. 17; H. David *supra* note 19, at chs. XIII, XIV; State's Brief on the Facts, *supra* note 16, at 1-2, 336-39, 342; State's Brief on the Law, *supra* note 18, at 2, 22-25, 36, 48, 65.

30. P. Avrich *supra* note 16, at 190.

31. *Id.* at 191.

32. P. Avrich *supra* note 16, at chs. 13, 17; H. David, *supra* note 19, at chs. VIII, XIII, XIV; D. Lum, *supra* note 26, at ch. VI.

33. Spies v. People, 122 Ill. 1, 80, 244-50 (1887); H.David, *supra* note 19, at chs. XIV, XVII.

34. *Id.* at ch. XVII.

35. H. David *supra* note 19, at 185, 206-209, 320, 323.

36. Gitlow v. New York, 268 U.S. 652, 666 (1925).

37. *See, e.g.* J.S. Mill, *On Liberty and Considerations on Representative Government* 13-48 (Oxford ed. 1946); T. Paine, *Common Sense and Other Political Writings* (Am. Her. ed. 1953).

38. D. Lum, *supra* note 26, at 186.

39. P. Avrich *supra* note 16, at chs. 5, 12; H. David, *supra* note 19, at 120.

40. P.Avrich, *supra* note 16, at 81-82; H. David, *supra* note 19, at 125-127; see *supra* notes 23 and 24.

41. Church, *supra* note 8, at 570; Filvaroff, *supra* note 4 at 200-201.

42. Church, *supra* note 8, at 575.

43. Schenck v. United States, 249 U.S. 47, 52 (1919).

44. *See, e.g.*, Schenck v. United States, 249 U.S. 47 (1919); Abrams v. United States, 249 U.S. 616 (1919); Pierce v. United States, 252 U.S. 239 (1920); Filvaroff, *supra* note 4, at 202-207.

45. Abrams v. United States, 250 U.S. 616, 627 (1919); Schaefer v. United States, 251 U.S. 466, 482 (1920); Pierce v. United States, 252 U.S. 239, 253 (1920); Filvaroff, *supra* note 4, at 205-207.

46. 341 U.S. 494, 497 (1951).

47. *Id.* at 510-11; Filvaroff, *supra* note 4, at 208-16.

48. Filvaroff, *supra* note 4, at 217.

49. *Id.*

50. 354 U.S. 298, 318, 324-25 (1957); Filvaroff, *supra* note 4, at 217-19.

51. 354 U.S. at 329.

52. 395 U.S. 444, 445 (1969).

53. *Id.* at 447 (emphasis added); Filvaroff, *supra* note 4, at 218.

54. See *supra* note 51.

55. The indictments were originally brought against eight defendants. The case is known as the "Chicago Seven," as Black Panther Party National Chairman Bobby Seale's case was severed from the other codefendants during trial. *The Conspiracy Trial* 188 (J. Clavir & J. Spitzer, ed. 1970) [hereafter *Transcript*]. *See also*, United States v. Spock, 416 F.2d 165 (1st Cir. 1969), where a jury found Dr. Benjamln Spock and three other defendants guilty of conspiracy to counsel, aid and abet individuals in refusing the draft. The Court of Appeats reversed all the convictions on grounds unrelated to sufficiency of the evidence, and directed acquittals of Spock and one other defendant on grounds of lack of evidence. *See*, Church, *supra* note 8, at 584-98.

56. 18 U.S.C. § 2101, 2102 (1982); A. Kinoy, H. Schwartz, D. Peterson, *Conspiracy on Appeal: Appellate Brief on Behalf of the Chicago Eight*, 41 (1971). [Thereafter *Appellate Brief*].

57. J. Epstein, *The Great Conspiracy Trial* 420-25 (1970).

58. *Appellate Brief*, *supra* note 56, at 133, 168, 181, 184; J. Epstein, *supra* note 57, at 77-82, 85, 159, 203, 207-08, 221-26, 236-37, 239-45, 280-86, 293-97, 386; *Transcript*, *supra* note 55, at 41-43, 69-70, 77-79, 101-02, 107-11, 116-17, 132, 139, 202, 205-06, 234-37.

59. United States v. Dellinger, 472 F.2d 340, 360, 392-407 (7th Cir. 1972), *cert. denied* 410 U.S. 910 (1973). The federal circuit court reversed the convictions and remanded for a new trial on grounds apart from the defendants' first amendment challenges to the Anti-Riot Act and its application to the defendants. *Id.* at 364-91.

60. *See*, Schauer, "Categories and the First Amendment: A Play in Three Acts," 34 *Vand. L. Rev.* 265, 271 n. 25 (1981).

61. Yates v. United States, 354 U.S. 298, 340 (1957) (Black & Douglas, JJ., concurring in part and dissenting in part).

Political Participation of the American Working Class at the End of the Nineteenth Century

Marie-France Toinet

At the end of the nineteenth century, the process of industrialization in the United States was in full swing; the country was being transformed from a rural, agricultural society into an urbanized, industrial one. Between 1860 and 1909, industrial production increased tenfold, from $2 billion to $20 billion. The railroad system, which covered around 30,000 miles in 1860, reached over 190,000 miles by the end of the century. In 1860, there were 150,000 industrial companies, and in 1900, there were over 500,000. The number of people working for these companies doubled every twenty years: the percentage of industrial (nonagricultural) workers in the labor force rose from 41% in 1860 to 61% in 1900.

Industrialization was accompanied by rapid and chaotic urbanization. In 1860, 94% of the population of 31 million people lived in the country or in towns of less than 8,000 inhabitants. In 1900, the total population numbered 76 million, one-third of whom lived in cities of more than 8,000 inhabitants. According to the title of a book by Arthur Schlesinger, Sr., this period can be characterized as the period of *The Rise of the City*. Urban growth is indeed stupendous: Chicago had 350 inhabitants in 1830; 112,000 in 1860; and 1,099,000 in 1890. It is not difficult to imagine that living conditions would have been less than ideal. Many people lived in slums, in the same filthy conditions and lack of comfort at home as in the factory, home, and workplace sometimes being the same.

Table 1. Employment of people over the age of 10 (in thousands)

	Agriculture	Manufact'ing	Mining	Construct'n	Trade	Railways	Domestics
1860	5,900	2,500	176	1,520	900	80	600
1880	8,900	4,400	280	900	1,900	416	1,100
1900	11,700	8,300	637	1,665	4,000	1,040	2,100

Source: These figures, as well as those used in Tables 2 and 3 are from the Bureau of Census, *Historical Statistics of the United States* (Washington, D.C.; Government Printing Office, 1975), 1:139.

At the same time, however, the economic development of this period was accompanied by a rapid accumulation of wealth and its unprecedented concentration in the hands of a few. There was hardly any sector of the American economy that was not dominated by one of a handful of magnates – from raw materials to transportation, from finance, to industry, from farming to food production, all were dominated by the inner circle of major American capitalists. Their methods were simple: cutthroat competitiveness, price manipulation (especially by means of the railroad system), and unmerciful exploitation of small farmers and laborers.

According to some surveys of the period, living conditions for workers were considerably worse than during the antebellum period and often only reach survival level because women and children made their own contributions to the family budget. In 1880, about one child out of every six was already working (1,118,000), and it was not unusual for these children to work ten hours or more each day.

These are all factors that form the background for the entry of the working class into American politics at the end of the nineteenth century. It has been said that this political insertion was fundamentally different from the one taking place at the same time in Europe, that America was "exceptional": the absence of class consciousness, ideological empiricism, democratic traditions, internal divisions within the working class, and basic ethnic, religious, regional, and professional differences are considered to explain the lack of success of any large socialist party. It is said that the workers were manipulated, especially by the political party machines, and that they were either unable to or did not want to use their votes autonomously because the crucial socioeconomic problems of the day were never formulated as issues for political debate. In sum, it has been said that there was a split, even a contradiction, between the intense social battles that sometimes escalated into open insurrection and the ritualized political life that supposedly did not reflect the experience of daily life.

This perception of reality, especially so far as the differences with Europe are concerned, seems debatable. Was the U.S. in this period truly an exception to the rest of Western industrial society? If this exceptionalism does exist, it only appeared much later on. At the time in question, if anything, there were only American "peculiarities." And these in themselves are not to be considered distinguishing characteristics – only the fact that they occur together makes the United States a special case.

Let's study the presumed causes of this American exceptionalism – first of all, the basic differences, in particular the ethnic ones. The massive importation of immigrant workers is said to have divided the American working class and radicalized it. We must analyze each of the words in this statement carefully. While it is true that there was massive immigration, this took place more toward the end of the nineteenth century, and on a greater scale at the beginning of the twentieth century.

It must be emphasized that the percentage of people in the total population who were "born in foreign countries" barely changed from the beginning to the end of the period being studied: 20% in 1870 and 18% in 1890. But there were more of them in the working class: they accounted for over one-third of all the workers. Even though the "native stock" is very upset by the "new" immigrants who are different from the traditional immigrants from northwestern Europe, from whom they themselves descended, it must be pointed out, however, that in the decade 1890-1900 a turning-point for American political life, people from northwestern Europe still form the majority if the Germans are included.

Table 2 — Number of immigrants (in millions)

1861-1870	2.3
1871-1880	2.8
1881-1890	5.2
1891-1900	3.6
1901-1910	8.7

It is true that the number of Germans includes socialists (Jewish) who along with the anarchists (Italians) supposedly threatened the political tranquility of the United States.

Table 3 – Country of origin for people "born in foreign countries" (in millions)

	Born in foreign countries	Great Britain and Ireland	Percentage	Germany	%	Italy and Russia	%
1870	5.6	3.1	65%	1.7	30%		
1890	9.2	4.4	48%	4.4	30%	0.4	5%

But we must not forget that it was businessmen themselves who wanted the immigrants to come in the first place. Immigrants were assumed to be more malleable than American workers, especially given that in the workplace care was taken to make sure that a Russian worker was put between an Irishman and an Italian rather than between two other Russians. Political and union organization for the working class was thus made more difficult, but as Philip Foner remarks, there was nothing to stop pamphlets from being printed in several languages, nothing to keep "locals" based on nationality from being set up, and nothing to stop multilingual "organizers" from being sent in. And this was exactly what the socialists and the Knights of Labor did in the 1880s. The immigrants themselves frequently insisted on maintaining their own languages even though they thereby lost all possibility of collective effectiveness – Engels accused the German socialists of being politically inept and hopeless because they stubbornly refused to learn English.[1] Were American workers, who very clearly realized that immigrants were often hired as strikebreakers, any more racist than their European counterparts? With the exception of attitudes towards the Chinese, there really was no systematically xenophobic behavior within the working class at that time – at least, no more than we see in the French working class during the same period.

In fact, union and political leaders born in foreign countries were found in the United States, and their number corresponded fairly closely to the proportion of their own nationality in the working class. The other basic differences that existed in the United States do not appear to be unique to this nation either. Religious or regional differences, disagreement between craftsmen's unions and industrial unions, and tensions between skilled and unskilled workers were just as strong in Europe at the same period in time.

What was supposedly different in the United States compared to Europe were the characteristics of political behavior, for example, the absence of class consciousness in the United States. But this assumption deserves closer scrutiny. Aren't there signs of class consciousness when workers question the stranglehold put on the government by private interests, or when they demand, according to an *Atlantic Monthly* reporter, in 1878, that government become the workers' employer through extensive programs of public works, feeling that it should run the railways, canals, and telegraph system for the benefit of all and supporting the idea that land ownership should be public and the concentration of wealth in the hands of a few should be legally prohibited?[2] On this subject, Friedrich Engels makes an instructive comparison with Europe:

> In European countries, it took the working class years and years before they fully realized the fact that they formed a distinct and, under the existing social conditions, a permanent class of modern society; and it took many more years before this class consciousness led them to form themselves into a distinct political party, independent of, and opposed to, all the old political parties formed by the various sectors of the ruling classes. On the more favored soil of America, where no medieval ruins barred the way, where history begins with the elements of the modern

> bourgeois society as evolved in the seventeenth century, the working class passed through these two stages of its development within ten months.[3]

Class consciousness is therefore not the exclusive property of European workers at the end of the nineteenth century. It is true, though, that in the United States, this class consciousness was accompanied by an ideological empiricism. Workers' demands were pragmatic in nature and very closely tied to living and working conditions: better salaries, shorter working hours, accident pay and, if applicable, indemnization for work-related accidents, better working conditions (especially regarding safety in the workplace), and so on. But even if these demands were of a practical nature, they were also political. To understand this, all we have to do is to take notice of the huge electoral and legal battles that the workers' demands unleased at the end of the century. The more directly ideological debate is no less important so far as the demands themselves are concerned: what should be the attitude of the working class toward government? This is really the heart of the matter in the strategic quarrel about the best means to achieve satisfaction. Should the government be brought down or taken over? Would it be better to work through the traditional parties or create working-class parties? Should the working class take action alone or should it work with allies, for example, the farmers? Should union activity be separate from political action or could they be used to help each other? All these different questions turned into quarrels that tore the workers apart, just as they did in Europe. Don't American socialists talk about the split between Lasallians and Marxists? As Leon Fink quite rightly comments: "Ironically, the worker's relation to politics, which has long served as an important explanation of why class consciousness failed to develop in the United States, might better be addressed by reassimilating American political culture into an international framework."[4] And he adds: "It is against this European background of contending and changing strategies for the working-class movement that the assumptions and practices of the North American labor movement are to be studied. On reexamination, American labor radicals and the Knights of Labor in particular do not seem far removed from the major currents of thought affecting their European contemporaries."[5]

This is indeed quite true, and we can go even further in describing the similarity between European and American political behavior. The well-known democratic tradition, embodied in universal suffrage, is thought to be unique to the United States and is supposed to have resisted any revolutionary impulse. But at the end of the century, universal male suffrage existed in France and Germany under the same conditions. Even though workers widely exercised the right to vote, this did not stop them from mounting massive insurrectional strikes that stand out as landmarks in the worker movement between 1877 and 1914, particularly in the United States.

But it was precisely the large worker participation in elections – and the not-to-be ignored results it achieved that irritated the "haves." The latter reacted to this by limiting access to the voting booths – that of blacks, which has drawn a lot of attention, but also that of the "dangerous" classes, which is rarely mentioned, even though it was very effective. Two figures show the extent of the change that was accomplished: the average voter participation (based on the number of potential voters)[6] between 1872 and 1900 during presidential elections is 77.1%; in the next eight elections, between 1904 and 1932, it falls to 57.9%, one-fourth less.[7] In the nineteenth century, there were scarcely any differences in voting participation linked to the social origin of the voters: blue- collar workers and members of the upper-middle class voted equally often in the United States, France, and Germany.[8] One century later, this was no longer true. Nothing had changed in France or in Germany, but things were quite different in the United States – the higher one was on the social ladder and the higher one's income the greater the chances that that person would go to the polls to vote. The lower one was on the social ladder and the lower one's income, the greater the chances that that person would not vote. Walter Dean Burnham shows this perfectly in a study of the polling precincts in 1960: in those where 40% of the white, male adults are in professional or managerial positions, voter participation reaches 71%; in those where these positions represent only 10%, it falls to 52% of the white, male adults and 41% of the black, male adults.[9] As Walter Dean Burnham stresses for the contemporary period, "on the whole, the upper half of the American class structure votes in elections, the lower half does not."[10]

At the end of the nineteenth century, American voters and in particular, the working class, were politicized in the dual sense of the term: they were politically educated and they were interested in politics.

Even if education was still determined by social factors, where was, at this point in time, an explosion in schooling. The number of children attending school rose 57% in 1870 to 72% in 1900, and only 11% of the population was illiterate in 1900, compared to 20% thirty years earlier. This movement goes hand in hand with the explosive growth of print communication. The number of daily newspapers published in English quadrupled between 1870 and 1900 (1,976 in 1900), and this advance was not at the expense of foreign language publications, since there were still 140 daily newspapers published in German, Yiddish, Italian, and other languages. The number of daily copies printed goes from 2.6 million in 1870 to 15 million in 1900. And the other periodicals were not to be ignored – the number of weekly publications tripled during this same period: 12,000 were being published in 1900.[11]

Obviously, not all the press was political – the taste for scandal and crime that makes for the success of "yellow" journalism was still quite apparent. But the press of that time was more politicized and more ideologically divided than the press of today. There were many publications representing the leftist political parties and the unions.

Philip Foner points out that in 1885, according to widely accepted estimates, the labor press included 17 monthlies, 400 weeklies, and a few daily newspapers (among them the socialist *Volkszeitung* and the *Irish World and American Industrial Liberator*).[12] Despite attempts by employers to limit the influence of the labor press – in particular, the firing of workers who were caught reading it[13] – its influence cannot be denied. This is due in large part to the libraries and reading rooms that unions and political movements or circles created at that time. The workers were aware of contemporary issues.

Politically educated, workers were also interested in politics. Political participation was not only electoral. It was also seen in political rallies: 750,000 people are said to have gone to McKinley's home during the 1896 campaign to listen to the candidate speak.[14] This represents 5% of the people who voted in 1896. Voter participation in candidates' election was equally striking: in 1880, political parties in New York had to organize 72 primary elections and 111 local conventions in order to settle on a final list of candidates.[15]

And candidacies from the working class were seen much more frequently then than they are today. In all the studies on the workers' movement, fragmentary, but meaningful data are found. Sydney Lens points out that in the 1870s, Irish miners from Pennsylvania succeeded in electing their own people to offices as country commissioners, tax collectors, school directors, and police chiefs or constables.[16] David Montgomery, who retraced the political career of several "VIPs" of American unions, stresses the number of them who held elected office from 1880 to 1890; out of 96 important union figures, 44 of them were involved in party activities; and half of this activity occurred within the main traditional parties, Republicans (13) and Democrats (9). Twenty-six of them held elected office (16 in state legislatures, 3 as city councilmen, 3 as mayors, and 4 as members of Congress), and 15 of them received political appointments (7 in the labor statistics offices which were politically very important for the working class and appointed by the employers).[17] Leon Fink points out that in 1886, working-class tickets appeared on the ballots in 189 cities in 34 (out of 38) states and were successful in one-third of them. From Congress to City Council (Henry George almost won a mayoral race in New York), with a certain number in state legislatures, dozens of workers were elected, not counting those whom the traditional parties were forced to put on the ballot because of how strong, even irresistible, the working-class movement had become.[18] Lastly, Philip Foner gives details, election by election, of the hundreds of members of the working class who were elected to various offices, including the most important ones (governors or members of Congress).[19]

It is outside the scope of this study to analyze the reasons, inside the labor movement, why the process of political insertion that started so brilliantly stopped in its tracks. Yet it is a fact that the ideological differences among farmers and the working class and disagreements within the labor movement over the strategy to be followed (creation of a workers' party or takeover of an already existing party) do not alone explain this failure. Repression by the employers also played a role. However, it seems to us that there is too great a tendency to ignore the influence of limits placed on suffrage by an upper class afraid of the political progress of the working class and the completion of the projects of their elected officials. Both Leon Fink and Philip Foner have emphasized this latter aspect. Fink in particular was stressed how much more advanced these reforms were compared to the situation in Europe at the same time. And Foner writes: "As a result of labor pressure, social legislation of various kinds slowly started to emerge. In 1877 Massachusetts passed the first American law requiring factory safeguards, and by 1887, 15 states had passed laws providing elementary safety measures in factories. By the same time, several states had restricted the labor of women and children. It was also during this period that a number of states established bureaus of labor or bureaus of labor statistics. The United States Bureau of Labor was founded in 1884."[20]

Of course, these laws would not be very widely enforced or else would be declared null and void by the Courts. But these laws symbolized the influence of the working class, which the upper classes feared would become greater. It had to be brought under control and limited. Under the pretext of "cleaning up" corrupt election procedures (which did exist), the extent of electoral democracy was reduced.

It is important to state that the political machines that were a symbol of corruption at the time, and the target of these reforms, were not so much in the hands of the working class as in the hands of the upper class. When exactly did the "machine" get its start? To say that there were signs of it from the very beginning of the American republic would be to shatter the myth of a machine created by the non-English immigrants who were not trained in the ways of democracy in their native countries. And this also implies that the English of the WASPs had highly democratic traditions, with well-established religious and political tolerance.

In fact, the machine was created even before Independence by the upper classes, who wanted to increase and then maintain its own power. For example, Tammany Hall is the machine in New York and as such the symbol of all the city machines. In fact, it was founded around 1732 in Philadelphia, as a patriotic society. The society grew and was established in New York in 1789. According to Alexander Callow: "The 'best' people were attracted to its ranks and the society assumed a prominent position in the social life of the city; its festivals were events of considerable pageantry, attracting large audiences."[21] Very quickly, this society became politically directed and at Jefferson's request, gave him its support. It foreshadowed the first organized parties while at the same time continuing the charity activities that it had carried out from its beginnings. This combination of charity and politics would only take on its full meaning later, when the leaders of the organization realized the benefits they could reap by organizing poor people. But, contrary to the myth, for many years it was the privileged class which controlled the "society," hesitating neither to corrupt, nor to be corrupted – and they refused immigration just as they refused to let poor people vote. Only when the poor put pressure on the society did it give in and become the defender of immigrants and the working class. Since the latter could no longer be ignored, it was better to live alongside them . . . and control them. Only very slowly and quite some time after the Civil War did aliens from other countries, more recently immigrated than the "old stock" Anglo-Saxons, rise to positions of responsibility. But let there be no mistake – when we study the situation in detail, we realize that there were never, at any time, many working-class people in positions of power. Immigrants and their descendants ("ethnics") progressively replaced the Anglo-Saxons, but they were in no way "poor immigrants."

The political machine has been seen as the preferred mode of political participation among immigrants. This perception is correct to a certain extent: new arrivals were politically initiated and educated by the machines. But on the other hand, contrary to this widely accepted view, it was the lower classes who suffered most under this system, and far from being captivated by it, they were the ones who made it possible to check its power and influence. As Alexander Callow notes, "Ironically, it was the very people the reformers despised the most, the immigrants and the native poor, who, because of their great numbers, put the reformers into office by splitting their vote between Tammany and the men running on the Democratic reform ticket" in 1871.[22]

In any case, the influence previously exerted by the traditional parties through their manipulation of political machines and patronage was reduced. The "reformers" gradually introduced nonpartisan and at-large elections, principally at the local level. They also developed the form of municipal government now known as the city manager system, which is headed by a nonelected professional administrator appointed by the city council. Since up to that time the different political parties, and particularly the smaller parties, had printed and distributed their own ballots for elections, the "Australian ballot" became an essential instrument of election reform. First used in Massachusetts in 1889, it was adopted by all the states except the Carolinas and Georgia by the end of the 1890s; it was in this period that the government assumed the responsibilities of printing and distributing ballots and established eligibility requirements and qualifying rules for third-party candidates.[23] These changes were taken a step further in many states: candidates' names appeared on the ballot according to the position or office they sought instead of by party affiliation, making straight-ticket voting difficult. Some politicians were well aware of the underlying motives for these measures: Governor David Hill twice vetoed the introduction of the Australian ballot in the state of New York because "it would tend to undermine both democracy and the organization of political parties."[24] Finally, tasks of governing that had been carried out previously by elected officials – or by ordinary citizens, in the case of jury members – were taken out of their hands. Appointed commissions assumed control of economic organization (regulation of banking and insurance, administration of public services and utilities, and decisions on zoning, urban planning, and other restrictions on land use), and working-class citizens considered too willing to come to the defense of organized labor were no longer called on to serve in jury trials against unionists: in their attempts to hamper union activity, employers had learned that it was more effective to seek injunctions against organizers from a single judge than to take a conspiracy case before a full jury.

This setback to the possibilities of worker representation would have been enough to make the workers feel less interested in political matters and to lessen their desire to participate in the electoral process.[25] But at the same time, the numerous, ultrapartisan, politically-active press was replaced by the modern press for the masses, which prides itself on being apolitical and above political parties, thereby reinforcing the depolitization desired by the upper classes. Even though this evolution of the press was not due to legal measures, it was still significant of the mood of the day, particularly since the great magnates of print journalism who decided the direction the press would take were all members of the upper class.

But this was not enough. Even the right to vote was restricted, first of all for the black, of course, but in a more subtle way for the entire working class, both white and black. In the decade following the Civil War, the United States experienced a remarkable extension of male suffrage. The right to vote was no longer limited for reasons of property, race, or religion. In fact, in some states immigrants were allowed to vote so long as they had been residents for several years and/or had expressed a desire to be naturalized. This did not make the United States the only democratic nation but it did make it one of the most democratic.

Beginning at the end of the 1870s, however, a series of legal measures seriously restricted electoral participation. At the end of the century, this process was almost entirely completed. The undeniable consequence of this was a decrease in voting, especially by the working class voters.

The first people whose right to vote was restricted were the immigrants who were not yet naturalized. Twenty-two states (out of 37 states in 1875) had at least allowed immigrants to vote. From 1875 on, state after state abolished this possibility. In 1900, there were only 11 states left which allowed immigrants to vote.[26]

The second group of people to lose the franchise were blacks – but at the same time, since the state legislators could not or would not control the ramifications of their decision, the poor whites, especially the working class, also lost their right to vote. As V. O. Key remarks, the timing of the decision to limit the right to vote "makes this interpretation plausible, for the poll tax is adopted at about the time when the Populists, the Farmers' Alliance, and other opposition groups are threatening the oligarchies which are in power."[27] Poor whites were often fully aware of the ambiguous consequences of legal decisions that do not really concern them and that are not really directed at them. In the South they opposed ratification of laws limiting the right to vote.[28] Two methods were used to set the limits: poll taxes and literacy tests. The poll tax was adopted for the first time in Florida in 1889. All the southern states (except Kentucky and Oklahoma) would adopt it. In some states, this tax was quite high. For example, Georgia demanded that the total accumulated tax from all previous years be paid before one could vote. The date on which this payment was due also restricted the number of people who could pay it.[29] "When the tax is due six months or more in advance of a campaign, before the candidates have announced and before political interest is aroused, the natural result is a smaller degree of payment than would occur if collection continued until a shorter time before the voting. The restriction of the electorate is of the same type as that effected by variations in the period between registration and election in nonpoll-tax states."[30] Literacy tests were first introduced in Connecticut (as early as 1855) and in Massachusetts (in 1857), then in New Hampshire with the very specific goal of excluding immigrants from the polls (whether they were U.S. citizens or not). Other Northern states adopted them for the same reasons: Wyoming (1889), California (1894), Washington (1896), Delaware and Maine (1897), among others. As a writer of the time remarked: "The influence of that great mass of ignorant and vicious voters, on whom we have so thoughtlessly conferred the right of suffrage" should be limited. Those tests were directed against blacks and the poor whites as well. When these two restrictions were used together, the effect was devastating, as is shown by Jerrold Rusk and John Stucker's study[31] on voting participation in the various Southern states during the presidential elections between 1892 and 1916 (see Table 4) – at the extremities, the difference reaches 48%. Other measures were used throughout the country to limit the right to vote. The first was the obligation of being registered to vote. This practice was used in all the states at the end of the century (except for states like Texas and Arkansas which instead demanded a receipt proving payment of the poll tax). It is true that the earlier practice of allowing people to vote if they were "recognized" when they came to the polls left the way open for all kinds of fraud, especially in the cities. But as Walter Dean Burnham stresses, "The original impetus to the adoption of person-registration requirements clearly grew out of that old-stock nativist and corporate-minded hostility to the political machine, the polyglot city, and the immigrant which was so important a component of the progressive mentality."[32]

Table 4 – Effect of the poll tax and literacy tests on voter participation (n = 101)

	Literacy test	No literacy test
Poll tax	24.2% (33)	40.2% (28)
No poll tax	57.2% (2)	72.1% (38)

This desire to control the dangerous classes' access to the polls is clearly apparent, for example, in the obligation for those voters living in the city of New York, but not the rest of the state, to renew their registration periodically. Once again the result of this would be less voter participation in cities, without a corresponding reduction of electoral fraud.

The strategy of voter registration was perfected by the establishment of a minimum length of residence before a person could register. Once again, these rules were set up only at the end of the century in most of the states. In most cases, a voter must have lived in the state for one year before being allowed to register; in some states, like Alabama and Mississippi, the time limit was even longer – two years. In France, after having proclaimed universal male suffrage in March 1848, the Second Republic set a residence requirement of two years, openly intended to eliminate the working-class vote. The Second Empire abolished the minimum residence requirement by proclamation on December 2, 1851, and it would never be reestablished in France. The objective of the Second Republic was similar to that of the upper classes in the United States: since workers were often looking for jobs or following the jobs where they could be found, they were migrants and consequently the targets of this requirement.

Lastly, gerrymandering, an old political practice, took on a new dimension. It was a matter of reducing the influence of working-class cities and of giving the advantage to rural localities which were thought to be less revolutionary. Thus in 1894, the State of New York systematically showed favoritism toward the "real Americans" in the northern part of the state, to the detriment of the "immigrant masses" in the New York City metropolitan area.[33]

In sum, as has been emphasized earlier in this study, electoral participation took a dramatic plunge between the end of the nineteenth century and the beginning of the twentieth century, especially in urban and working-class localities. The electoral influence of the "dangerous" classes was severely limited. Of course, as is often true in the history of the United States, one single element was responsible for this phenomenon. It was the accumulation of restrictive factors, which when taken individually are harmless enough, but which all worked in the same restrictive direction, that calls for a more subtle analysis of a system that is more ambiguous and less democratic than is usually believed.

Lastly, we must try to understand why the working class did not react to such an outright attack on its political influence. On the one hand, it would appear that it was difficult for them to realize the true objective behind the measures enacted (limiting the working-class vote). This was hardly obvious. The admitted objective was to reform the electoral system, to clean it up, and to eliminate fraud and corruption. How could the working class say "no" to such noble intentions? The workers were even more in favor of these objectives since they themselves had lost elections through electoral fraud. Moreover, people tend to think that the other (especially if he is black) is the one being targeted. On the other hand, what is new and original in the United States was perhaps the talent the ruling class had for handing out punishment and praise at the same time – a strike might be put down one day (and with what violence!), and the next day, minimum reforms granted; the third day, ways would quickly be found to neutralize the reforms or to keep them from being applied. Workers' candidacies were accepted at the same time as union activists were jailed. Latent xenophobia was used to advantage or even encouraged (including in the working class), while at the same time the importation of immigrants intended to act as strikebreakers was made easier. Some were accepted so that it was easier to reject the others. Democracy was proclaimed at the same time as the right to vote became limited. Weakened by its internal battles over strategy and by the repression it suffered, and more responsive to the repression than to losing the right to vote, the working class passively witnessed its elimination from the political process. Undoubtedly, their submission proved disastrous, but that is another issue altogether.

Notes

1. Philip S. Foner, *History of the Labor Movement in the United States*, 3 vols., 2nd ed. (New York: International Publishers, 1975), 2:42-43 and 57-58.

2. *Atlantic Monthly*, November 1878, 524.

3. Friedrich Engels, quoted in *Workingmen's Democracy: The Knights of Labor and American Politics* (Urbana: University of Illinois Press, 1983), 6.

4. Fink, 21.

5. Fink, 23.

6. The number of potential voters is made up of the voters who meet the legal conditions for participating in the election.

7. The figures are based on data from Walter Dean Burnham, *Critical Elections and the Mainspring of American Politics* (New York: Norton, 1970), 80. If we check statistics for individual states, things are even more striking. In Virginia, an extreme case, the participation rate fell from a record high in 1888 (83.2%) to a record low (25.7%) in 1912. Since women were still not allowed to vote, they cannot be held responsible for the change. In 1888, even if we consider that *all* white males voted, which is improbable, still only about 56% of black males voted. In 1912, even if *all* black males were prevented from voting, which is not impossible, only about 38% of white males voted.

8. Compare, for example, the study we have done after each election since 1978 for the Parisian polling places – there is no significant difference between the upper-middle class polls and the polls in working-class neighborhoods. Françoise Subileau and M.-F. Toinet, "L'abstentionnisme en France et aux Etats-Unis," in Daniel Gaxie, ed., *Explication du vote* (Paris: Presses de la FNSP: 1986), 175-198.

9. Burnham, *Critical Elections*, 82.

10. Walter Dean Burnham, "Fighting the Image War," *New Republic*, October 20, 1976, 21.

11. These figures are from Edwin and Michael Emery, *The Press and America*, 4th ed. (Englewood Cliffs: Prentice Hall, 1978), 574.

12. Foner, 2:29-30. Foner gives no figure for the overall circulation.

13. Ibid.

14. Quoted by Burnham, *Critical Elections*, 73.

15. Morton Keller, *Affairs of State* (Cambridge: Harvard University Press, 1977), 240.

16. Sydney Lens, *The Labor Wars* (Garden City: Anchor Press, Doubleday, 1974), 19.

17. David Montgomery, *Beyond Quality* (New York: Random House, 1976), 208-209.

18. Fink, 26.

19. Foner, 127-31, 145-46, 309-10, and 324-26.

20. Foner, 2:24.

21. Alexander Callow, *The Tweed Ring* (London-New York: Oxford University Press, 1977), 94.

22. Callow, 278.

23. It was only in 1980 that, for the first time in a century, a presidential candidate, John Anderson, would appear on the ballot in all the states of the Union, and he had a difficult time doing it.

24. Burnham, *Critical Elections*, 75.

25. In 1974, when asked why he did not vote, a sugar laborer explained: "I don't vote because whoever wins will not be interested in me anyway. What difference will it make if I vote?" R. Shaffer, "Left Behind," *Wall Street Journal*, October 17, 1974. It is because of reactions like this one that some American political scientists describe Americans' abstention as "apathetic" or "passive."

26. In 1925, Arkansas was the only state where this privilege still existed. In 1926, it was totally abolished. In 1928, for the first time ever, not a single non-American voted in any national, state, or local election. See Leon E. Aylsworth, "The Passing of Alien Suffrage," *American Political Science Review* (Spring 1931): 114-116.

27. V. O. Key, Jr., *Politics, Parties, and Pressure Groups* 5th ed. (New York: Thomas Y. Crowell, 1964), 618.

28. See V. O. Key, *Southern Politics* 1st ed. (Knoxville: University of Tennessee Press, 1986), pp. 549 et seq.

29. Key, *Southern Politics*, 586.

30. Quoted in Keller, 529.

31. Jerrold Rusk and John Stucker, "Effects of Southern Election Laws on Voting Participation," in John Silbey *et al.*, The History of American Electoral Behavior (Princeton: Princeton University Press, 1978), 198-250.

32. Burnham, *Critical Elections*, 79-81.

33. Burnham, *Critical Elections*, 81.

Summaries

Dirk Hoerder: German Immigrant Workers' View of "America" in the 1880s

In nineteenth-century Germany and among German immigrants America was not so much a "country" as a model Republic, a better world. This "construct" became the object of a kind of secular religion which migrant workers seem to have adopted. The critic of America became sharper as social and economic changes took place and close contacts between social-democrats in Europe and America opened new channels of information. Yet the myth of America was kept alive in spite of attacks on American capitalism in the labor press.

Rudolph Vecoli: "Free Country": The American Republic Viewed by the Italian Left, 1880-1920

America occupied a special place in the Italian radical imagination. Between 1880 and 1920 there was a shift in the view of the Italian left from America as the model of republicanism to America as the epitome of the evils of capitalism. This changing image of America was shaped by the experience of Italian immigrants and had its roots in Italian political culture. It testifies to the vitality of Italian radicalism in the U.S.

Lars-Göran Tedebrand: America in the Swedish Labor Press, 1880s to 1920s

In the late nineteenth century, Swedish immigrants were no longer peasants but industrial workers. Among the pioneers of Swedish socialism and trade unionism who immigrated to America, a small minority remained very active in the early twentieth century. The American-Swedish socialist press represented all currents of socialism and many contacts were made between organized labor in Sweden and Swedish-Americans. In the labor press the image of America as a land of political freedom, justice and religious tolerance was gradually replaced by that of America as a "proletarian hell."

Ivan Cizmić: The Experience of South Slav Immigrants on Ellis Island and the Establishment of the Slavonic Immigrant Society in New York

South Slav Immigrants were victims of discrimination on Ellis Island and the newspaper *Narodni List* played an active role in the defense of their rights. The efforts of the Croatian community to improve the treatment of Croat immigrants make it clear that citizenship became a stake in the struggle for social recognition.

Adam Walaszek: "For in America Poles Work Like Cattle": Polish Peasant Immigrants and Work in America, 1890-1891

Using emigrants' letters as its source, this paper aims at reaching the subjective experience of immigrant workers. It explores the relationship between their expectations and their actual experience. Walaszek examines the difficulties they had making sense of the modern organization of work in big industry, concluding that for them work was not something to be proud of but only a means of survival.

Ferdinando Fasce: Freedom in the Workplace? Immigrants at the Scoville Manufacturing Company, 1915-1921

The author focuses on the role played by private firms in developing the patriotism and loyalty of immigrants workers in industry at the time of World War I. Employers tried to impose the model of the employee-citizen whose efficiency in his job and loyalty to his employer was proof of allegiance to his new country, but many immigrants rejected this perception of citizenship and fought instead for greater workplace freedom.

Bruno Cartosio: Sicilian Radicals in Two Worlds

Emigration from Sicily was not simply a question of subsistence but a gesture of protest and a quest for freedom. The struggle carried on by Sicilian radicals – farm workers, tenant farmers, artisans and intellectuals – was not brought to an end by emigration. The article brings into relief the political culture of so-called illiterate peasants. The itineraries of radicals from Sicily to the U.S. and back show the international dimension of militancy linked to emigration and the need to explore the interactions between social movements on both sides of the Atlantic.

Julianna Puskas: Hungarian Immigration and Socialism

Most Hungarians who migrated to the U.S. intended to stay only temporarily. They did not form a homogeneous group but, contrary to widely held ideas, most knew how to read and write. Those who were socialists were divided on questions of political theory and strategy, as can be seen from their relationship to the American labor movement and to political organizations. They were critical of the pragmatism of the American labor movement and of its electoral tactics, but they realized they would be accepted in the movement only if they became Americanized.

Ronald Creagh: Socialism in America: The French-speaking Coalminers in the Late Nineteenth Century

In American immigration history French immigrants have remained invisible though their presence has been constant since the eighteenth century. In the 1880s, French-speaking miners in Pennsylvania played an important part in the creation of militant networks and in the publishing of anarchist and socialist newspapers. The article focuses on the influence and personality of some of these immigrant agitators.

Hubert Perrier and Michel Cordillot: The Origins of May Day: The American Connection

The decision taken by the International Socialist Congress in Paris in July 1889 to select the First of May as an international workers' holiday and a day of struggle reveals the complex interactions between American and European labor and socialist organizations at the time. Officially, there was no reference to the Haymarket tragedy but the decision did reveal its impact on the European labor and socialist movements. In the 1890s, the discrepancy between the type of action undertaken by Gompers and that suggested by the European Marxists, the deterioration of relations between the AFL and the SLP and finally the estrangement of the mainstream of American trade-unionism from the Second International, all contributed to the AFL's retreat from involvement and loss of interest in the First of May. Yet the legacy of the Haymarket tragedy – which meant different things to different political groups – remained very much alive in Europe, especially in Spain and France.

Linda Schneider: Republicanism Reinterpreted: American Ironworkers, 1860-1892

Throughout the nineteenth century there have been successive interpretations of Republicanism. In the early part of the century it served as a tool for the artisans of a radical critic of certain aspects of the capitalistic system, but from the 1880s on it turned into a more conservative defense of a stable community life built upon well-paid skills. This reinterpretation was accompanied by a change in the self-image of workers and by an increasing recognition of the institutional power wielded by unions.

Nick Salvatore: Some Thoughts on Class and Citizenship in America in the Late Nineteenth Century

This paper discusses the meaning of republicanism as a political tradition, a social experience and a prophetic vision. Salvatore does not believe that working-class republicanism provided a viable definition for American workers as a separate and distinct group within society. Analyzing the growing complexity of the Republican tradition after the Civil War he focuses on some of its contradictions. Thus racist attitudes and a commitment to egalitarian democracy were not antithetical within the political culture. The reinterpretation of Republicanism in the late nineteenth century – a reinterpretation that emphasized the exceptional nature of the American case – built up resistance to the social changes that industrialization and immigration called for.

Catherine Collomp: Unions, Civics, and National Identity: Organized Labor's Reaction to Immigration, 1881-1897

Labor organizations played an important part in the enactment of laws restricting entry of "new" immigrants into the U.S. The author focuses on the literacy test bill which the Knights of Labor and the American Federation of Labor came to support in the 1890s. Labor's desire to restrict immigration can be seen as a consequence of its narrow conception of unionization and its craft union structure. It was also strongly motivated by the AFL's shift towards increasing integration within the dominant ideology and the two-party system.

Hartmut Keil: An Ambivalent Identity: The Attitude of German Socialist Immigrants toward American Political Institutions and American Citizenship

German Socialists shared a long liberal republican tradition dating back to the American as well as to the French Revolution. German Socialist immigrants, who had high hopes for the positive development of the American Republic after the abolition of slavery, observed the widening gap between political ideals and social and political reality. In spite of their criticism of American society the German-American socialists sought the rights offered them as citizens of the Republic. They attempted to Americanize the socialist movement but feared diluting its radicalism.

Risa Lieberwitz: The Use of Criminal Conspiracy Prosecutions to Restrict Freedom of Speech

In the Haymarket trial the state government stretched the conspiracy doctrine to its utmost extreme. The state based its case on the cumulative effect of the defendants' advocacy of revolutionary doctrine since 1883, alleging that the bomb thrower had been persuaded to act by revolutionary teachings. What was at stake then in the trial was the scope of freedom of speech. By resorting to criminal conspiracy the government aimed at silencing radicals and discouraging individuals from taking part in political activity.

Marie-France Toinet: Political Participation of the American Working Class at the End of the Nineteenth Century

Questioning the thesis of American exceptionalism the author underlines the similarities between the political behavior of American and European workers at the end of the nineteenth century. It was the politicization of the American working-class and its active role in elections that spurred the dominant classes to find ways of restricting working-class political participation. Through the adoption of new measures procedures citizenship was made increasingly selective in the United States in the beginning of the twentieth century.

Notes on Contributors

Bruno Cartosio teaches American studies at the University of Milan. He has published numerous essays on the history of American workers and has edited, among other volumes, *Dentro l'America in Crisi* (1980) and *Tute e Technicolor* (1980). He has just completed a book on American culture and society from Truman to Kennedy.

Ivan Cizmić received his doctorate from the Faculty of Arts in Zagreb and has served as senior scientific advisor with the Institute for Migrations and Nationalities. His research in the field of Yugoslav emigration has appeared in numerous articles published in scholarly journals. He is the author of three books on Yugoslav immigrants in the United States.

Catherine Collomp teaches American social history at the University of Paris-XII. She received her *Doctorat d'Etat* from the University of Paris-VIII in 1985. Her doctoral dissertation dealt with the relation between immigration and labor in the United States from 1881 to 1900. She has published articles in *La Revue Française d'Etudes Américaines*, *Encrages* (Paris-VIII) and *International Labor and Working Class History*.

Michel Cordillot teaches at the University of Paris-VIII. He received his *Doctorat d'Etat* from that university in 1984. The title of his doctoral dissertation was *The Origins of the Labor Movement in the South*. His most recent article appeared in *Le Mouvement Social* in 1987. He is contributor to *Internationalism in the Labor Movement (1830-1940)* edited by F. van Holtoon and M. van der Linden

(1988) and the editor of *Les Révolutions du XIXe siécle, 1852-1872: du coup d'état a la IIIe République* (1988). He is currently working with a group of scholars on a biographical dictionary of French exiles and political immigrants in the United States, 1848-1914.

Ronald Creagh, professor at the Université Paul Valery in Montpellier, is the author of *Histoire de l'anarchisme aux Etats-Unis* (1981), *Laboratoires de l'utopie: les communautés libertaires aux Etats-Unis* (1983) and *Sacco et Vanzetti* (1984). His book on French immigration to the United States, *Nos cousins d'Amérique*, was published in 1989.

Marianne Debouzy teaches American social history at the University of Paris-VIII. Her articles have appeared in *Le Mouvement Social, Cahiers Internationaux de Sociologie, Travail* and *Reviews in American History*. Her latest work includes *Travail et Travailleurs aux Etat-Unis* (1984) and an introduction to *Les Salariés dans l'Amérique de Reagan* (1987) coedited with Catherine Collomp and Sylvie Le Bars.

Ferdinando Fasce is research fellow at the Instituto de Storia Moderna e Contemporanea, University of Genoa. He is the author of *Dal Mestiere alla Catena: Lavoro e Controllo Sociale in America, 1877-1920* (1983). He is currently working on a book about the development of corporate culture in a large U.S. metal firm, the Scovill Manufacturing Company at Waterbury, Conn., during the period 1900-1925.

Dirk Hoerder is professor of North American social history at the University of Bremen in West Germany. He coordinates the International Labor Migration Project and has recently published a three-volume bibliography of the non-English labor press in the United States and Canada as well as collections of essays on labor migration (*Labor Migration in the Atlantic Economies*, 1985) and on working-class immigrants (*"Struggle a Hard Battle,"* 1986).

Hartmut Keil teaches U.S. social and cultural history at the America Institute, University of Munich in West Germany. He has worked on McCarthyism and on the German-American labor movement. His publications include articles, a documentary history of German workers in Chicago, and collections of essays on the German- American labor movement as well as a monograph on German socialist immigration to the U.S.

Risa Lieberwitz is assistant professor of Labor Law at Cornell University in the School of Industrial and Labor Relations. She has published several articles on constitutional issues in labor law, in particular on freedom of speech and due process rights.

Hubert Perrier, professor of American studies at the University of Paris-XIII, specializes in United States working class and radical history. His articles have appeared in various periodicals, including *Labor History* and *International Labor and Working Class History*. His doctoral dissertation will be published by Presses Universitaires de Nancy as *Les Socialistes et la République: Etats-Unis, 1848-1898*. He is currently working on a study of working-class activists' discourse in Gilded Age America.

Julianna Puskas is a senior researcher at the Institute of History of the Hungarian Academy of Sciences. Her articles on migration and ethnic problems have appeared in scholarly reviews both in Hungary and abroad. Her two monographs *From Hungary to the United States, 1880-1914* (in English) and *Kivándorló magyarok az Egyesült Allamokba, 1880-1940* (Hungarian Emigrants to the United States, 1880-1940) were published in Budapest in 1982.

Nick Salvatore teaches American social history at the New York State School of Industrial and Labor Relations, Cornell University. He is author of *Eugene V. Debs: Citizen and Socialist* (1982). He has edited an abridged version of Samuel Gompers, *Seventy Years of Life and Labor* (1984), and is currently writing a history of urban Afro-Americans in the post–Civil War North (forthcoming).

Linda Schneider is professor of sociology, Nassau Community College. Her article "The Citizen-striker: Workers' Ideology in the Homestead Strike of 1892" appeared in *Labor History* (Winter 1982). She is currently completing a book on American working-class republicanism from 1873 to 1919.

Lars-Göran Tedebrand, born in 1939, has been teaching in the history department of Uppsala University since 1969 and was appointed to the Swedish Humanistic-Social Science Research Council Professorship in Historical Demography at Umea University in 1982. His publications include *Västernorrland och Nordamerika, 1875-1913, Utvandring och återinvandring* (Emigration from the Province of Västernorrland to North America and re-immigration) (1982) and *Selánger. En sockens historia* (Selánger: the history of a parish) (1983). At present, he is directing a project dealing with the decline of mortality in Sweden between 1750 and 1950.

Marie-France Toinet is "directeur de recherche" (research fellow) at the Foundation Nationale des Sciences Politiques in Paris. Her articles have appeared in *Le Monde Diplomatique*, *La Revue Française de Science Politique*, *Pouvoirs*, *Etudes*, etc. Her most recent books include *La Chasse aux Sorcières* (The witch-hunt) (1984), *Le Système Politique des Etats-Unis* (1987), *L'Amérique dans les têtes* (The changing image of the U.S. in French life and politics) coedited with Denis Lacorne and Jacques Rupnik (1986).

Rudolph J. Vecoli is professor of history and director of the Immigration Research Center at the University of Minnesota. His work includes *A Century of American Immigration, 1884-1984*, co-authored with Joy Lintelm (1984); "The Search for an Italian American Identity: Continuity and Change" in *Italian Americans: New Perspectives in Italian Immigration and Ethnicity*, (Lydio Tomasi ed.) (1985); "The Italian Immigrants in the United States Labor Movement from 1880 to 1929" in *Gli Italiani fuori d'Italia. Gli emigrati Italiani nei movimenti operai dei paesi d'adozione, 1880-1940* (B. Bezzo ed.) (1983) and "The Formation of Chicago's Little Italies" in *Migration Across Time and Nations* (Ira Grazer and Luigi De Rosa eds.) (1986). He has edited and contributed to *Italian Immigrants in Rural and Small Town America* (1987).

Born in 1951, **Adam Walaszek** is assistant professor at the Polonia Research Institute of the Jagiellonian University. He has published articles in *Przeglad Polonijny and Studia Historyczne*. He is the author of *Reemigracja ze Stanów Zjednoczonych do Polski po I wojnie swatowej* (Return migration from the United States to Poland after World War I) (1983) and *Stubborn Newcomers: Polish Workers, Work and Trade Unions in the United States, 1880-1920, Krnabrni przybysze: polscy robotnicy, praca i zwiazki zawodowe w Stanach Zjednoczonych Ameryki, 1880-1920* (forthcoming in Polish and English).